BASEBALL'S MOST MEMORABLE TRADES

By Fred Eisenhammer
and Eric B. Sondheimer

*College Football's Most Memorable Games, 1913 Through 1990:
The Stories of 54 History-Making Contests*
(McFarland, 1992)

BASEBALL'S MOST MEMORABLE TRADES

Superstars Swapped, All-Stars Copped and Megadeals That Flopped

by FRED EISENHAMMER *and*
JIM BINKLEY

McFarland & Company, Inc., Publishers
Jefferson, North Carolina, and London

Front cover photograph: When perennial home run champion Ralph Kiner was traded from the Pittsburgh Pirates to the Chicago Cubs in 1953, it was part of a blockbuster 10-player deal. In the end, the trade had little effect on either team (George Brace photograph).

British Library Cataloguing-in-Publication data are available

Library of Congress Cataloguing-in-Publication Data

Eisenhammer, Fred.
    Baseball's most memorable trades : superstars swapped, all-stars copped, and megadeals that flopped / by Fred Eisenhammer and Jim Binkley.
      p. cm.
    Includes index.
    ISBN 0-7864-0198-2 (sewn softcover : 50# alkaline paper) ∞
    1. Baseball players—Trading of—United States—History.
I. Binkley, Jim, 1952–   II. Title.
GV880.3.E37 1997
796.357'64—dc21   96-40943
                                   CIP

Manufactured in the United States of America

McFarland & Company, Inc., Publishers
  Box 611, Jefferson, North Carolina 28640

To my beloved mother, Paula, and my father,
Henry, and my wife, Arlene —F.E.

To all of the former ballplayers, whose cooperation
made this project interesting. And to Connie and
Timothy, whose cooperation made this project possible.
And thanks to Bob Vanderberg for his involvement —J.B.

Table of Contents

Preface

Each year baseball fans are fascinated by trades that major league teams pull off in an attempt to better their fortunes. Sometimes these trades are big, sometimes small. Sometimes these trades occur during the season and sometimes during the off-season, bringing baseball storming back into the news. In any event, fans often rejoice or despair when they learn about these transactions, although the outcome typically isn't known for years.

For our book, we've considered trades that took place from 1900 through 1993. All the trades we've selected created a stir among fans and major league teams either at the time of the transaction or later when the results of the trade became apparent. We have tried to explain why the trades were consummated and we have analyzed the results.

Having the benefit of hindsight, we have looked back at some of the more interesting trades. Using newspapers, magazines, the wire services, the *Baseball Encyclopedia* and conversations with former and current players and officials, we have painstakingly arrived at 25 notable trades that have left their mark on baseball. These trades come from each decade of the 20th century.

We are particularly thankful for the completeness of the *Baseball Encyclopedia*, which lists among its contents every player and manager who has reached the majors. It also includes every trade ever made at the major league level.

Generally, we've focused on pivotal trades involving players with Hall of Fame ability, such as Babe Ruth, who is known even to those who are not sports fans. Other players, such as Kiki Cuyler and Chuck Klein, are not as well known. They played more than fifty years ago but their feats were magnificent in their own right and were well documented during their era. One of the trades we cite does not even include any players but instead recounts the zany, unprecedented trade involving two managers.

What all these trades have in common is that they were memorable in one way or another. And they all created a lasting impression among baseball followers.

Introduction

After 10 seasons during which he averaged more than 30 home runs and claimed the National League's Most Valuable Player award in 1961 for the Cincinnati Reds, Frank Robinson could well have expected a big-bucks, lifetime contract.

Instead, he was traded.

Robinson, one of the greatest hitters in Cincinnati history, was dealt to the Baltimore Orioles in December 1965 for pitchers Milt Pappas and Jack Baldschun and outfielder Dick Simpson. The Reds dispatched the 30-year-old Robinson because they believed he was "an old 30," but the hard-hitting outfielder didn't slow down a step with the Orioles. In fact, Robinson picked up the pace. He enjoyed his best season in 1966, winning the Triple Crown with a .316 batting average, 49 home runs and 122 runs batted in, becoming the only player to capture the Most Valuable Player award in both leagues.

Robinson concluded his career with 586 homers, fourth on the all-time list, and 2,943 hits and was selected to the Hall of Fame. Pappas, Baldschun and Simpson never lived up to expectations with the Reds and now are dredged up only as answers to a trivia question: whom did the Orioles trade to obtain Robinson from the Reds?

For this book, we selected trades—such as the Robinson one—that typically were one-sided and involved well known players, either at the time of the trade or later in their careers.

Another classic one-sided deal came in 1920 when the New York Yankees secured Babe Ruth—arguably baseball's top all-time player—for $100,000 plus a $300,000 loan to Boston Red Sox owner Harry Frazee. Ruth had set a home run record in 1919 with a then-astonishing 29. But that was small potatoes compared to Ruth's future accomplishments that included 60 homers in 1927, 59 in 1921 and 54 in 1920 and 1928. Frazee's deal was a stinker of classic proportions.

We considered the Ruth transaction as a trade although some people might debate the matter, arguing that the deal was a sale and not truly a trade. However, a trade occurs when two commodities are exchanged and this is what occurred in the Ruth transaction. The venerable *Baseball Encyclopedia* lists the Ruth deal among its trades.

Highly talked about trades also were subject to selection to our list of elite trades. One such deal that falls in this category included Harvey Kuenn being sent from the Detroit Tigers to the Cleveland Indians in exchange for Rocky Colavito in a blockbuster trade in 1960. In 1959 Kuenn led the league in batting at .353. Colavito had tied for the league lead in home runs with 42 the previous year. Although both players would enjoy other good years—Colavito swatted 45 homers in 1961—neither player led the league in his respective category at any other time in his career.

Trades didn't always have to draw big headlines to rate among the most memorable of all time. In 1982, the Chicago Cubs traded shortstop Ivan DeJesus to Philadelphia for shortstop Larry Bowa. But there was another player in the trade, a throw-in named Ryne Sandberg, who the Cubs insisted on receiving before they would consummate the deal. At the time, Sandberg had a total of six major league at-bats and one hit, a single. A few months later, though, Sandberg would embark on a spectacular major league career in which he would become recognized as one of the top second basemen in the game.

This was a sweet trade for the Cubs, but they have made their share of disastrous ones as well. Who could forget the Cubs trade of Lou Brock to the St. Louis Cardinals for Ernie Broglio in 1964? There were other names in the trade but Brock and Broglio were the principals. Broglio was no slouch with the Cardinals, winning a league-high 21 games in 1960 and compiling an impressive 70–55 record with St. Louis. But with the Cubs, he won seven games in 2½ seasons, while losing 19.

And Brock? The speedy outfielder went on to distinguish himself as one of the top players of all time, leading the National League in steals eight times, including a record 118 in 1974. Brock, who closed out his 19 year major league career with 3,023 hits, tormented long-suffering Cubs fans for 16 seasons with St. Louis. Chicago fans were not disappointed at all when Brock retired after the 1979 season, as they tried to put one of the most unfortunate trades in history behind them.

Matty Gets
the Run-Around

*December 15, 1900: The Cincinnati Reds
trade Christy Mathewson to the
New York Giants for Amos Rusie*

Very, very peculiar. That's about the only way to describe what happened to young Christy Mathewson shortly after the turn of the century.

Here was a promising pitcher who would someday rule the National League. He would win 373 games in a magnificent 17-year career that lasted until 1916. He would help the New York Giants win five pennants and turn in perhaps the greatest pitching performance in World Series history. And he would add to the game a special dignity that made him one of the game's most beloved figures.

As Grantland Rice later wrote, "There have been others who had as great an arm, others with as much nerve, and probably a few just as smart, but when it comes to concentrating all these things, there will never be another Matty ... Christy Mathewson brought something to baseball no one else had ever given the game—not even Babe Ruth or Ty Cobb—he handed the game a certain touch of class, an indefinable lift in culture, brains, personality...."[1]

Yet, at the very start of his major league career, Mathewson was treated in the most curious manner. During the final month of 1900 and the beginning of 1901, his contract was bounced around like a Ping-Pong ball. Mathewson was the property of three teams—or perhaps as many as five—before he finally ended up with the Giants to stay. The trade that put him there was initiated on December 15, 1900, when the Cincinnati Reds acquired Amos Rusie, a washed-up former star, and then sent Mathewson to New York in exchange.

Why was Matty given the run-around during this brief period? And why was he finally traded for someone like Rusie? Most likely, he was an unknowing pawn in a carefully orchestrated con game played by a couple of scheming magnates. But we'll get back to that later. First, the facts.

Christy Mathewson first caught the eye of Giants management as a hot-shot minor leaguer with Norfolk of the Virginia State League during the first half of the 1900 season. According to varying reports, Mathewson's record was either 20–2 or 21–2 by the middle of July when the Giants and Philadelphia Phillies both offered to buy his contract. Norfolk owner E.H. Cunningham said it was up to Mathewson to decide which team he wanted to join.

"At first I wanted to go to Philadelphia, because it was nearer my home," Mathewson recalled some years later. "But after studying the pitching staffs of both clubs, I decided that the opportunity in New York was better. The Phillies looked strong in the box. So I selected New York."[2]

Giants owner Andrew Freedman and Cunningham agreed to a conditional deal, which gave Freedman the option to return the 19-year-old Mathewson to Norfolk if things did not work out. If Freedman wanted to keep Mathewson, he reportedly had to pay Cunningham $2,000 by October 15.

Mathewson showed a few flashes of his potential during his first taste of the big leagues, but overall was pretty much of a bust. In his debut on July 17 against Brooklyn, he came on in the fifth inning of a tie game and promptly let things slip away in a 13–7 loss. In his final appearance of the season, September 26 against Boston, he again came on in relief with the Giants leading 7–4 and ended up walking six batters to lose the game 8–7. In his six appearances with the Giants in 1900, Mathewson was 0–3 with a lackluster 5.08 earned run average. Even worse, he showed very little control as he walked 20 batters in 33⅔ innings.

Freedman must not have been too impressed, but he wasn't quite willing to give up on Mathewson. When the October 15 deadline passed, Freedman had neither returned Mathewson to Norfolk nor paid Norfolk for his contract. That's when things started to get interesting.

During the baseball owners' meeting in early December, Cunningham met with Freedman. According to reports in the *Norfolk Virginia Pilot*, when Cunningham asked about the $2,000 as noted in the contract, Freedman said he never even read the contract. Freedman offered to pay $1,000, but Cunningham refused to accept any compromise. Cunningham, thinking he had reacquired the rights to Mathewson, then sold the pitcher's contract to Toronto of the Eastern League.

Little did Cunningham know, but Freedman had already hatched a plot to keep Mathewson in New York at a minimal cost. To make it all work, he contacted his old pal John Brush, who was owner of the Cincinnati Reds as well as a stockholder in the Giants. (This was a conflict of interest to be sure, but the business of baseball was a lot different at the turn of the century.)

Freedman and Brush were about to play what was referred to at the time as "syndicate baseball," and Cunningham was going to be caught out in left field. As noted in an article in *Sporting Life*, Cunningham received notice on December 19 that the Giants were returning Mathewson to Norfolk. The

Christy Mathewson won 373 games after the New York Giants acquired him in a trade with the Cincinnati Reds after the 1900 season (George Brace photograph).

following day, Cincinnati drafted Mathewson for the paltry $100 selection fee required by the Virginia League. As pointed out in the article, "Pretty quick work, don't you think? I wonder how the Cincinnati club knew that Christy Mathewson's name was going to be taken off the New York club's reserve list."[3] Brush then sent Mathewson back to New York in exchange for Amos Rusie—a hard-throwing pitcher who had already won 246 games but had not played for two years—to complete a deal made on December 15.

By putting Mathewson on the New York–to–Norfolk–to–Cincinnati–to–New York shuttle, Freedman and Brush bamboozled Norfolk out of a tidy sum of money. It was certainly unethical, and Cunningham cried foul when he learned what was happening. His complaints basically went unnoticed.

After the rapid-fire series of transactions, Freedman and Brush were amazingly successful in keeping the whole episode a secret. At the time, nobody knew Mathewson was involved in the transaction involving Rusie. In fact, few people even knew Matty was briefly the property of the Reds. Mathewson himself didn't even know.

To show the extent of the cover-up, check out this odd, little exchange between Brush and a reporter from the *Cincinnati Enquirer* on the day the Reds acquired Rusie:

Q: Did you give New York money or players for him?

Brush: "My, the sun is shining."

Q: Which players?

Brush: "I'll bet it is dark and muggy in Cincinnati."[4]

The deception continued a week later when Giants manager George Davis gave the phony story that Rusie was sent to the Reds in a belated exchange for pitcher Pink Hawley and outfielder Kip Selbach. In reality, Hawley and Selbach were sold from the Reds to the Giants the previous February and had played the 1900 season with New York. But as Davis tried to explain, the two were traded to New York "with the understanding that Rusie was to pitch one more year here and then join the Reds."[5] Again, no mention of Mathewson.

From Freedman's perspective, the scheme worked like a charm. But it almost backfired when Mathewson—who didn't realize he was still in the Giants' plans—started talking to Philadelphia Athletics founder Connie Mack about jumping to the new American League in 1901.

"I didn't know where I stood," Mathewson recalled. "Therefore, when Connie Mack offered me $1,200 to pitch for the Athletics and sent me $50 advance money, I signed with him."[6] When Freedman heard about the plan to join the Athletics, he convinced Mathewson—using assorted threats, according to some historians—to stay with the Giants.

As late as April 4, newspapers were listing Mathewson on the rosters of both the Giants and the Athletics. The Toronto ballclub also thought it had Mathewson in line as late as March 2. In the end, of course, Freedman got what he wanted and Mathewson was on hand with the Giants at the start of spring training.

Mathewson got off to a fast start in 1901, winning his first eight games. He then gained national attention on July 15 by pitching a no-hitter against St. Louis. He finished the season with a 20–17 record, the first of 13 seasons in which he would win at least 20 games.

The 1902 season was a mixed bag. Although Mathewson pitched well—posting a 2.11 ERA and leading the league with eight shutouts—he finished with a disappointing 14–17 record for a team that was headed for a last-place finish. But the midseason arrival of new manager John McGraw signaled a change of fortunes for both Mathewson and the Giants.

Another big change took place at the end of the 1902 season when Freedman sold the Giants to none other than John Brush. This led to a theory that Brush was planning all along to buy the Giants, and had actually made the Mathewson-Rusie trade so Matty would be waiting in New York when he took over. That seems rather far-fetched, but whether or not it's true, Brush was about to profit handsomely from that original swap.

Between 1903 and 1914, Matty won at least 22 games each season as he helped the Giants win five pennants and one World Series title. The star right-hander won 30 or more games four times, posting records of 30–13, 33–12 and 31–8 between 1903 and 1905 and then adding a 37–11 season in 1908. His 373–188 career record still makes him the National League's winningest pitcher, a position he shares with Grover Cleveland Alexander (373–208). His career ERA of 2.13 is the fifth lowest of all time.

Mathewson became master of what he called the fadeaway—a pitch that broke uncharacteristically in on right-handed hitters, like the modern-day screwball. He found the pinpoint control that was missing during his first shot with the Giants and ended up leading the league in strikeouts five times. He also pitched his second no-hitter on June 13, 1905, when he blanked Chicago 1–0.

For anyone looking for proof of how effective Mathewson could be, his performance in the 1905 World Series will always be the standard by which other pitchers are measured. Over a span of six days, Matty faced Connie Mack's Athletics three times. He pitched three shutouts and gave up just 14 total hits. His third shutout gave the Giants the championship 4 games to 1.

"Mathewson was an easy worker," said Roger Bresnahan, the Giants catcher from 1905 to 1908. "You could catch him sittin' in a chair. If you held up your glove, he'd hit it and likely wouldn't be an inch off plumb center."[7]

Mathewson remained a fierce competitor throughout his career, yet was admired for never acting less than a gentleman. In fact, he was quite religious and made points with the public when he said he would not pitch on Sundays.

"How we loved to play for him!" noted Chief Meyers, another of

Mathewson's catchers with the Giants. "We'd break our necks for that guy. If you made an error behind him, or anything of that sort, he'd never get mad or sulk. He'd come over and pat you on the back. He had the sweetest, most gentle nature."[8]

While Mathewson was marching down a path that would lead him into the Hall of Fame as one of the five original inductees, it was a different story for the other player involved in that original Reds-Giants trade. Amos Rusie came to the Reds with a pretty impressive past but, unfortunately, not much of a future.

Rusie had been a flame-throwing star in the early and mid–1890s, when he became known as the Hoosier Thunderbolt. Rusie averaged 29 wins in each of his eight seasons with the Giants, and in 1893 pitched 50 complete games to set a record that still stands. It was said that Rusie's intimidating fastball was one of the reasons the mound was moved back from 50 feet to 60 feet 6 inches in 1893. But Rusie's career began to unravel in 1898, when he started to have arm trouble. He also had contract problems with the Giants ownership and did not even play in 1899 and 1900.

During his extended layoff, Rusie publicly announced he never wanted to play again for the Giants. So Freedman actually was getting rid of some dead weight when he shrewdly made Rusie part of his plan to retain Mathewson.

Many observers believed the 29-year-old Rusie, who came to the Reds with a 246–173 record, would never pitch effectively again because his arm was shot. "In '97, when I was managing the Giants, Rusie showed signs of decay," Bill Joyce said at the time of the trade. "I cannot for the life of me see how he can get out and make good in the spring."[9]

Brush, who supposedly was a great admirer of Rusie, was hoping the big right-hander still had some life left in his arm. Rusie also thought he could make a comeback. "I'll be in condition, and that comes from the heart," he told a reporter. "I'll be better than I ever was."[10]

Rusie was wrong. The Hoosier Thunderbolt never got on track and pitched in only three games for the Reds in 1901. He gave up 43 hits in 22 innings and posted an 0–1 record. He never appeared in another major league game.

Notes

1. Jack Sher, "Christy Mathewson—The Immortal 'Big Six'," *Sport* (October 1949).

2. *New York Evening Telegram*, undated clipping, National Baseball Hall of Fame, Cooperstown, N.Y.

3. *Sporting Life*, 5 January 1901.

4. *Cincinnati Enquirer*, 15 December 1900.

5. *Cincinnati Enquirer*, 23 December 1900.

6. *New York Evening Telegram,* undated clipping, National Baseball Hall of Fame, Cooperstown, N.Y.

7. John P. Carmichael, "Roger Bresnahan—'You could catch Matty sittin' in a chair'," *Baseball Digest* (October 1943). Condensed from the *Chicago Daily News*.

8. Lawrence S. Ritter, *The Glory of Their Times* (New York: William Morrow, 1984).

9. *Sporting Life*, 29 December 1900.

10. *Cincinnati Enquirer*, 20 December 1900.

Catch Me If You Can

June, 1902: The Philadelphia Athletics
sell Napoleon Lajoie to the Cleveland Blues for cash

For one glorious and bizarre season, Napoleon "Larry" Lajoie was baseball's most wanted man. Lajoie, quite naturally, was coveted by many teams because he could hit and field with such skill that he is regarded as one of the finest second basemen of all time. But in the unpredictable season of 1902, Lajoie was also wanted by law enforcement officers in Pennsylvania because of a trade—perhaps "transfer" is a better word—which sent him from the Philadelphia Athletics to the Cleveland American League franchise known at that time as the Blues.

Lajoie's intriguing saga began shortly before the 1901 season, when he defected from the Philadelphia Phillies of the established National League to the Athletics of the newly formed American League. The big Frenchman had put in four standout seasons with the Phillies—never batting less than .324—but he opted to join the Athletics because he had a contract disagreement with Phillies owner John Rogers. Besides that, Athletics founder and manager Connie Mack offered considerably more money than the National League limit of $2,400 per season.

Lajoie was joined in his jump across town by pitchers Bill Bernhard and Chick Fraser, and they were immediately caught up in the war between the leagues. The Phillies went to court over the matter, claiming that the National League's reserve clause was legal and binding and that the three were still their property.

A judge in the Philadephia Common Pleas Court disagreed, and refused to grant an injunction that would have prevented the players from joining Mack's ballclub. Lajoie and the others had survived their first skirmish in the courts, and they went on to play the 1901 season with the Athletics without incident.

Lajoie wasted no time establishing himself as the league's number one offensive threat. Hitting against pitching staffs diluted somewhat by the expansion, Lajoie won the Triple Crown with a .422 batting average (which remains a league record to this day), 14 home runs and 125 runs batted in. As dangerous as he was at the plate, he was just as graceful in the field.

Before Lajoie had a chance for an encore, however, the courts stepped in again. On April 21, 1902, just two days before the start of the season, the Pennsylvania Supreme Court reversed the lower decision and ruled that the National League's reserve clause—at least in Lajoie's case—was indeed binding. The Supreme Court's decision was based on a legal principle concerning employees who possess special skills, and the court made the determination that Lajoie's talents were so unique that they were impossible for the Phillies to replace. The judge said, in effect, that if Lajoie wanted to play baseball, it had to be with the Phillies.

Lajoie played in the Athletics' season opener at Baltimore, but that was the end of the line. While that first game was in progress, the courts issued a temporary injunction against Lajoie, threatening him with legal action if he ever suited up again for a team besides the Phillies. Word of the injunction reached Athletics manager Connie Mack in the eighth inning, and he immediately pulled Lajoie out of the game.

Five days later, the Phillies obtained a permanent injunction in the case, and this time it included Bernhard and Fraser as well. For the time being, the careers of Napoleon Lajoie, Bill Bernhard and Chick Fraser were put on hold.

"I felt as though they had swept my ballclub right from under me," Mack said.[1]

The following week, American League president Ban Johnson announced that the league would appeal the ruling. "This battle has just begun," he said, "and we are ready to give the National League all the trouble it desires."[2]

The Athletics returned to Philadelphia for their home opener on May 2, and the fans let Lajoie know they were on his side. When Lajoie entered the ballpark in his street clothes, the band struck up "Ain't that a shame." Lajoie was also presented a bouquet of flowers and later came out on the field to acknowledge the cheering crowd.

In the meantime, other American League teams started looking into acquiring Lajoie's services instead of waiting for the courts to sort out this mess. After all, the Pennsylvania Supreme Court had no jurisdiction outside the state.

Detroit was the first club to make a serious bid for Lajoie, reportedly offering to pick up his salary and give veteran second baseman Kid Gleason in return. Rogers, the Phillies owner, also made repeated efforts to bring Lajoie and the others back into the fold. Rogers did succeed in getting Fraser to jump back, but the salary negotiations with Lajoie and Bernhard reached a stalemate.

Then, on Friday, May 23, Cleveland owner Charles Somers arrived in Philadelphia with one task in mind: Sign Lajoie. Somers had money to burn. This was no secret, because his financial backing had helped the American

Napoleon Lajoie became Cleveland's first genuine star after he was acquired from the Philadelphia Athletics in 1902 (George Brace photograph).

League get off the ground in the first place. Somers also had a last-place ballclub which needed a shot in the arm, something a star like Lajoie could provide.

Somers met with Lajoie twice within hours after arriving in Philadelphia. Within a few days, Lajoie and Bernhard were in Cleveland hammering out the details of their new contracts.

"If I play anywhere in the American League, it will be with Cleveland," Lajoie told reporters at the time. "Will I go back to Col. Rogers? I hardly think I will. He had his chance to get me and failed to take advantage of the opportunity."[3]

By June 1, Lajoie and Bernhard had officially signed with Cleveland. In exchange for the two ballplayers, Somers eventually sent the Athletics an undisclosed amount of cash plus catcher Ossee Schreckengost and infielder Frank Bonner.[4]

Ban Johnson, who had a hand in just about everything that went on in the American League at the time, helped arrange the players' transfer. It is generally believed that Johnson did this to repay Somers for his earlier financial assistance with the league.

Lajoie's first day with the Blues was like Christmas. Extra bleachers were put up at Cleveland's League Park and more than 10,000 fans showed up on June 4 to watch the team's new savior on "Lajoie Day." Lajoie had one hit—a ringing double off the wall in left—in three at-bats as the Blues beat Boston 4–3. As noted in the *Cleveland Plain Dealer,* "It was in the field, however, that Nap distinguished himself, being the pivotal point of two of the fastest double plays ever witnessed on the local diamond."

Among the onlookers that afternoon in Cleveland was Frank Robison, president of the St. Louis National League team. Robison was an unofficial representative of his league, and was there merely to watch the game and report back to the Phillies management that Lajoie had defied the court order by playing.

The Phillies then filed an appeal in the Ohio courts, seeking to have that state enforce their injunction. But the U.S. Circuit Court in Cleveland dismissed the case, claiming it had no jurisdiction because the players were not citizens of Ohio.

"That case of mine helped decide the fate of the American League," Lajoie later said. "If they had beaten us in the courts outside Pennsylvania, I don't believe there would have been a rival league to the National."[5]

As a result of that ruling in Cleveland, Lajoie and Bernhard got the o.k. to continue playing. The Phillies could do nothing about it as long as the players stayed out of Pennsylvania. And that's how the cat-and-mouse game started between Lajoie and the law.

For the rest of the 1902 season, deputy sheriffs—hoping to bring Lajoie and Bernhard into custody for contempt of court—were supposedly on hand to greet the train whenever the Blues came to Philadelphia. The constables also staked out the team's hotel there. But they never caught the two ballplayers, who took a short vacation whenever their team played in Philadelphia.

"I have always regretted that I couldn't witness one of those receptions," Lajoie said in an interview for *The Sporting News* forty years later. "The boys entertained me with many a funny story of the futile searches, but I would have liked to have been a spectator."[6]

During that interview, Lajoie went on to explain how he even had to sneak around back in Cleveland.

"On occasions when the Blues were scheduled to open an Eastern trip in Philadelphia, officers would come to Cleveland several days in advance and sit in the stands," Lajoie recalled. "They tried to follow me when I left the park, but I always managed to shake them off my trail.

"Several times I left the game in about the sixth inning and the players stalled around until I had time to leave the park. At least twice I took batting practice and then skipped. The officers didn't wake up until our team went out to start the game. Then it was too late."

As it turns out, when his teammates were playing in Philadelphia, Lajoie was often 60 miles away on the beach in Atlantic City. And he admits he didn't always travel in comfort as he passed through Pennsylvania on his way to the ocean.

"They kept a pretty close watch on the passenger trains, so I had to give my business to the freights," Lajoie explained. "I usually was quite a sight when I arrived at Atlantic City. If my father had seen me, he would have considered himself a prophet. When I was a boy in Rhode Island and talked about becoming a professional ballplayer, my father would say, 'I'd hate to see my boy become a tramp.' And, after long rides on freight trains, I'm afraid that I looked the part of a hobo."[7]

Lajoie also had to take roundabout train rides through Virginia and West Virginia whenever the Blues traveled to Washington or Baltimore. Sometimes, on trips to Boston, he risked getting caught by taking trains that passed through the small strip of Pennsylvania that separates Ohio from New York. Throughout his travels, the deputies—just like the pitchers of his era— never could figure out a way to handcuff Lajoie.

Due mostly to the legal entanglements, Lajoie played in only 87 games in 1902. He still batted .366 to finish second in the batting race to Washington's Ed Delahanty, his old friend and former Phillies teammate. It was the start of 13 seasons in Cleveland during which Lajoie was the undisputed team leader.

Bernhard, by the way, also made a big contribution to the Blues in 1902 as he posted a 17–5 record. He would remain one of the team's top starters for two more seasons before his career tailed off.

In 1903, the shenanigans and wayward train rides were over. The National

League and American League negotiated a settlement, keeping the leagues separate but allowing the AL teams to retain most of the players they had taken from their rival circuit. Lajoie and Bernhard were allowed to stay with Cleveland, and the injunction against them was lifted.

Lajoie soon added his second and third American League batting titles, hitting .355 in 1903 and .381 in 1904. He also became the team's player-manager in 1905, and by this time the team had changed its nickname to the Naps in honor of its star.

Lajoie later admitted that being player-manager left a lot to be desired because it adversely affected his on-field performance. He gave up his managerial duties late in the 1909 season but stayed on as the team's second baseman. This set the stage for one of Lajoie's greatest seasons and one of baseball's biggest controversies.

In 1910, Lajoie and Detroit Tigers great Ty Cobb were involved in a two-man race for the batting crown that went right down to the wire. Heading into the final day of the season, Cobb led with a .385 average, while Lajoie was at .376. Cobb had decided to sit out the final two games of the season, leaving it up to Lajoie to play catch-up.

The Naps were to finish with a doubleheader at St. Louis, and it became obvious that the Browns were willing to do anything that day to keep the unpopular Cobb from winning the title. "The players were in my corner," Lajoie admitted. "At any rate, they didn't try too hard to get me out."[8]

Before the doubleheader, St. Louis manager Jack O'Connor supposedly gave some advice to his rookie third baseman, Red Corriden: "Better play Lajoie deep. He'll tear your head off with a line drive." So Corriden dutifully played way back, almost on the outfield grass.[9]

Corriden's positioning did not matter on Lajoie's first at-bat as he ripped a triple to center. But as the afternoon wore on, Lajoie collected six base hits on bunts down the third-base line. Lajoie finished the day with eight hits in eight at-bats. When all the figures were tabulated, Lajoie had finished with a .384 average to barely miss overtaking Cobb.

Still, there was quite a furor over the Browns' actions on that final day of the season, and Ban Johnson ordered an investigation into the matter. It was uncovered that St. Louis coach Harry Howell had made several trips to the press box during the afternoon to make sure Lajoie's bunts were being recorded as hits. During the investigation, Howell and O'Connor claimed there was no harm in trying to help Lajoie win the batting title because the pennant race was already settled and the games' outcome would not affect the standings.

When Johnson was finished with his inquiry, he insisted that the St. Louis ballclub fire both O'Connor and Howell because of their conduct. Corriden was cleared of any wrongdoing because he was just a rookie following his manager's directions. And Lajoie was allowed to keep his 8-for-8 performance because, in the end, it didn't allow him to overtake Cobb.

After that wild finale in 1910, Lajoie played four more seasons in Cleveland before the team ran into financial problems. Lajoie was then sold back to the Athletics, where he played two more seasons. The Cleveland ballclub, for which Lajoie had given his sweat as well as his name for 13 years, then changed its nickname to the Indians.

When Lajoie finished his major league career after the 1916 season at the age of 42, he had collected 3,244 hits for a lifetime batting average of .338. He batted at least .350 in 10 of his 21 seasons. He was also noted as being the first major league player to get an intentional walk with the bases loaded. Most impressively, he accomplished everything in baseball's so-called dead-ball era.

"Nap Lajoie could have hit .300 one-handed against the present jackrabbit ball," Ty Cobb noted in 1961.[10]

Unfortunately, Lajoie never played on a championship team. In fact, he missed out on playing on the Athletics teams that won six pennants between 1902 and 1914. But that's about the only thing Lajoie missed out on during his career.

Shortly before Lajoie was voted into the Hall of Fame in 1937 as one of the first eight members, Arch Ward, the famous Chicago newspaperman who came up with idea for the All-Star Game, wrote about what had made Lajoie so special:

> Mention of Lajoie as the all-time greatest second baseman usually arouses a storm of protest. There were other good second sackers, notably John Evers, Eddie Collins and Rogers Hornsby. But in the opinion of this department, Lajoie had something on all of them. Although a big man and not speedy afoot, he was an amazing fielder, accomplishing with no apparent effort plays that other second basemen couldn't make without running out from under their caps. It was a habit with him to flip out runners at first base without even looking in the direction in which he was throwing.
>
> As a hitter, Lajoie probably was one of the most powerful of them all. He didn't have the speed that in the course of a season means a large total of hits. He didn't put together an amazing batting average over a stretch of 21 seasons by banging drives over short fences. Neither did he have a lively ball such as the present day batters enjoy hitting. In his own leisurely, quiet way, he simply was good.[11]

Notes

1. Frederick G. Lieb, *Connie Mack, Grand Old Man of Baseball* (New York: G.P. Putnam's Sons, 1945).
2. *Chicago Tribune*, 1 May 1902.
3. *Cleveland Plain Dealer*, 28 May 1902.
4. *The Baseball Encyclopedia* (New York: Macmillan Publishing Company, 1993).

5. *Cleveland Plain Dealer*, 18 April 1949.
6. *The Sporting News*, 19 February 1942.
7. Ibid.
8. *The Sporting News*, 26 February 1942.
9. Associated Press, 26 May 1956.
10. Ty Cobb, with Al Stump, *My Life in Baseball: The True Record* (New York: Doubleday, 1961).
11. *Chicago Tribune*, 6 January 1937.

A Cardinal Mistake

*December 12, 1903: The St. Louis Cardinals
trade Three-Finger Brown and Jack O'Neill to
the Chicago Cubs for Jack Taylor and Larry McLean*

In autumn of 1903, the St. Louis Cardinals were a desperate team. They had just finished the season with a 43–94 record, one of the worst in franchise history. They had one of the weakest hitting lineups in the National League, and not one of their pitchers finished with a winning record. In short, they needed a complete overhaul.

Since the beginning of baseball, desperate teams such as this have often made matters worse by making ill-advised trades in an attempt at a quick fix. That's exactly what happened to Cardinals president Frank Robison. When the opportunity came to trade for an established, frontline pitcher, Robison jumped at the chance. To complete the deal, however, he gave up his team's future—promising right-handed pitcher Mordecai "Three-Finger" Brown.

As sportswriter Fred Lieb wrote in 1944, it was "the worst deal ever made by the Cardinal ballclub."[1] A lot has happened since Lieb made that remark, but that trade on December 12, 1903, still ranks as one of the team's all-time stinkers.

The established pitcher who attracted Robison's attention back then was Jack Taylor, who had turned in five solid seasons with the Chicago Cubs. Taylor had led his team in wins in 1902 and 1903, posting records of 22–11 and 21–14. He was also noted for his iron-man efforts, having completed 165 of 167 starts since coming up to the big leagues.

Despite the fact that Taylor was considered one of the league's premier pitchers, Cubs president James Hart put him on the market after the 1903 season. At the time, manager Frank Selee said that Taylor had grown tired of playing in Chicago.

In reality, Taylor had gotten into trouble with ownership as a result of his performance in the postseason exhibition series against the White Sox. Taylor was uncharacteristically roughed up in his four starts and finished with a 1–3 record. After the series—which ended in a 7–7 tie—Hart became suspicious that Taylor had "thrown" the games for profit. Although Hart did not

Mordecai "Three-Finger" Brown averaged about 21 wins a season with the Chicago Cubs after he was traded by the St. Louis Cardinals in 1903 (George Brace photograph).

push for charges against Taylor, the Chicago magnate obviously was no longer interested in his services.

When Hart went to the owners' meeting in December with the intention of dealing Taylor, he found a willing listener in the Cardinals' Robison. The trade was made on December 12, with the teams exchanging batteries: The Cardinals received Taylor and backup catcher Larry McLean, while the Cubs acquired Brown and starting catcher Jack O'Neill.

At the time, St. Louis fans didn't seem too concerned about losing the 27-year-old Brown. After all, he had been in the big leagues for just one season and had finished 9–13. To the Cardinals' faithful, the bigger news was the loss of the popular O'Neill and the acquisition of the talented Taylor.

A story in the *St. Louis Post-Dispatch* described how Taylor was "one man whose merit is tried and who certainly can be relied upon for good work." But the reporter also hinted that the trade might not have been in the Cardinals' best interests after all: "In the end, Chicago may get the better of it for O'Neill can catch and Brown may prove a pitching 'find.'"[2]

Taylor was indeed a reliable addition to the Cardinals that first season, as he finished 21–19 and helped them climb from last place to fifth. But he slumped to 15–21 in 1905, and was then traded in 1906 back to the Cubs who had new owners who were willing to forget his alleged past indiscretions. By 1907, Taylor's major league career was over. Also by 1907, the Cardinals were back in last place and as desperate as ever.

The Cubs, on the other hand, discovered right away that Brown was precisely the pitching "find" that the St. Louis reporter said he might be. Although Brown lost his first two starts for his new team in 1904, he came on to finish the season with a 15–10 record.

After posting an 18–12 mark in 1905, he began a six-year stretch during which he was never less than superb. From 1906 to 1911, he had records of 26–6, 20–6, 29–9, 27–9, 25–13 and 21–11. His pitching—combined with the fabled infield play of Joe Tinker, Johnny Evers and Frank Chance—helped the Cubs win pennants in 1906, 1907, 1908 and 1910 and World Series titles in 1907 and 1908.

The 1906 season was one for the record books, as Brown helped the Cubs finish 116–36, the best record in major league history. The following year, Brown and four teammates—Orval Overall, Carl Lundgren, Jack Pfiester, and Ed Reulbach—each won at least 15 games with an earned run average of less than 2.00. The Cubs had a team ERA of 1.73, the lowest recorded this century.

Just as noteworthy as Brown's statistics was the fact that he accomplished it all with a physical handicap. Due to a couple of farm accidents when he was a youngster, Brown had lost most of the index finger on his pitching hand, and two other fingers on the same hand were left gnarled. The disfigurement actually allowed him to put a unique spin on the ball, and he took full advantage of it.

"Gee, he was one of the wonders of baseball," noted shortstop Al Bridwell, who played for several National League teams during Brown's career. "Just as good as Matty, in my book. Better, maybe."[3]

Ah, the comparison between Brown and Christy Mathewson. There have been many great pitching rivalries over the years, but the granddaddy of them all is Three-Finger vs. the New York Giants legendary pitcher. Here were two Hall of Fame pitchers whose careers covered pretty much the same period. Mathewson usually won more games and as a result gained more fame, but Brown was never far behind. When Mathewson had his biggest season with 37 wins in 1908, Brown finished second in the league with 29 wins. When Mathewson pitched a no-hitter against the Cubs on June 13, 1905, Brown took the loss in the 1–0 game.

During the six years when Brown was at his best, he averaged almost 25 victories with a 1.41 ERA while Mathewson averaged 27 wins with a 1.87 ERA. In head-to-head competition, Brown certainly held his own against Mathewson. Brown won 13 of their 24 matchups, including nine straight between July 1905, and October 1908.

The last game of that streak, by the way, is the game for which Brown is probably best remembered. It took place on October 8, 1908, in a one-game playoff to determine the National League champion.

The game was made necessary because of Giant rookie Fred Merkle's infamous "boner" made against the Cubs two weeks earlier. In the bottom of the ninth inning of the game played on September 23, the Giants had two runners on base—Merkle on first and Moose McCormick on third—with the score tied 1–1. When Al Bridwell hit an apparent game-winning single, Merkle ran straight to the clubhouse instead of touching second. While the crowd ran onto the Polo Grounds field to celebrate, the Cubs players tracked down the ball and relayed it back to the infield, where Johnny Evers touched second for the forceout. Amid the confusion, Merkle was called out, and the game was ruled a 1–1 tie.

When the regular season ended, the Cubs and Giants finished with identical 98–55 records. League officials then ordered the playoff game in the Polo Grounds.

Mathewson, naturally, was slated to start for the Giants. Cubs player-manager Frank Chance decided to go with the left-handed Pfiester, because of the lefty-dominated Giants lineup. Brown was told by Chance and club owner Charley Murphy to be ready in case Pfiester faltered.

"I told them that it was apparent to me that they didn't have much confidence in Pfiester and why not let me start," Brown recalled some years later. "They discussed it for a moment and decided to go through with their first plans."[4]

The game was not for the fainthearted. The New York fans, still bristling over the Merkle incident, were rowdy from the moment they arrived. They hurled insults and other objects at the Cubs players, and the police had to spray down some fans with a fire hose to keep them in check. "It was as near a lunatic asylum as I ever saw," Brown noted.[5]

As Chance had feared, Pfiester got off to a shaky start. A hit-batsman, a walk and a double gave the Giants a quick run. When Pfiester walked the next batter, Chance had seen enough. Brown was called in from the bullpen with two runners on and two outs.

Brown struck out Art Devlin to get out of the first inning mess, and he then shut down the Giants on one run and four hits the rest of the way. When the Cubs walked off with a 4–2 victory and the NL pennant, Brown had defeated Mathewson once more.

"I was about as good that day as I ever was in my life," said Brown.[6]

"We never had a chance against Brown," Mathewson recalled. "His curve was breaking sharply, and his control was microscopic."[7]

Brown had started or relieved in seven of the Cubs' final 14 games to lead their late season charge. And within a week of the wild playoff game, Brown earned two more wins in the World Series as he helped the Cubs defeat the Tigers four games to one.

Brown played with the Cubs through 1912. He finished his major league career in 1916 with a 239–129 lifetime record. His career ERA of 2.06 is the third lowest of all time. During his nine years in Chicago, the Cubs never won fewer than 91 games or finished lower than third. The Cardinals, meanwhile, never even got out of the second division until 1914. And they had to wait until 1926 before winning their first pennant.

Throughout this period, Cub fans had reason to gloat over the trade that blindsided the rival Cardinals. But things always seem to even out in the end. For Cardinal fans, pay-back time came in 1964. It came in the person of Lou Brock.

Notes

1. Frederick G. Lieb, *The St. Louis Cardinals* (New York: G.P. Putnam's Sons, 1944).

2. *St. Louis Post-Dispatch*, 14 December 1903.

3. Lawrence S. Ritter, *The Glory of Their Times* (New York: William Morrow and Company Inc., 1984).

4. *Chicago Tribune*, 1 May 1937.

5. Mordecai Brown, with Jack Ryan, "Mordecai Brown," *My Greatest Day in Baseball* (New York: Barnes, 1945).

6. Ibid.

7. Undated clipping, National Baseball Hall of Fame, Cooperstown, N.Y.

Break Up the A's

1914-15, 1932-33, 1976:
The Athletics dissolve three championship ballclubs
with a series of blockbuster trades

Eddie Collins. Frank "Home Run" Baker. Eddie Plank. Charles "Chief" Bender. Al Simmons. Mickey Cochrane. Robert Moses "Lefty" Grove. Jimmie Foxx. Reggie Jackson. Jim "Catfish" Hunter. Rollie Fingers.

These are some of the greatest players of the 20th century, Hall of Famers every one of them. During three separate eras, they all were stars on the individual level in addition to playing on some of the most imposing teams ever assembled. There is another common denominator that sets these players apart from all others: They were all key figures with championship Athletics ballclubs that were systematically dismantled by ownership.

Call it bad luck or call it bad timing. But for one reason or another, the Athletics franchise has had to purge itself every 20 years or so.

The first breakup came in 1914, when Connie Mack split up a team which had won three World Series championships in five years. Then in the early 1930s, Mack traded away his best players after they had proven themselves. There was no personnel shuffle in the 1950s, but the team underwent a change when new owners moved the A's from Philadelphia to Kansas City. Finally, it was Charlie Finley's turn in the mid–1970s, when he presided over the unraveling of a team that had won three straight World Series titles.

Although each of the three roster shakeups resulted from a different set of circumstances, money was the central issue in each case. It offers dramatic evidence of what most fans like to forget—that despite the sheer joy of having grown men playing essentially a little boy's game, major league baseball is still a business. And, as Connie Mack wrote in his autobiography in 1950, "No one can continue in business when operating at a loss."[1]

The First Breakup

Connie Mack's Philadelphia Athletics were one of the top teams in the American League from the moment the league began in 1901. But it was not until 1910 that Mack put together a truly great team.

He had a pitching staff with three top-flight starters: Jack Coombs, Eddie Plank and Chief Bender. Coombs was at his best for three seasons starting in 1910, when he posted records of 31–9, 28–12 and 21–10; Plank was 23–8 and 26–6 in 1911 and 1912 and would go on to collect 327 career wins; and Bender, a Chippewa Indian who had grown up on a reservation, had a 91–31 record from 1910 to 1914. This group helped the A's compile a team earned run average of 1.79 in 1910, which is the lowest in American League history.

The offense was centered around second baseman Eddie Collins, who was just getting started on one of the most distinguished careers ever. He would end up with a .333 lifetime batting average and 3,313 hits.

Collins was part of what became known as Mack's "$100,000 infield," which also featured first baseman Stuffy McInnis, shortstop Jack Barry and third baseman Frank Baker. McInnis batted over .300 for six straight seasons beginning in 1910; "Home Run" Baker was a lifetime .307 hitter who acquired his nickname when he hit homers in successive games against the New York Giants in the 1911 World Series; and Barry, while not as good a hitter as the others, was an intelligent role player who helped hold the group together.

With a pitching staff and infield second to none, the A's won pennants in 1910, 1911, 1913 and 1914. They also won the World Series in 1910, 1911 and 1913, beating the Chicago Cubs and then twice defeating the Giants.

In 1914, however, things began to fall apart for Mack's powerhouse ballclub. The reason was the large sums of money being offered by teams of the Federal League, which was just getting under way that season and was trying to steal away some of the game's brightest stars.

"They waved the 'long green' in front of our players' eyes," Mack recalled in his autobiography. "Our team was divided into two factions: One for jumping to the rich Federal League, and the other for remaining loyal to the American League."[2]

During the 1914 season, Mack tried to fight the Federal League threat by giving new contracts to Collins, Baker and some other regulars. But as the season wore on, Mack knew he was losing the good fight.

"After giving the crisis much careful thought, I decided that the war had gone too far to stop it by trying to outbid the Federal moneybags," Mack wrote. "Nothing could be more disastrous at this time than a salary war.

"There was but one thing to do: To refuse to be drawn into this bitter conflict, and to let those who wanted to risk their fate with the Federals to go with the Federals."[3]

Mack's own financial situation had a great deal to do with this decision. Although the Athletics had the best record in major league baseball, the fans were not supporting the team as they had in previous seasons. Attendance dropped from 571,896 in 1913 to 346,641 in 1914, giving Mack significantly less capital with which to work.

As Mack noted, "It is a curious fact that Philadelphians will turn out in greater numbers to see their home team fight to become champions than they will to see them fight to remain champions."[4]

Mack's financial problems were so great in 1914 that he had to turn down a chance to purchase a promising young pitcher named Babe Ruth at a bargain-basement price. Mack was given the offer at midseason, when the owner of the Baltimore franchise of the International League started selling off his top prospects to solve his own money problems.

The Athletics managed to win the 1914 pennant with ease, but the World Series that followed was a disaster. The A's were swept by the Boston Braves four games to none, and Mack blamed the players' lack of unity for the poor showing.

Shortly after the Series, Mack began the house-cleaning by placing his three veteran pitchers—Bender, Plank and Coombs—on waivers so they could make deals with the Federals. Bender and Plank did jump leagues right away, while Coombs talked with the Federals before eventually signing with Brooklyn of the National League.

Next came the trade that shook the foundation of the Athletics franchise. On December 8, Mack sold the great Eddie Collins to the White Sox for $50,000. The 27-year-old Collins, nicknamed "Cocky" because of the self-assured manner in which he handled himself on the field, had batted .346, .322, .365, .348, .345 and .344 in his six previous seasons. He was the league's Most Valuable Player in 1914.

"Collins cost a heap of money," White Sox owner Charles A. Comiskey told reporters. "For years I have been spending money for players from the minors and paying high prices for some of them who lacked class. I was tired of throwing away coin that way, and made up my mind that if I ever got into the same room with a club owner who could be induced to fix a price on a real ballplayer, I would pay that price. That's how I got Collins."[5]

At the time of the trade, Mack kept rather tight-lipped about his motives. But Collins told reporters that "Mr. Mack had no desire to sever our connections except for financial reasons."[6]

To put it simply, Mack could no longer afford his number one man. Although Collins had signed a new contract with the A's at midseason, the Federals had continued to offer more money in an attempt to lure him. When Mack couldn't match the Federals' offer, he approached American League president Ban Johnson about the situation. It was Johnson, the iron-fisted ruler who was committed to his league's survival, who actually handled the deal for Collins.

Here is Johnson's story of the negotiations: "I learned Mack's price was $50,000, and as I realized the attraction Collins would be in New York, I went to [Yankees owners Jacob Ruppert and Tillinghast L'Hommedieu Huston] and advised them to make the purchase. They regarded $50,000 as an excessive figure. Then I told Comiskey of the contemplated sale, and after we had discussed what Collins' presence in a Chicago uniform might mean, we decided to go over to Philadelphia and talk to the player."[7]

As it turned out, Collins did not want to play in Chicago. But he agreed to the trade when Johnson gave him a $5,000 bonus out of his own pocket.

Collins spent the next 12 seasons with Comiskey's ballclub as he continued to build on his reputation as one of the top second basemen of all time. He hit better than .300 during 10 of his seasons with the White Sox and helped them win pennants in 1917 and 1919. It wasn't always the best of times in Chicago—some teammates resented Collins' high salary and the ballclub eventually broke into factions, leading to the Black Sox scandal in which eight of Collins' teammates were indicted for fixing the 1919 World Series— but considering the length of Collins' service, Comiskey certainly got his money's worth.

Mack, on the other hand, saw things go downhill right away after the departure of Collins and the three pitchers. Baker asked for a new contract for the 1915 season, and he then temporarily retired when he did not get it. Mack later sold him to the Yankees for $37,500. Once the season got under way, Barry said he wanted to be traded to Boston, and Mack obliged him by selling him to the Red Sox for $8,000. Promising young pitchers Herb Pennock and Bob Shawkey were also sold off—Pennock going to the Red Sox for the waiver price, and Shawkey to the Yankees for $18,000—and outfielder Eddie Murphy went to the White Sox for $13,500.

"If the players were going to 'cash in' and leave me to hold the bag, there was nothing for me to do but cash in too," Mack explained.[8]

Although the Philadelphia fans lamented the loss of their heroes, some observers understood why Mack had taken such drastic measures. An editorial at that time in the *Cleveland Plain Dealer* noted: "Connie Mack was the first to read the handwriting on the wall. He saw the financial abyss that was ahead of the national pastime because of the tremendous overhead expenses."[9]

With their roster pretty well gutted, the Athletics slumped to 43–109 in 1915 as they posted the first of seven straight last-place finishes. Mack later admitted it was his decision to completely break up his championship team rather than start rebuilding with some of his old regulars: "When a team starts to disintegrate, it is like trying to plug up the hole in a dam to stop the flood. The boys who are left have lost their high spirits and they want to go where they think the future looks brighter."[10]

For most of the players who left, the future was not as bright as those glory days with the Athletics. Bender and Plank each played one season with the Federal League before it folded. They then added a couple more undistinguished seasons with other ballclubs before retiring. Coombs had two decent seasons with Brooklyn, and managed to play in the 1916 World Series before his career quickly tailed off. Barry also got into one World Series with the Red Sox.

Besides Collins, the players who really did find bright futures outside Philadelphia were Pennock, Shawkey and Baker. These three ended up teammates with the Yankees in the early 1920s and helped begin the dynasty there that would last for years to come.

Mack, meanwhile, had to start from scratch with his Athletics. It took a decade for them to become contenders once more.

The Second Breakup

By 1925, Mack had once again assembled a young, formidable team. Outfielder Al Simmons—a .334 career hitter—had come up the year before, and now catcher Mickey Cochrane and pitcher Lefty Grove were added to the mix. Jimmie Foxx, who would go on to hit 534 home runs, also made his first appearance in an Athletics uniform, although it would be another two seasons before he became a regular.

The A's finished near the top for four seasons before breaking through and winning the pennant in 1929. The fabled Yankees finished 18 games behind. Philadelphia also won pennants in 1930 and 1931 and averaged 104 victories over those three championship seasons. In World Series play, Mack's team defeated the Cubs in 1929 and the Cardinals in 1930, but then lost to the Cardinals in 1931.

Although the Yankees are remembered as having the most fearsome lineup of the era, these Athletics teams were almost as explosive. During the three pennant-winning seasons, Simmons batted .365, .381 and .390; Cochrane batted .331, .357 and .349; outfielder Mule Haas batted .313, .299 and .323; infielder Jimmie Dykes batted .327, .301 and .273; and Foxx batted .354, .335 and .291 while averaging 33 home runs a season.

On the mound, Grove and George Earnshaw were also in their prime during the championship years. Grove finished 20–6, 28–5 and 31–4 and was named the American League Most Valuable Player in 1931. During the same three seasons, Earnshaw was 24–8, 22–13 and 21–7.

But, just like in 1914, things weren't perfect in Philadelphia. About 20 years earlier, the Federal League was the thorn in Mack's side. Now, his nemesis was the Great Depression. Attendance was down everywhere in baseball, and Mack really took a financial beating. Attendance reached 839,176 during that first pennant season of 1929, but it then dropped by about 100,000 during each of the next two seasons. Compounding the problems, Mack now had to deal with the higher salaries that befitted a championship ballclub.

"We were going up while the stocks were going down," Mack noted. "With our heavy investment and the expenses of building Shibe Park and operating the costliest team in our national game, we had to borrow $700,000 from one of our banks.

"We had spent a great deal of money to build a championship team, and we didn't have the bankroll of some of the financial magnates in New York and Boston and Chicago."[11]

The Athletics' pennant run ended in 1932 when they finished second to the Yankees. The A's still had all of their marquee players—Foxx, in fact, led the league with 58 home runs and was named MVP—but attendance plummeted to 405,500. When the banks started calling on Mack to repay the loans, he knew something had to give.

On September 28, 1932, just three days after the end of the regular season, Mack sold three of his regulars—left fielder Simmons, center fielder Haas and third baseman Dykes—to the White Sox for $100,000. The Sox were in the market for some hitting because they had not recovered from the Black Sox scandal and had been residing in the second division ever since 1921.

In explaining his reasons for the sale, Mack told reporters, "We played to empty parks most of last season. You can't imagine how deep in the red we are."[12] Simmons emphasized that he and Mack did not have a falling out: "The White Sox probably offered a lot of money and Mack gave in, I think, because he and the other owners need cash."[13]

Although there were rumors that Mack was going to dispose of some of his other stars, he promised not to make any additional sales or trades until after the 1933 season. He then added, "If I should break this promise, you can take a scythe and cut my legs from under me."[14]

Although Mack had not completely dismantled his club, the Athletics started to teeter in 1933. There were still some wondrous individual efforts—Foxx won his second straight MVP award and the Triple Crown by batting .356 with 48 home runs and 163 runs batted in, and Grove finished 24–8—but the Athletics were never in contention and finished 79–72. Worse yet, attendance fell to less than 300,000.

Mack had vowed to wait a year before making further changes, and he kept his word. But after the 1933 season ended, he again had to do something radical to ease his sorry financial situation.

According to Mack, he had a meeting with Grove and told his star pitcher he could not continue to pay him the same salary. Mack offered Grove a contract with a cut in pay and told him to think it over, but Grove never came back to discuss it.[15]

The word was soon out that Mack was getting ready for another fire sale, and trade rumors filled the newspapers. The Tigers were especially interested in acquiring Cochrane to be their manager. When Mack finally did pull the trigger on the deals, it struck like a thunderbolt. It all happened on December 12, 1933:

• Cochrane was sent to the Tigers for backup catcher Johnny Pasek and $100,000.

• Grove plus pitcher Rube Walberg and second baseman Max Bishop were traded to the Red Sox for reliever Bob Kline, second baseman Rabbit Warstler and $125,000. Interestingly, the Red Sox vice president at the time was Eddie Collins, the focal point of the 1914 breakup.

• Earnshaw and Pasek went to the White Sox for catcher Charlie Berry and $20,000.

When the 70-year-old Mack announced the trades, he allowed only Philadelphia reporters into the press conference so he wouldn't have to share his sentimentality with strangers. And when the day was over, the Athletics were through as a first-division ballclub.

"Having gone through the heartache of breaking up our earlier championship club, I disliked doing it again," Mack said, "but we had to do it to live."[16]

The only big-name player to escape the 1933 bombshell was Foxx. But he, too, was traded to the Red Sox two years later for a couple of lesser players and $150,000.

The long-range results of the deals were pretty much the same as after the Athletics' first breakup. The ballclub fell to fifth place in 1934 and then last place in 1935. They went on to finish last eight times in the next 11 seasons as Mack tried without success to put together another winner.

The group of players that Mack sold off had been nearly unbeatable as a unit, but they had mixed results after being shuffled to other teams. The only one who recaptured the old World Series magic was Cochrane, who led the Tigers to pennants as player-manager in 1934 and 1935. He was the MVP in 1934 when he batted .320.

Simmons, Haas and Dykes all played a few years with the White Sox, but they didn't immediately reverse their new team's fortunes. It wasn't until 1936 that Chicago finally cracked the first division, as Dykes managed the team to a third-place showing. That was as high as they would get.

Grove pitched for the Red Sox for eight seasons and never had a losing record. But his biggest seasons were behind him and he had only one more 20-win season. He never played on a pennant-winner in Boston and finished his career with a 300–141 record.

Like Grove, Foxx never played in a World Series after leaving Philadelphia despite putting up more big numbers in his six seasons with the Red Sox. He added another MVP award in 1938, when he batted .349 and hit 50 home runs. Through the years that followed, Mack spoke often about his desire to win just one more pennant before retiring as manager of his beloved Athletics. He never finished on top again.

The Third Breakup

The next time the Athletics put together a championship team, in the early 1970s, it was definitely a new breed. Mack had been dead for nearly 20 years and now the owner was the very un–Mack-like Charlie Finley. The franchise had moved into and out of Kansas City and now was in Oakland. And the players wore colorful green and gold uniforms with white shoes, reflecting the flamboyant personality of their owner. But there was one big similarity between these baby-boomer Athletics and the Athletics of long ago. When they finally did put a winner on the field, it was nothing short of spectacular.

After climbing into contention with second-place showings in 1969 and 1970, Finley's A's won five straight division championships. They won the World Series in 1972, 1973 and 1974, beating first the Reds, then the Mets and finally the Dodgers. Leading the way were two of the biggest stars of the era: outfielder Reggie Jackson and pitcher Catfish Hunter.

Jackson was one of the game's great big-play artists. He hit .300 only once in his career and he ended up striking out more than anyone in history, but he was the player pitchers feared most when the Athletics desperately needed the long ball. During the Athletics' pennant-winning seasons, Jackson averaged 31 home runs a year. He was named the league's MVP in 1973 when he led the league with 32 homers and 117 RBIs.

Hunter was baseball's most consistent winner between 1971 and 1974, posting records of 21–11, 21–7, 21–5 and 25–12. Wilbur Wood of the White Sox was the only pitcher to win more games over this period, but Wood's composite record of 90–69 doesn't come close to Hunter's 88–35. In Hunter's three World Series with the Athletics, he never lost a game.

Although Jackson and Hunter were the most celebrated players on the Athletics, it was a team loaded with solid role players. Third baseman Sal Bando was the team captain who regularly dueled Jackson for the team lead in RBIs; shortstop Bert Campaneris was a top-notch base stealer; catcher/first baseman Gene Tenace developed into a consistent home run hitter; and outfielder Joe Rudi was one of the top defensive players in the game as well as an outstanding clutch hitter. The pitching staff also featured Kenny Holtzman, who won at least 18 games a season with the A's after coming over in a trade in 1972; the promising young Vida Blue, whose 24–8 record in 1971 earned him the MVP and Cy Young awards; and reliever Rollie Fingers, who led the team in saves every season between 1971 and 1975 as his earned run average never got above 3.00.

It's kind of funny, but despite their domination of the early 1970s, the Athletics were never quite viewed as being invincible. "They give you an idea that you can beat them, and then you find out you've lost 12 out of 18," Angels General Manager Harry Dalton said in 1974. "They do just what is necessary to beat you."[17]

Although the A's were champions on the field, they were far from a happy family off it. The players fought among themselves, but mostly they fought with the tightfisted Finley over money. In 1974, for example, nine Oakland players went to arbitration to have their contracts settled. And after the A's had won their third straight world championship that season, Jackson claims Finley did not even offer him a raise.

"If they ever have a 'Tough SOB Wing in the Hall of Fame,' he [Finley] will be the very first person in it," Jackson noted in his autobiography. "He could be vindictive and he could be impossible, but I always thought Charlie was honorable at the core, a businessman who was mostly interested in the bottom line. Looking back, just about every one of our fights was about money. If Charlie could pinch a nickel on you, he would. Once he got away with pinching the nickel, he'd shoot for a dime. Then a quarter. In that sense, you had to battle him every step of the way. But it was his nature.

"We were always mad at Charlie because we were the best baseball team in the world and we knew he was paying us slave wages."[18]

These salary battles were just the beginning of Finley's headaches. He was about to encounter his biggest challenge: free agency. It would have the same consequences as those earlier times when Mack had to deal with the Federal League and the Great Depression.

The first Oakland player to be declared a free agent was Hunter, who was set free after the 1974 season on a technicality. He won a breach-of-contract hearing because Finley had failed to defer half of his $100,000 salary into insurance annuities as written into his contract. When Hunter signed a five-year deal with the Yankees for about $3.5 million, it showed his former A's teammates that there was plenty of money out there if they could get away from the A's.

After Hunter's departure, the Athletics held together for another division championship in 1975. But when they were swept by the Red Sox in the playoffs, it was the first sign that the new dynasty was starting to crumble.

Heading into the 1976 season, Finley knew something was about to give. Due to the landmark ruling of the Andy Messersmith case, this was the first year in which players had the legitimate opportunity to play out their options and become free agents. Seven of the Athletics' big-name players—Bando, Campaneris, Fingers, Holtzman, Jackson, Rudi and Tenace—were eligible to be free agents after the season. They finally had Finley backed into a corner and they were ready to cash in one way or another. The big question was whether Finley would break open his piggy bank and give the players what they wanted.

Finley fired off his answer on April 2, just a week before the season opener. He traded two of his heavyweights—Jackson and Holtzman—plus minor-league pitcher Bill Van Bommel to Baltimore for outfielder Don Baylor and pitchers Mike Torrez and Paul Mitchell. Baylor had shown considerable promise with the Orioles, batting .282 with 25 home runs the year before. Torrez was coming off the best season of his career, when he posted a 20–9 record.

When Holtzman was told about the trade, he said, "I never thought I'd get away from Charlie Finley that easily."[19]

Although Jackson admitted he was shaken up emotionally by the trade, he understood Finley's motives: "It was so clear what Charlie was doing. He was making examples out of Holtzman and me. The deck had gone cold on Charlie, and he was playing it the only way he knew how. Hard-line."[20]

A few days later, Finley sounded off to reporters: "No athlete is going to bankrupt me. Free agency gives the athlete a double-edged sword, a shotgun and a hammer to hold over your head. I had two choices. Let them play out their options, or trade while I still could demand something in exchange."[21]

Finley fired his next volley on June 15, just hours before the trading deadline. It was perhaps his most controversial act and it would keep Finley in court for several years to come. In two separate deals, he sent Rudi and Fingers to the Red Sox for $1 million each and Blue to the Yankees for $1.5 million. Finley also reportedly offered Tenace, Bando and Campaneris to the White Sox for $1 million each, but Sox owner Bill Veeck turned down the offer. Veeck told reporters, "It looks as if he's pulling another Connie Mack."[22]

Finley said he made the deals because he could not afford to meet the players' salary demands, and that he only sold them after he called every team in the league in an attempt to make an acceptable trade. Finley also explained, like Connie Mack did years beforehand, that part of the reason he could not pay the high salaries was a lack of support by the home fans which kept his profits down.

The Athletics' attendance figures support Finley's claim. The Athletics drew a million fans only twice during their championship run, at a time when other teams such as the Dodgers and Reds were attracting 2 million a year. The most glaring example of this lack of support came during the 1973 American League playoffs, when only 24,265 fans—less than half of capacity in Oakland's stadium—showed up for the fifth and deciding game against the Orioles.

Despite Finley's arguments, Commissioner Bowie Kuhn issued a landmark ruling three days later that voided the sale of Rudi, Fingers and Blue. Kuhn said he made his decision in the best interests of baseball because Finley—in exchange for money—had weakened his team to the extent that it jeopardized the integrity of the game.

Finley said Kuhn was "talking like the village idiot,"[23] and sued the commissioner for $3.5 million. It was a lawsuit that netted Finley nothing. Finley later said that Kuhn's ruling was the beginning of the end for him in Oakland.

At any rate, Rudi, Fingers and Blue returned to the Athletics to finish out the 1976 season. And after the season was over and the Athletics had managed a second place finish, the long-expected breakup took shape.

It started on November 5 when Finley traded Chuck Tanner, his manager for just one season, to the Pirates for catcher Manny Sanguillen and $100,000. Then the free agents took flight: Bando signed with the Brewers, Campaneris signed with the Rangers, Fingers and Tenace signed with the Padres, and Rudi and newcomer Baylor signed with the Angels. Before the 1977 season started, Finley also traded away outfielder Claudell Washington and pitcher Paul Lindblad to the Rangers and pitcher Jim Todd to the Cubs. In those deals, he received a few fringe players plus more cash.

Sal Bando, for one, had no sympathy for his old boss regarding the breakup. "I look back at it all, and I can't help but thinking that Charlie Finley blew it," Bando said a year after he left the A's. "He had the best baseball team of modern time in Oakland, the guys he had playing for him wanted to stay there, and he blew it…. I used to think he was concerned about winning, and for a while he was. But there came a point where I realized Charlie was interested only in making money and putting it in his pockets."[24]

Alvin Dark, who managed the A's in 1974 and 1975, perhaps put it best: "A snap of the fingers and that great team was history."[25]

Of the players who left that great team, Jackson and Hunter fared the best in the following seasons. That was certainly no surprise.

Jackson played just one season with Baltimore after his trade, and he then signed with the Yankees as a free agent. He helped the Yankees win pennants in 1977, 1978 and 1981, and the World Series continued to be his showplace. His most electrifying performance, of course, came when he hit three straight home runs against the Dodgers in the clinching game of the 1977 Series. He finished his career with a .357 batting average in his six World Series appearances, justifying his nickname "Mr. October." Jackson retired after the 1987 season with 563 home runs.

Hunter played with the Yankees for five years before he retired at the relatively young age of 33 with a 224–166 record. His best season in New York was 1975, when he was 23–14 and led the league in wins. Like Jackson, Hunter appeared in three World Series with the Yankees.

Although Fingers never played in another World Series after leaving the A's (he was on the Brewers' pennant-winning team in 1982, but missed the playoffs due to an injury), he did prosper on an individual level. He led the league in saves three times and won the MVP and Cy Young awards in 1981. By the time he finished his career in 1985, he had a major league record 341 saves.

Back in Oakland, meanwhile, Finley watched the bottom drop out from underneath his Athletics after the key players departed just like it had happened twice before in earlier times. The A's finished in last place in 1977 and stayed near the bottom for two more seasons. Finley then started to rebuild his team, and the A's were contending again by the time he sold the ballclub in August 1980.

When Finley left Oakland, he didn't go quietly: "I'm leaving the game because I can no longer compete financially—because of the idiotic, astronomical, unjustified salaries today."[26]

Connie Mack would have understood.

Notes

1. Connie Mack, *My 66 Years in the Big Leagues* (Philadelphia: The John C. Winston Company, 1950).

2. Ibid.

3. Ibid.

4. Ibid.

5. *Chicago Tribune*, 10 December 1914.

6. *Philadelphia Inquirer*, 9 December 1914.

7. *Chicago Tribune*, 3 March 1929.

8. Mack, *My 66 Years in the Big Leagues*.

9. *Cleveland Plain Dealer*, 11 July 1915.

10. Mack, *My 66 Years in the Big Leagues*.

11. Ibid.

12. *Philadelphia Inquirer*, 5 October 1932.

13. *Chicago Tribune*, 29 September 1932.

14. *Philadelphia Inquirer*, 5 October 1932.

15. Associated Press, 19 December 1933.

16. Frederick G. Lieb, *Connie Mack, Grand Old Man of Baseball* (New York: G.P. Putnam's Sons, 1945).

17. *Los Angeles Times*, 18 October 1974.

18. Reggie Jackson, with Mike Lupica, *Reggie: The Autobiography* (New York: Villard Books, 1984).

19. *Chicago Tribune*, 3 April 1976.

20. Jackson, *Reggie: The Autobiography*.

21. *Chicago Tribune*, 6 April 1976.

22. *Chicago Tribune/wire service report*, 16 June 1976.

23. *Chicago Tribune*, 19 June 1976.

24 *Chicago Tribune*, 28 August 1977.

25. Alvin Dark and John Underwood, *When in Doubt, Fire the Manager: My Life and Times in Baseball* (New York: Dutton, 1980).

26. *Chicago Tribune/wire service report*, 24 August 1980.

Into the Eye of the Storm

*August 21, 1915: The Cleveland Indians
trade Shoeless Joe Jackson to
the Chicago White Sox for Ed Klepfer,
Bob Roth, Larry Chappell and $31,500*

Was Shoeless Joe Jackson guilty, or was he unfairly banned from base-ball?

It is a question that has been asked over and over again, ever since Jackson and seven teammates were implicated in the infamous Black Sox scandal of 1919. It is a question that remains part of baseball's texture, just like debating whether Babe Ruth actually called his shot in the 1932 World Series.

In the case of Joe Jackson, the question of innocence or guilt exists only because of the transaction made in August 1915, which brought Jackson from the Cleveland Indians to the Chicago White Sox for three lesser ballplayers and a bundle of cash. The trade allowed Jackson to become the key player on one of the most talented teams of that era, and as a result wind up one of baseball's most tragic figures.

Jackson played in the big leagues for parts of 13 seasons, and he certainly packed a lot into that span. In fact, so much about the man—including what he did or did not do—is simply myth that it's difficult to know where the real Joe Jackson ends and the fictional Joe Jackson begins.

The most undeniable fact about Joe Jackson is that he was one of the finest natural hitters to ever pick up a bat. Jackson's black-finished bat, in fact, was part of the legend because it had a special name: Black Betsy.

Jackson was a notorious line-drive hitter whose .356 lifetime batting average is the third highest ever—trailing only Ty Cobb's .367 and Rogers Hornsby's .358. After he became a regular in 1911, Jackson hit at least .300 every season.

He also displayed the kind of power that was rare in baseball's dead-ball era. In June 1913, for example, Jackson became the first player to hit a home run over the right-field roof at the famed Polo Grounds.

Babe Ruth was so impressed with Jackson's hitting that he copied Shoeless Joe's batting stance. "I wanted to improve my batting, so I decided to study the best hitter I could find," Ruth told sportswriter Grantland Rice. "Naturally, Ty Cobb was a great hitter, but I wanted to take a fuller swing at the ball and not choke up the bat. After looking them all over, I decided Joe Jackson was at the top of the class."[1] Hall of Fame umpire Billy Evans, in comparing players of Jackson's era with the likes of Joe DiMaggio and Ted Williams, said in 1942 that "no hitter had more perfect coordination than Jackson. He could have hit fourth on my all-time team of great hitters of the game."[2]

Jackson started to gain his reputation as a natural hitter by playing semi-pro ball back home in South Carolina. It was also during this early period that Jackson acquired his nickname. As the often-repeated story goes, he became Shoeless Joe after playing a minor-league game in his socks because he had sore feet after breaking in a new pair of spikes.

Jackson's hitting eventually was called to the attention of Philadelphia Athletics manager Connie Mack, who gave Jackson his first big break by signing him in 1908. Jackson, however, never made his mark with Mack's Athletics. Jackson was an uneducated Southerner who felt uncomfortable in Philadelphia from the very beginning, and his teammates made matters worse by making fun of him. As noted in the book *Say it Ain't So, Joe!*, Jackson said that his Athletics teammates made him feel as bad as he had ever felt in his entire life.[3]

After brief stays with the A's in 1908 and 1909, it was obvious Jackson could not fit in. So Mack gave the promising young outfielder his second big break. He traded Jackson, who was playing minor-league ball at the time, to Cleveland in July 1910.

Jackson played in 20 games with Cleveland at the end of that 1910 season and hit .387. The 22-year-old hopeful was in the major leagues to stay.

In 1911, Jackson's first full year in the big leagues, he came into his own and showed why Mack had originally brought him up north. He banged out 233 hits and finished with a career-high .408 batting average.

In that season's American League batting race, Jackson finished second-best to Detroit Tiger star Ty Cobb, who batted a career-best .420. It was the beginning of a familiar pattern between the two friendly rivals.

That wild battle for the 1911 batting crown also set the stage for one of the first myths involving Jackson. In his autobiography *My Life in Baseball*, Cobb claimed he had to play mind games with Jackson to beat him out for the title. As the tale goes, when Cobb trailed in the batting race late in the season, he pretended to snub Jackson by not talking to him. This made Jackson think that Cobb was mad at him for some unknown reason, which in turn took Jackson's mind off his hitting. As a result, Jackson went into a slump and Cobb whizzed past him for the title.[4]

In reality, Cobb never had to play such mind games because he was always comfortably ahead of Jackson. Cobb was batting around .420 the entire

After being traded from the Cleveland Indians to the Chicago White Sox in 1915, Shoeless Joe Jackson batted at least .300 for five seasons and helped his team win two pennants. But he is better known today for what happened in a Chicago courtroom after the Black Sox scandal broke in 1920 (George Brace photograph).

month of September, while Jackson had to finish with a rush just to get to .408.

Another often-repeated story concerning Jackson supposedly took place about this time, and this one owes its origins to Jackson's lack of education and the ribbing he took because of it. According to legend, as Jackson stood on third base after hitting a triple one afternoon, an opposing fan yelled out,

"Hey Jackson, can you spell 'cat'?" Jackson turned to the fan and spit back, "Hey mister, can you spell 'shit'?" Whether this actually happened is anybody's guess, but it does add some color to the Joe Jackson we like to think actually existed.

For the next three years after his breakthrough season of 1911, Jackson gave Cleveland fans just about everything they hoped for as he batted .395, .373 and .338. He was second in the league batting race in 1912 and 1913, again finishing behind the incomparable Cobb. At the time, Jackson supposedly told a reporter, "What a hell of a league this is. I hit .408, .395 and .373 the last three years, and I ain't won nothin' yet."

Despite his batting skills, the one thing Jackson could not do was help Cleveland win a pennant. The ballclub finished no higher than third during his stay there, and wound up in last place in 1914 with a 51–102 record. The franchise would never again have such a low winning percentage. Worse yet, home attendance dropped to 185,997 that season, an average of less than 3,000 per game.

Due to the lack of fan support, Cleveland owner Charles Somers found himself in financial trouble after the 1914 season. Things were so bleak that a committee of Cleveland bankers took control of Somers' affairs. This was a complete turnabout for Somers, who had used his seemingly limitless assets to help bankroll the American League when it was organized some 14 years beforehand. In January 1915, Somers sold longtime star Napoleon Lajoie to the Philadelphia Athletics to help ease the financial situation.

When the Indians continued to flounder and attendance continued to decline in 1915, Somers' concerns about his team's financial outlook became even more serious. Somers also was worried about the new Federal League, which had started up the previous season and was trying to steal away some established big-name players. These were the conditions which led to Jackson's trade to the White Sox.

In early August 1915, there was a report in the *Chicago Evening American* that the White Sox were going to make a serious bid for Jackson, offering several players plus $20,000. This was not surprising, considering White Sox owner Charles A. Comiskey was attempting to buy a pennant winner. Before the season started, he had paid the unheard of sum of $50,000 to the Athletics for second baseman Eddie Collins. The Indians, however, denied that a trade involving Jackson was in the works.

On Sunday, August 15, Joe Tinker came to Cleveland and things started to change. Tinker was manager of the Chicago team of the Federal League, and he met with Jackson in an attempt to get him to jump leagues. Tinker supposedly offered a three-year deal for $10,000 a year, considerably more than Jackson would ever make during his career. Jackson refused Tinker's offer.

"I told him that I was satisfied with the treatment I had received from

Mr. Somers and the Cleveland fans," Jackson told reporters, "and I thought I would stick right here until my contract expired [after the 1916 season]."[5]

In reality, Jackson was not as happy as he appeared in public. Shortly after Tinker's visit, he told Somers that despite his .330 average, "I think I am in a rut here in Cleveland, and could play better ball somewhere else."[6] Somers said he would put Jackson on the auction block.

Comiskey immediately sent his team secretary, Harry Grabiner, to Cleveland to outbid all comers. American League rivals Boston, Washington and New York were also interested in acquiring Jackson, and Washington's reported bid of $20,000 plus two players—shortstop George McBride and second baseman Ray Morgan—seemed to be the best offer. But in the end, Grabiner brought Jackson to Chicago in a trade announced August 21, 1915.

"Because of a bad financial year, I was forced to let Jackson go," Somers said at the time. "Attendance had fallen off to such an extent that it was up to me to take some radical move to relieve the pressure."[7]

American League president Ban Johnson, who was well aware of Somers' crisis, said he tried to keep Jackson in Cleveland. "I protested to the bankers against this move as I wished to keep the club intact. But the bankers wanted cash, so Jackson was sold."[8]

In exchange for Jackson, Somers received $31,500 plus three players—pitcher Ed Klepfer and outfielders Bob "Braggo" Roth and Larry Chappell. As it turned out, none of the three lasted very long in Cleveland. Klepfer stayed with the Indians through 1919 and finished with a 22–17 career record; Roth became Cleveland's regular right fielder, but he was traded away after the 1918 season; and Chappell played only three games with the Indians before he was traded away in 1916. The financially strapped Somers was also gone soon, as he was forced to sell the ballclub after the 1915 season.

On the other hand, when Jackson arrived in Chicago he joined a group of players that was destined for greatness. That, by the way, is undisputed fact. Jackson's teammates included three future Hall of Famers in second baseman Eddie Collins, catcher Ray Schalk and pitcher Red Faber. A couple of other players—pitcher Eddie Cicotte and third baseman Buck Weaver— were on the brink of stardom.

Most of the White Sox players had something in common besides their talent: a bitterness toward Comiskey, who was known to do anything to keep his profits up. Comiskey reportedly kept salaries notoriously low and, as was later disclosed in court, even charged players 50 cents to have their uniforms cleaned.

In 1916, Jackson's first full season in Chicago, he batted .341 and added a league-leading 21 triples (a club record that still stands) to help the Sox finish second, just two games behind Boston. In 1917, everything fell into place for Comiskey's ballclub. Although Jackson batted just .301, his lowest average for any full season, the Sox finished 100–54 and won the pennant by nine games over Boston. The White Sox then beat the New York Giants in the World Series four games to two.

Jackson missed most of the 1918 season when he went to work for a shipbuilder near Philadelphia to fulfill his wartime obligations. In 1919, Jackson returned to the White Sox and helped them put together what seemed to be a dream season. Jackson batted .351 as the Sox went 88–52 to again win the AL pennant. When the World Series began against the underdog Cincinnati Reds, however, it opened the door for what would become one of the bleakest episodes—as well as biggest mysteries—in baseball history.

Before the first game was played in Cincinnati on October 1, rumors were flying that some of the White Sox players had conspired with gamblers to "fix" the Series. The results of the World Series—which was the debut of an experimental best-of-nine format—seemed to bear out the rumors. The Reds won the first two games before the Sox returned to Comiskey Park to win game three. The teams then split the next four games. In game eight, the Reds jumped on Sox pitcher Lefty Williams for four runs in the first inning and went on to win 10–5 and wrap up the Series five games to three.

The day after the Series ended, sportswriter Hugh Fullerton made this startling prediction in the *Chicago Herald-Examiner*: "Yesterday's, in all probability, is the last game that will be played in any World Series. If the club owners, and those who have the interest of the game at heart, have listened during the Series, they will call off the annual interleague contest. If they value the good name of the sport, they will do so beyond doubt. Yesterday's game also means the disruption of the Chicago White Sox ballclub. There are seven men on the team who will not be there when the gong sounds next spring."[9]

Fullerton's prediction was a bit heavy-handed, and baseball did nothing officially. The 1919 season melted away and 1920 became another banner season for Jackson and the White Sox. Jackson batted .382 with a league-leading 20 triples, and three Sox players—Jackson, Eddie Collins and Buck Weaver—all finished with more than 200 hits. The ballclub also had four 20-game winners—Eddie Cicotte, Lefty Williams, Red Faber and Dickie Kerr. With this impressive array of talent, the Chicagoans were able to stay in a tight pennant race until the end of September.

That's when all hell broke loose for the White Sox.

In September 1920, a grand jury had convened in Chicago to look into a Chicago Cubs game from that season that seemed to have been fixed. On September 22, some of the National League players being investigated said they were aware of a fix in the 1919 World Series, and the grand jury's focus suddenly switched to the White Sox. Within a week—after exhaustive testimony and a number of player confessions—it became known that two groups of gamblers had plotted with eight White Sox players to throw the Series.

The eight players were pitchers Eddie Cicotte and Claude "Lefty" Williams, first baseman Arnold "Chick" Gandil, shortstop Charles "Swede" Risberg, third baseman George "Buck" Weaver, left fielder Joe Jackson, center fielder Oscar "Happy" Felsch, and utility infielder Fred McMullin. These eight would forever be known as the Black Sox.

The acknowledged ringleader of the Black Sox was Gandil. In a 1956 *Sports Illustrated* story, Gandil gave the reasons for the plot: "There was a common bond among most of us—our dislike for Comiskey. I would like to blame the trouble we got into on Comiskey's cheapness, but my conscience won't let me. We had no one to blame except ourselves. But, so help me, this fellow was tight." According to Gandil, when the opportunity came to pick up some extra cash from the gamblers, he and the others jumped at the idea.[10]

Gandil did not approach Collins or some of the other players because they did not get along. In fact, Gandil and Collins reportedly did not even talk to each other.

As painstakingly detailed in the book *Eight Men Out*, the fix ended up a confusing ordeal because neither the gamblers nor the players trusted one another. The plot disintegrated into a series of misunderstandings and double-crosses. To begin with, the gamblers supposedly promised the players between $80,000 and $100,000, but then held back some of the money to make bigger bets on the Reds. And when the Sox won game three, it came as an unpleasant surprise to one group of gamblers who had made their bets with the understanding the Sox were going to lose that game. By the time the Series was over, the players apparently received nowhere near the amount of money they had been promised.[11]

Where did Joe Jackson fit into this intriguing mess? Well, this is where it really becomes difficult separating fact from fiction.

One view is that Jackson was totally innocent and never wanted any part of the conspiracy to begin with. He played his hardest every game, and in fact tried to tell Comiskey about the fix. It was the other crooked players who linked his name with the deal. For those who believe in statistics, this view rings true. Jackson batted .375 in the World Series, did not make an error and hit the only series home run. This image of an innocent Shoeless Joe Jackson is what we see emerging from the cornfield in the movie, *Field of Dreams*.

The other view is that Jackson was no better than any of the other players who took money and did a number of things to help the Reds win the championship.

Some of the details of Jackson's actual involvement can be uncovered in the events of September 28, 1920. The infamous day began with a guilt-ridden Cicotte giving voluntary testimony before the grand jury. When Cicotte was through, Jackson took the stand and made his confession.

After so many years, piecing together the actual statements in front of the grand jury is like trying to put together an enormous jigsaw puzzle with some of the pieces missing. Although the grand jury testimony was conducted behind closed doors, all of the local newspapers printed what they described as accurate accounts. The newspaper reports agreed on many points; disagreed on others. Later, the players repudiated the confessions. To top it off, the official documentary evidence of the testimony mysteriously vanished from the state's attorney's office shortly after the grand jury adjourned.

When Cicotte testified, it was the first time any player admitted that there indeed had been a fix. According to most reports, Cicotte began by telling how Gandil had gathered the eight players and gotten them to agree to lose the World Series. Cicotte also testified that he said he would not get involved unless he received $10,000 before he pitched the first game. According to the *Chicago Tribune*, Cicotte then said, "The day before I went to Cincinnati, I put it up to them squarely for the last time that there would be nothing doing unless I got the money. That night I found the money under my pillow. There was $10,000. I counted it. I don't know who put it there. But it was there."[12]

Cicotte went on to explain how he helped the Sox lose the first game. Here is that account as it appeared in several papers: "There was a man on first and the Reds batter hit a slow grounder to me. I could have made a double play out of it without any trouble at all. But I was slow—slow enough to permit the batter to get to first and the man on first to get to second. [After the play, the Reds went on to score five runs.] It did not necessarily look crooked on my part. It is hard to tell when a game is on the square and when it is not. A player can make a crooked error that will look on the square as easy as he can make a square one."[13]

When it was Jackson's turn to talk, he reportedly gave a rambling statement that at times professed his innocence and at other times admitted his guilt. As he said later, he was half-drunk at the time.

Several newspapers quoted Jackson: "I got in there and I said, 'I got $5,000 and they promised me $20,000. All I got was $5,000 that Lefty Williams handed me in a dirty envelope. I never got the other $15,000.'"[14] This was corroborated the following day, when Williams gave his confession.

According to the *Chicago Herald-Examiner*, Jackson also testified how he helped the Sox lose: "When a Cincinnati player would bat a ball out to my territory, I'd muff it if I could—that is, fail to catch it. But if it would look too much like crooked work to do that, I'd be slow and make a throw to the infield that would be too short. My work netted the Cincinnati team several runs that they would never have made if I had been playing on the square."[15]

In the *Chicago American*, however, Jackson was quoted as saying he took the $5,000, but "did nothing to throw any game in the Series."[16] This was later verified by Henry Brigham, foreman of the grand jury, who claimed that when Jackson testified, he denied being in on the conspiracy.

A few years later, in fact, Jackson testified at a different trial that he did not know why Williams gave him the $5,000. According to Jackson, Williams said that the conspirators had used Jackson's name to help convince the gamblers the plot would work, so they thought he deserved a small share of the money even though he was not involved. Jackson then supposedly went to Comiskey the day after the Series to presumably talk about the scandal and the $5,000 he received. But Jackson said he was informed by team secretary Harry Grabiner that "the old man was not feeling good" and would not see him.[17]

Regardless of what Jackson actually told the grand jury on that autumn afternoon in 1920, his appearance there set up perhaps the most enduring myth about Shoeless Joe. Here is the poignant account, as it appeared in the *Chicago Herald-Examiner*, of what happened when he left the courthouse:

> As Jackson stepped out of the building, one little urchin in the crowd grabbed him by his coat sleeve.
> "It ain't true, is it, Joe?" he said.
> "Yes, kid, I'm afraid it is," Jackson replied.[18]

As you read this little slice of life, you can almost see the tears running down the boy's cheeks. It was a nice bit of story-telling, but according to Jackson, that touching little moment never took place. As Jackson noted in an interview for *Sport* magazine in 1949, "I guess the biggest joke of all was that story that got out about 'Say it ain't so, Joe.' There weren't any words passed between anybody except me and a deputy sheriff. When I came out of the building, this deputy asked me where I was going , and I told him to the South Side. He asked me for a ride and we got in the car together and left. There was a big crowd hanging around in front of the building, but nobody else said anything to me."[19]

By the time that day of testimony was over, the Black Sox players were indicted by the grand jury and suspended by Comiskey. In his statement to the players, Comiskey said, "If you are innocent of any wrongdoing you and each of you will be reinstated; if you are guilty you will be retired from organized baseball for the rest of your lives, if I can accomplish it."[20]

The suspensions virtually ended the White Sox's chances for the 1920 pennant. Trailing the Indians by a half-game, the "clean" White Sox went to St. Louis for the final series of the season and lost two of the three games. They finished 96–58, two games behind.

It was not until the following summer that the Black Sox went on trial for conspiracy to throw the World Series and defraud the public. The proceedings opened on Monday, July 18, 1921, and it was once again a media circus that featured any number of unexpected twists.

To begin with, Assistant State's Attorney George Gorman came to court on July 22 and said that his office—in addition to losing the original grand jury testimony—was now missing the waivers of immunity the players had signed the previous September. Gorman said he was unable to account for the loss. Cicotte, Jackson and Williams were then put on the stand and each said he had been promised immunity before confessing to the grand jury. Judge Hugo Friend, however, allowed the state to enter copies of the testimony as evidence.

In the end, the trial went over much of the same ground that was covered during the grand jury proceedings. The jurors heard from a battery of witnesses, including Comiskey and some of the gamblers who had organized the conspiracy. But they never heard from the Black Sox themselves, as the defense shrewdly chose not to put the indicted players on the stand. The attorneys knew that while the witnesses had testified that the players had agreed to take money for their own benefit, there was no evidence that they had done so with specific intent to defraud the public or the baseball owners.

The jury apparently agreed. On August 2, the jurors deliberated only 2 hours and 47 minutes before finding the Black Sox players innocent. The announcement of the verdict kicked off a wild celebration like those seen in an old Frank Capra movie. Onlookers in the courtroom cheered and jumped about, while the players hugged one another and the jurors.

After learning of his acquittal, Jackson told reporters that he was going to concentrate on running his store in Chicago or look into a coaching job in Japan. "I'm through with organized baseball," he said.[21] Jackson probably had no idea how accurate his comment was. Right after the trial ended, Judge Kenesaw Mountain Landis, who had been named to fill the newly created position of baseball commissioner, issued his famous statement: "Regardless of the verdict of jurors, no player that throws a game, no player that entertains proposals or promises to throw a game, no player that sits in a conference with a bunch of crooked gamblers, where the ways and means of throwing games are discussed, and does not promptly tell his club about it, will ever play professional baseball."[22]

With that announcement, 33-year-old Joe Jackson and the other seven Black Sox players were banned from professional baseball for life.

Chicago author James T. Farrell, a young White Sox fan at the time, later wrote about how he and others viewed Jackson's alleged involvement in the scandal: "He was a subject of particular pride to White Sox fans. In him, they had on their team one of the greatest of all baseball players. The defection of Joe Jackson hurt Chicago fans more than did that of any of the others."[23]

Jackson did continue to play after Judge Landis' ruling, but he was limited to semipro games down South. He reportedly played semipro baseball into his 40s, when he was slow and overweight but could still put a charge into the ball.

Over the years, Jackson continued to maintain his innocence. "I went out and played my heart out against Cincinnati," he said in that 1949 interview for *Sport* magazine. "I can say that my conscience is clear and I'll stand on my record in that World Series."

There were several attempts to have Jackson's ban overturned, which would have cleared his name as well as made him eligible for the Hall of Fame. But Jackson remained a baseball outcast until his death on December 5, 1951. He died just 11 days before he was to appear on national television, where he was to be honored for being selected into the Cleveland baseball Hall of Fame.

Notes

1. Grantland Rice, "Shoeless Joe: Fame That Survives Shame," *Collier's*, January 23, 1932.

2. Billy Evans, "Baseball's 13 Best Batters," *Esquire* (June 1942).

3. Donald Gropman, *Say It Ain't So, Joe! The Story of Shoeless Joe Jackson* (Boston: Little, Brown, 1979).

4. Ty Cobb, with Al Stump, *My Life in Baseball: The True Record* (New York: Doubleday, 1961).

5. *Cleveland Plain Dealer*, 16 August 1915.

6. *Cleveland Plain Dealer*, 21 August 1915.

7. Ibid.

8. *Chicago Tribune*, 3 March 1929.

9. *Chicago Herald-Examiner*, 10 October 1919.

10. Arnold "Chick" Gandil, with Melvin Durslag, "This Is My Story of the Black Sox Series," *Sports Illustrated* (September 17, 1956).

11. Eliot Asinof, *Eight Men Out: The Black Sox and the 1919 World Series* (New York: Holt, Rinehart and Winston, 1963).

12. *Chicago Tribune*, 29 September 1920.

13. *Chicago Daily News*, 29 September 1920.

14. *Chicago Tribune*, 29 September 1920.

15. *Chicago Herald-Examiner*, 29 September 1920.

16. *Chicago American*, 18 July 1921.

17. *Chicago Herald-Examiner*, 30 January 1924.

18. *Chicago Herald-Examiner*, 29 September 1920.

19. Shoeless Joe Jackson, with Furman Bisher, "This is the Truth!" *Sport* (October 1949).

20. *Chicago Tribune*, 29 September 1920.

21. *Chicago Tribune*, 3 August 1921.

22. *Chicago Tribune*, 4 August 1921.

23. James T. Farrell, "I Remember the Black Sox," *My Baseball Diary* (New York: A.S. Barnes and Company, 1957).

A Dynasty Is Born

December 26, 1919:
The Boston Red Sox sell Babe Ruth
to the New York Yankees for $100,000

For Babe Ruth, baseball was a passion. Nobody loved to play the game as much as the Sultan of Swat.

For Harry Frazee, who owned the Boston Red Sox from 1916 to 1923, baseball was merely a business.

As the saying goes, business comes before pleasure. And that is why Frazee traded Ruth to the New York Yankees after the 1919 season in perhaps the most significant deal in baseball history.

Ruth was shipped to the Yankees in a straight cash transaction. Frazee received $100,000 plus a $300,000 loan from Yankees owners Jacob Ruppert and Tillinghast L'Hommedieu Huston. That was the largest sum ever paid for a ballplayer at the time, and Frazee needed it to make up for his financial losses, mostly incurred from ventures outside baseball.

In return for the cash, the Yankees received a legend. In the most simple terms, Babe Ruth has to be regarded as one of the greatest ballplayers of all time. His 714 home runs, 2,211 runs batted in and .342 lifetime batting average are testament to his hitting prowess. He was the most powerful bat in a thunderous lineup that helped the Yankees win seven American League pennants from 1921 to 1932. He even held his own defensively, as he spent most of his years in New York patrolling right field. Ruth also was the catalyst for a Yankee dynasty that would stay at or near the top of the American League for 45 years.

Statistics, however, do not begin to tell the whole story of Ruth's career in New York. In addition to getting a player whose hitting would forever change the face of baseball, the Yankees acquired probably the greatest showman the game ever produced.

Ruth did everything to the extreme. He hit 50 home runs in an era when other power hitters were cranking out maybe 20. He was a superstar in the sexual arena as well, as his late-night escapades with whores were legendary. He could eat frightful amounts of food and was known to down 15 hot dogs

The most significant deal in baseball history took place after the 1919 season, when the Boston Red Sox sold budding superstar Babe Ruth to the New York Yankees (George Brace photograph).

and 15 sodas at a sitting. And, during his finest moments, he could spend countless hours with children, showing them how to play the game he loved.

The public adored every minute of it. By the time he retired in 1935, Ruth was known all over the world. And when he died of cancer in 1948 at age 53, the entire nation mourned his loss.

"You know, I saw it all happen, from beginning to end," said Hall of Famer Harry Hooper, who played with Ruth early in the Babe's career. "But sometimes I can't believe what I saw: this 19-year-old kid , crude, poorly educated, only lightly brushed by the social veneer we call civilization, gradually transformed into the idol of American youth and the symbol of baseball the world over—a man loved by more people and with an intensity of feeling that perhaps has never been equaled before or since. I saw a man transformed from a human being into something pretty close to a god."[1]

Frazee surely knew he was giving up something special when he sent Ruth packing after the 1919 season. Frazee, who had made his money as a New York theatrical producer, had owned the Red Sox for three seasons and had seen the Babe's career take off.

When Ruth came to Boston in 1914, he was used exclusively as a pitcher. He was a star in his own right on the mound, posting records of 23–12 in 1916 and 24–13 in 1917. He also set a World Series record by pitching 29⅔ consecutive scoreless innings in a stretch that started in the 1916 Series against Brooklyn and continued in the 1918 Series against Chicago.

As Ruth wrote in his autobiography shortly before his death, "I'm still prouder of my achievement of pitching 29 consecutive World Series scoreless innings than I am of my subsequent home run records with the Yankees."[2]

In 1918, Red Sox Manager Ed Barrow started using Ruth in the outfield on days when he did not pitch to take advantage of the hitting talent he had shown during his limited plate appearances. Early in the 1919 season, Barrow made the switch permanent and Ruth became the regular left fielder.

Billy Evans, the Hall of Fame umpire from that era, recalled some years later that he originally doubted the wisdom of Barrow's decision: "As the best left-handed pitcher of his era, Ruth every now and then would make you gasp at the distance he would drive some pitch to his liking. However, he was often a strikeout victim, and there was a serious question in my mind whether Ruth, because of his penchant for striking out, wouldn't be a bust as an everyday hitter. However, Barrow saw possibilities in Ruth that others couldn't see."[3]

It didn't take long before Ruth convinced Evans and any other doubters. He finished the 1919 season with a .322 batting average and 29 home runs. That total of 29 home runs pales in comparison with Ruth's later seasons, but at the time it set a major league record and astonished the baseball world. This was still the so-called dead-ball era, and Ruth had belted the most home runs since Ned Williamson hit 27 for the Chicago White Stockings in 1884.

In fact, between the turn of the century and 1919, only two players had hit as many as 20 home runs in a season—Gavvy Cravath hit 24 for the 1915 Philadelphia Phillies and Wildfire Schulte hit 21 for the 1911 Chicago Cubs.

It was also during these early seasons with the Red Sox that Ruth developed his reputation as a playboy off the field and a hard-to-control youngster on it. There was that famous incident on June 23, 1917, when he punched umpire Brick Owens during a disagreement after the ump had called four straight balls to start the game. Ruth was ejected from the game, and Ernie Shore came in and retired the next 26 batters after that first baserunner was thrown out trying to steal. At the time, Shore was credited with a perfect game. Ruth also had a number of run-ins with his manager, Barrow, including one episode in 1919 that came close to fisticuffs in the Red Sox clubhouse. In the end, Ruth and Barrow settled their differences and became long-time friends.

"In my three successful years with the Red Sox, I had plenty of fun and did my share of hell-raising," Ruth admitted.[4]

Considering Ruth was only 24 years old after the 1919 season, his talent and ever-increasing popularity probably would have kept the Red Sox competitive and brought fans into Fenway Park for years to come. But this promising scenario was compromised by three financial considerations: 1. Ruth asked for a raise from $10,000 to $20,000 for the 1920 season; 2. Harry Frazee needed money; and 3. Ruth's value on the open market was at an all-time high.

At this same time, Yankees owners Ruppert and Huston were trying to build a championship team in New York. As the story goes, after the Yankees' third-place finish in 1919, Ruppert had a meeting with manager Miller Huggins to discuss the team's future. In an interview with New York sportswriter Daniel Daniel, Ruppert described what happened next:

"I asked, 'Miller, what can we do to win?' He replied, 'Get this man Ruth from Boston. Frazee is hard up. Ruth hit 29 home runs this season. Bring him into the Polo Grounds and he will make 35, at least.'

"I told Huggins to see Frazee, and a week later Miller brought me word that Harry would 'begin talking business if you will recognize $100,000 as a fair price for the player.'

"I exclaimed, 'Huggins, you are crazy, and this man Frazee is even crazier. Who ever heard of a ballplayer being worth $100,000 in cash? I could have bought both Eddie Collins and Tris Speaker for that!'

"Huggins laughed and said: 'Take my advice. Buy Ruth. Frazee is crazy, yes. He's crazy to let you have the Babe for so little.'"[5]

Ruppert finally went along with his manager and the contract was signed on December 26, 1919, sending Ruth to Gotham for $25,000 cash and three $25,000 promissory notes to be paid over the next three years, plus 6 percent interest. Frazee later received a $300,000 loan, and he put up the mortgage on Fenway Park as collateral.

Before word of the trade was released to the public on January 5, 1920, Frazee let Barrow in on the news. In Barrow's autobiography, he recounted that meeting with Frazee at the Hotel Knickerbocker in New York:

"I'm going to sell Ruth to the Yankees," Frazee began.

"I thought as much," Barrow answered. "I could feel it in my bones. But you ought to know that you're making a mistake."

"Maybe I am," Frazee said. "But I can't help it. [Previous Red Sox owner Joe] Lannin is after me to make good on my notes. And my [Broadway] shows aren't going so good. Ruppert and Huston will give me $100,000 for Ruth. I can't turn that down."[6]

Meanwhile, Huggins went to talk to Ruth to make sure the young slugger could be signed.

"We haven't put through the deal yet, but I want to know whether you will behave yourself if we do obtain your services," Huggins told Ruth. "I know you've been a pretty wild boy in Boston, and if you come to New York, it's got to be strictly business."[7]

Ruth did not say he would turn into an angel overnight, but he did assure Huggins that he would play as hard as he could. So they turned to financial matters, and Ruth agreed to play for about $20,000 a season for 1920 and 1921.

When the trade was finally announced, it was big news everywhere—partly because of the record sum of money, and partly because it involved the Colossus of Swat, as Ruth was called in newspaper articles at the time. When reporters asked Ruth about the trade, he said he was not surprised: "When I made my demand on the Red Sox for $20,000 a year, I had an idea they would choose to sell me rather than pay the increase."[8]

Frazee claimed that money was not the issue. Instead, he said, "Ruth had become simply impossible and the Boston club could no longer put up with his eccentricities. While Ruth, without question, is the greatest hitter that the game has ever seen, he is likewise one of the most selfish and inconsiderate men that ever wore a baseball uniform. Had he been willing to take orders and work for the good of the club like the other men on the team, I would never have dared let him go."[9] Frazee went on to say that he doubted Ruth would ever match his home run total of 1919.

As expected, Frazee took a lot of heat in Boston over the transaction. As noted in an editorial in the *Boston Post*: "This is not the first time that Boston baseball has been shocked by the sale of a wonderful player—Cy Young and Tris Speaker went their ways, much to the disgust of the faithful, but the club did not suffer materially. But Ruth is different. He is of a class of ballplayers that flashes across the firmament once in a great while and who alone brings the crowds to the park, whether the team is winning or losing."[10]

On the other hand, the New York faithful suddenly had genuine cause for optimism heading into the 1920 season. A New York Times commentary appeared a few days later: "Ruth would have been a 'good buy' at a figure higher than the sum disbursed. He should pay for himself in a few years at best, and it is barely possible that in one big year he may cross off the Ruppert-Huston slate the record sum paid for his services."[11]

Once the 1920 season started, however, everyone was wondering who actually got the better end of the bargain. During that first spring training with the Yankees, onlookers were awed not by Ruth's home runs, but by his strikeouts. Ruth was unconcerned. "I'll hit 50 this year," he boasted. "Spring training don't mean a thing."[12]

When the regular season started, things did not get much better. But Ruth finally hit his first home run on May 1—a blast over the roof of the Polo Grounds—and from that point on, there was no slowing him down. He finished the season with an eye-popping 54 home runs to go along with his .376 batting average, 158 runs scored and 137 RBIs. His slugging percentage of .847 is a record that still stands. To give an idea of what he had accomplished, the Philadelphia Phillies—with 64 home runs—were the only team to hit more round-trippers than Ruth did that season.

Although the Yankees finished third in 1920, Ruth made the impact that his new owners had hoped for. This was also true at the box office, as the Yankees became the first team to draw a million fans when 1,289,422 turned out at the Polo Grounds. Many of the fans no doubt showed up early to watch the Babe amuse himself by hitting home runs one-handed during batting practice.

That record attendance really hit a sore spot with the New York Giants management, which owned the Polo Grounds. Giants manager John McGraw, in particular, didn't enjoy seeing his team outdrawn by the Yankees. According to some historians, Ruppert and Huston were soon informed that their lease would not be renewed when it expired in 1922. Whether or not this was the case, work indeed started on Yankee Stadium, which was ready for the 1923 season and would be forever known as "The House That Ruth Built."

The big numbers that Ruth put up in 1920 had further significance because this was the season during which the Black Sox scandal broke. With widespread rumors of gamblers controlling baseball and eight members of the 1919 Chicago White Sox eventually being charged with throwing the World Series, the public needed a hero to restore its faith in the national pastime. Ruth was that hero, and fans turned out in droves to gawk at his mammoth blasts and his trademark home run trot. It may be too strong to say that Ruth saved baseball during that troubled time, as some authorities claim, but he certainly added some pizzazz to the game when it needed it most.

In 1921, Ruth was reunited with Ed Barrow, who left the Red Sox to become business manager of the Yankees. Barrow would remain in the Yankees' front office for 25 years. During that 1921 season, Ruth broke his home run record once again with 59, in addition to batting .378 with 171 RBIs. This time, the payoff was the Yankees' first pennant in franchise history. Although they lost to the neighboring Giants in the World Series, the pieces were starting to fall into place for a lineup that would be known as Murderers' Row.

What followed in Ruth's next 13 seasons with the Yankees was a little bit of everything. There were highlights, lowlights, stories that became part of American folklore, and salary figures that boggled the minds of Americans everywhere. Above all, there were home runs. Lots of home runs.

There were pennants won in 1922, 1923, 1926, 1927, 1928 and 1932, plus World Series championships in 1923, 1927, 1928 and 1932. The only season in which Ruth's Yankees finished lower than third was 1925, when they slumped to seventh as Ruth missed two months because of an intestinal abscess, reportedly caused by his wild lifestyle. Ruth surprisingly won only one Most Valuable Player award, when he batted .393 and hit 41 home runs in 1923.

The crowning jewel of Ruth's career was the 1927 season, when he teamed up with such stars as Lou Gehrig, Tony Lazzeri, Earle Combs and Bob Meusel in what is regarded by many as the greatest team of all time. These Yankees finished 110–44 and led the league in batting (.307), runs (975) and home runs (158, compared to second-place Philadelphia's total of 56).

Ruth towered above all others on the 1927 team, as he broke his home run record one final time with 60. To show just how dominating Ruth was in 1927, his 60 home runs represented almost 14 percent of those hit in the American League. By the time Roger Maris broke Ruth's mark in 1961, long-ball hitters were much more commonplace, and his 61 homers were just four percent of the league total.

Ruth's legendary status was also enhanced by the fact that, through all of his successes, he never seemed to miss out on having fun. As Yankee teammate and Hall of Fame pitcher Waite Hoyt recalled: "The guy just never grew up. The world was his, and its trials and tribulations were too minor to worry about. His love was baseball—the fans his friends—the world his playground."[13]

Umpire Billy Evans told a similar story: "When Ruth hit a home run, he let you know that he was just as delighted over the happening as his most loyal rooter. ... The crowd seemed to sense his enthusiasm and became part of it."[14]

Even when Ruth's career was tailing off, he still had a flair for the dramatic. His most talked-about act came in the 1932 World Series when, according to legend, he called his shot before hitting a home run against the Cubs in Wrigley Field. As with many of the tales involving Ruth, there was probably more fiction than fact to this story.

Considering everything that Ruth accomplished with the Yankees—and contributed to baseball in general—it was only fitting when he became one of the original five members of the Hall of Fame in 1936.

And what happened to Harry Frazee's Red Sox while Ruth was soaring to new heights? Well, things didn't go quite as well back in Boston.

When he traded Ruth, Frazee said that he would use the money obtained in the transaction to buy other players and keep the Red Sox contending. As it turned out, Frazee never did use the money for that purpose. Instead, he continued to sell off his best players, adding to a pattern that began even before the Ruth trade. In December 1918, for example, Frazee sent pitchers Dutch Leonard and Ernie Shore plus outfielder Duffy Lewis to the Yankees for four part-timers and $15,000. In July 1919, starting pitcher Carl Mays went to the Yankees for two rather forgettable pitchers and $40,000. In December 1920, catcher Wally Schang, second baseman Mike McNally and pitchers Waite Hoyt and Harry Harper were traded to New York. The Boston-to-New York express continued following the 1921 season, when Frazee traded starting pitchers Sad Sam Jones and Joe Bush and starting shortstop Everett Scott. In July 1922, third baseman Joe Dugan and outfielder Elmer Smith went to the Yankees for four part-timers and $50,000. And finally, in January 1923, future Hall of Fame pitcher Herb Pennock was traded to the Yankees for three little-used players and $50,000.

As Red Sox outfielder Harry Hooper recalled, "All Frazee wanted was the money. He was short of cash and he sold the whole team down the river to keep his dirty nose above water. What a way to end a wonderful ballclub!"[15]

Frazee finally sold the team in 1923, and two years later struck it rich when his production of "No, No, Nanette" was a hit on Broadway. The Red Sox were not so lucky. Frazee had pretty much cleaned out the cupboard by the time he left the ballclub, and it would finish last nine times between 1922 and 1932. The Red Sox didn't put together another contending team until 1938. Some say that was the Curse of the Bambino.

As Ruth noted, "They'll never build any monuments to Frazee in Boston."[16]

Notes

1. Lawrence S. Ritter, *The Glory of Their Times* (New York: William Morrow and Company Inc., 1984).

2. Babe Ruth, with Bob Considine, *The Babe Ruth Story* (New York: Dutton, 1948).

3. Billy Evans, "Baseball's 13 Best Batters," *Esquire* (June 1942).

4. Ruth, *The Babe Ruth Story.*

5. Daniel Daniel, *The Real Babe Ruth* (St. Louis: The Sporting News Publishing Co., 1948).

6. Edward Grant Barrow, with James M. Kahn, *My Fifty Years in Baseball* (New York. Coward-McCann, Inc., 1951).

7. Ruth, *The Babe Ruth Story.*

8. *New York Times*, 6 January 1920.

9. *Boston Post*, 6 January 1920.

10. Ibid.

11. *New York Times*, 12 January 1920.

12. Ken Sobol, *Babe Ruth and the American Dream* (New York: Random House, 1974).

13. Waite Hoyt, "The Babe Ruth His Teammates Knew," *Baseball Digest* (August 1961).

14. Evans, "Baseball's 13 Best Batters."

15. Ritter, *The Glory of Their Times.*

16. Ruth, *The Babe Ruth Story.*

The Rajah and the Flash

December 20, 1926:
The St. Louis Cardinals trade
Rogers Hornsby to the New York Giants
for Frankie Frisch and Jimmy Ring

Rogers Hornsby was by no means baseball's version of a "yes man." He was a belligerent, foul-mouthed fellow who seemed to take pride in the fact that he would stand up to anyone—from batboy to team owner—who got in his way. Near the end of the 1926 season, he made a mistake when he stood up to the wrong person.

Frankie Frisch made a different kind of mistake that same season. Although Frisch had a fiery personality himself, he ran away from a confrontation in a moment of weakness and, in the process, let down his unforgiving manager.

That, in a nutshell, is why the St. Louis Cardinals traded Hornsby to the New York Giants for Frisch just before Christmas of 1926. It was one of those rare swaps that involved two genuine stars who played the same position. The 30-year-old Hornsby and 28-year-old Frisch were among the game's premier second basemen, and both were destined for the Hall of Fame.

In Hornsby's 11 full seasons with the Cardinals before the trade, the "Rajah" won six league batting titles and hit over .400 three times. He would end up the greatest right-handed hitter of all time, compiling a lifetime .358 batting average.

In Frisch's eight seasons with the Giants before being traded, he batted at least .314 six times and had a high of .348 in 1923. By the time he retired, the "Fordham Flash" had collected 2,880 hits for a .316 career average and gained considerable acclaim for his defensive play.

Besides being a real blockbuster of a trade, the Hornsby-Frisch exchange ended up surprisingly one-sided. Although the fans in St. Louis raised quite a ruckus when they lost Hornsby, he never really made any mark with the Giants. Frisch, on the other hand, became one of the driving forces behind a Cardinal team that won four pennants. He was also the player-manager for that group of characters that gained everlasting fame as the Gas House Gang.

Rogers Hornsby. In 1926, it was believed that the New York Giants got the better end of the bargain when they traded Frankie Frisch to the St. Louis Cardinals for the great Rogers Hornsby (George Brace photograph).

Frankie Frisch. As it turned out, Frankie Frisch meant more to the Cardinals than Hornsby did to the Giants (George Brace photograph).

As St. Louis sportswriter Bob Broeg put it, "The Flash didn't make them forget Hornsby, but he certainly made them remember Frisch."[1]

Although few trades created the kind of fanfare as this one, it actually came as no surprise. That is because both players were so far into their management's dog house that there was no way out.

Frisch, the Giants' team captain, was the first to fall out of favor with his boss. And the incident that put him in that position coincidentally came in St. Louis, when the Giants played a weekend series there in August 1926.

During a key moment in the game on August 20, Frisch missed a sign flashed by manager John McGraw. With the score tied 2–2 with two outs in the fourth inning, the Cardinals had runners on first and third. McGraw signalled that in the event of a double steal, the catcher was to fire the ball to the pitcher—hoping to catch the runner off third—instead of throwing down to second base. The Cardinal runner at first did break with the pitch, and Frisch unwisely left his second base post to cover the base. The batter, Tommy Thevenow, hit a grounder through the area vacated by Frisch. The Cards took the lead and went on to a 6–2 victory.

At the time, Frisch was physically run down. His legs had been bothering him for much of the season and he had a bad cold. To top it off, he now had to listen to some of McGraw's blistering criticisms. The volatile McGraw also announced he was going to make some lineup changes, and Frisch was being moved to third base.

"Every man on the team caught that signal except the captain," McGraw told reporters in what most likely was a cleaned-up version of his postgame clubhouse discussion. "It's like every person on a train except the engineer having the signal."[2]

This was not the first time Frisch had been chewed out. He knew that his role as team captain meant he had to put up with considerable verbal abuse from McGraw whenever something went wrong. After all, that is the way McGraw motivated his players. But an individual can only take so much, and the verbal shredding Frisch absorbed that afternoon in St. Louis pushed him over the edge.

That night, Frisch went out drinking with teammates Bill Terry, George Kelly and Irish Meusel. As his sympathetic colleagues listened, Frisch told them he had had enough. The next morning, instead of heading out to the ballpark, Frisch checked out of the hotel and caught a train back to New York.

As Terry recalled, "Frisch never would've gone, but Kelly, Meusel and myself went with him to the train. Moral support."[3]

When Frisch got back to New York, he was ordered to stay in bed by his family doctor. He was suffering from a heavy cold and a rundown condition. While resting at home, he gave an interview to local reporters.

"I came home because I am all in," Frisch began. "My legs have bothered me all season and I am not in shape to play my best."

Q: Did you object to playing third base?

"I don't object to playing anywhere when I'm in shape, but I am not in shape now."

Q: Did you have any trouble with McGraw?

"No."

Q: Did you tell him you were leaving the team?

"No. I just packed my bags and got on a train."

Q: Has McGraw criticized your playing in a manner you regard as unduly severe?

"I don't want to talk about that."[4]

McGraw was surprisingly understanding of his AWOL captain—at least in public. Although he said he did not intend to "let any player think he can disobey any of the club's rules and get away with it," he also made it known he would be lenient with Frisch.[5]

Despite McGraw's outward appearance, there was speculation that Frisch's career with the Giants was all but over. New York columnist Joe Vila wrote, "In deserting the Giants, Capt. Frisch has committed a serious offense and probably will be traded by manager McGraw next winter, if not before that time. Frisch may have been 'ridden' severely by McGraw on certain occasions, but in justice to the Giants followers, who pay his salary, the team's captain should have stuck to his post, regardless of his personal feelings."[6]

While Frisch remained at home, his teammates continued on what turned out to be a distastrous road trip. With their morale reportedly shattered by Frisch's desertion, the Giants lost 11 of 13 games as their record fell below .500.

On September 2, McGraw announced he was fining Frisch $500 for leaving the club without permission. He also ordered Frisch to return to the team, which he did two days later. Frisch was back in the lineup on September 3 and went on to finish with a .314 batting average, his lowest since 1920.

Although the episode was over, things were never the same between Frisch and his manager. After all, running away was something you just did not do to John McGraw. Not to the man known as "Little Napoleon," who demanded more of his players—including loyalty—than perhaps any manager in history. As Mrs. McGraw wrote later in a biography about her husband, "John couldn't forgive [Frisch] for breaking just when his cooperation was needed most."[7] McGraw and Frisch stopped speaking to one another and their silence would last for several years.

At just about the time Frisch's two-week hiatus from the Giants was coming to an end, Hornsby was involved in an incident that led to his downfall with the Cardinals. It all happened after a Labor Day doubleheader in Pittsburgh, when player-manager Hornsby had an ugly confrontation in the clubhouse with team owner Sam Breadon.

Earlier, Hornsby had asked Breadon to try to cancel a September exhibition game in New Haven, Connecticut. The Cardinals were in the middle of a heated pennant race, and Hornsby thought his players needed every day off they could manage down the stretch.

Breadon, however, was unable to cancel the game in New Haven, and he unfortunately picked a bad moment to break the news to Hornsby. The Cards had just split the doubleheader with the Pirates, losing the nightcap 4–2 as their lead in the National League remained just one game over Cincinnati. While Breadon simply told Hornsby that the Cardinals would have to play the exhibition, what Hornsby told Breadon is not fit for print.

"It might have been different if Breadon had waited until we all cooled off, perhaps told me that evening after dinner," Hornsby noted years later in his autobiography: "A big steak might have taken some sting out of the defeat. But I was red hot, and the news about exhibitions made me hotter. I suppose I spoke more bluntly than I usually do. I told him what he could do with those exhibition games, and all exhibition games."[8]

Cardinal catcher Bob O'Farrell witnessed the verbal fireworks: "Those of us in the clubhouse at the time said among ourselves, 'That's the end of Rogers Hornsby here.'"[9]

The same thought was going through Breadon's mind. And when he saw Branch Rickey, his brilliant general manager, he was livid. "He's got to go, Branch! Nobody can talk to me that way."[10] For the time being, though, Breadon stayed out of Hornsby's hair. And the team's performance for the rest of the season set the city of St. Louis ablaze with excitement. The Cardinals won their first pennant in franchise history, edging the Reds by two games.

There were many heroes on that Cardinal team. Pitcher Flint Rhem finished 20–7 and tied for the league lead in wins; 39-year-old Grover Cleveland Alexander was picked up on waivers in June and provided added pitching strength by going 9–7; outfielder Billy Southworth came over in a mid-season trade with the Giants and batted .317; and O'Farrell was named the league's Most Valuable Player after batting .293 and providing invaluable leadership. But Hornsby, despite batting an unusually low .317, received the lion's share of the credit for ending the Cardinals' pennant drought.

The World Series against the Yankees also provided its share of unforgettable moments, especially in the seventh and final game. With the Cardinals leading 3–2 in the seventh inning, the veteran Alexander came in and struck out Tony Lazzeri with the bases loaded and two outs. Alexander finished the game, and O'Farrell capped off the 3–2 victory in dramatic fashion when he threw out Babe Ruth trying to steal second for the final out.

"That pennant and our victory over the Yankees combined to give me the greatest thrill of my baseball career," noted Hornsby. "It's a thrill to win any ballgame, but there's nothing that stands out in a ballplayer's life like that first pennant."[11]

Once the excitement of the World Series died down, Breadon went back to the business about solving the Hornsby situation. Hornsby thought he deserved a raise and a multi-year contract after his successful season, but Breadon refused to offer more than a one-year deal. They had a couple of conferences in early December to try to reach an agreement, but neither side gave an inch. Basically, Breadon was negotiating just for show. He knew Hornsby would not accept his offer, and he did not really care.

With the contract negotiations at a stalemate, Breadon paid a visit to John McGraw and Giants owner Charles Stoneham on December 13 to see if they might be interested in his hot-tempered star. Back in 1919, the Giants had offered the astounding sum of $300,000 for Hornsby, and the Cardinals had tried to buy Frisch as well. Neither team was willing to accept the other's offer at that time, but now conditions had changed.

This is the way McGraw remembered the conversation that took place in Stoneham's office:

"'I'm having trouble with Hornsby,' said Mr. Breadon. 'He wants a three-year contract. I have offered him a one-year contract, and that is as far as I will go. If he refuses, I am open to propositions for him. I will trade you Hornsby for Frisch and Terry.'

"I said I could not consider trading both of these men."

"'Will you give a pitcher with Frisch?' Breadon asked.

"I considered for a moment and then said I would give Frisch and [Jimmy] Ring or [Jack] Scott."

"We came to no agreement then. That is, Mr. Breadon didn't say which of the pitchers he would take."[12]

McGraw said he assumed nothing would come of the proposition, that Breadon was just gathering ammunition for his next talk with Hornsby. But a week later, the proposition became reality.

On December 20, Breadon met with Hornsby one last time and again offered the one-year contract. When Hornsby said no, Breadon got back in touch with Stoneham. The long-distance phone call lasted about five minutes, and when it was over Rogers Hornsby was no longer a Cardinal. Breadon had accepted the standing offer of Frankie Frisch and Jimmy Ring.

"I do not think I have been treated fairly by the owner of the Cardinal club," Hornsby said in a statement the following day. Hornsby also blasted Breadon for blaming him for the salary impasse and for telling reporters that he had requested a trade. "I never asked to be traded and never wanted to be traded," Hornsby concluded.[13]

Frisch, no doubt expecting to be dealt, had little to say: "It's pretty hot out there [in St. Louis], but I guess I'll play."[14]

In St. Louis, news of the transaction touched off a storm of protest. The

St. Louis Chamber of Commerce sent a telegram to Commissioner Kenesaw Mountain Landis, urging him to cancel the deal. He refused. Some angry fans even stopped Breadon's automobile and yelled insults at his wife until the police came and stopped the commotion. Other fans draped black crepe over Breadon's office door.

Breadon took it all in stride: "This will all quiet down in summertime. If Hornsby burns up the league and Frisch breaks a leg and Ring has a bad year, I'll catch it. They'll razz me to a fare-you-well. However, if Hornsby slips, as he gave evidence of doing last season, and Frisch and Ring play real ball, the fans will say, 'Well, Sam Breadon knew his ivory, after all.' It's just a gamble. Time will tell, and if time doesn't, the bleachers will."[15]

In New York, the consensus among the so-called experts was that McGraw had made out like a bandit. As one sportswriter pointed out, "Now he is prepared to put Hornsby against Ruth, confident that the presence of the most perfect hitter in his lineup will draw added thousands through the turnstyles at the Polo Grounds."[16]

Before Hornsby had a chance to show the fans of New York just how perfect he was, one matter had to be settled. Hornsby had bought a considerable amount of stock in the Cardinals when he became player-manager in 1925, and National League President John Heydler ruled that Hornsby could not play with the Giants as long as he held the stock.

When Hornsby demanded considerably more per share than Breadon was willing to pay, the remaining National League teams reportedly contributed a few thousand dollars apiece to make up the difference. The other owners knew full well they would recoup the loss because of Hornsby's drawing power at the gate.

Once the 1927 season got under way, Hornsby joined first baseman Bill Terry, shortstop Travis Jackson and third baseman Freddie Lindstrom to give the Giants a formidable infield composed of four future Hall of Famers. Hornsby also showed that his subpar batting average of the previous season was just a quirk as he rebounded with a .361 mark.

Still, the magic was missing from these Giants. They had to close with a rush to finish with a 92–62 record, in third place behind the Pirates and the second-place Cardinals.

It might have been surprising that the talent-laden Giants failed to win it all that season, but it was even a bigger surprise when Hornsby was sent packing three months later. When the Rajah was traded to the Boston Braves on January 10, 1928, for a couple of relative unknowns—catcher Shanty Hogan and outfielder Jimmy Welsh—the Giants simply released a statement saying it was "for the best interests of the New York Giants."[17]

It always remained a mystery why the Giants got rid of Hornsby after just one season. Hornsby thought it was because he mouthed off to traveling secretary Jim Tierney, who was one of Charles Stoneham's righthand men.

New York sportswriter Frank Graham claimed it was because Hornsby mouthed off to Stoneham. And Bill Terry said it was because Hornsby mouthed off to McGraw. Maybe all these views are correct.

At any rate, it wasn't the first time Hornsby's mouth had cost him a job. And it would not be the last.

"Nobody ever bothered to give me an explanation of why I was traded," Hornsby noted. "But they never do give you any explanation."[18]

While Hornsby was saying hello and good-bye to New York, the big story in St. Louis in 1927 was whether Frisch could fill Hornsby's shoes at second base. As it turned out, he filled them better than anyone could possibly imagine.

Playing with the kind of pressure only a few ballplayers experience—trying to replace a local legend—the switch-hitting Frisch put up some numbers that first season that were nothing short of sensational. He batted .337 with 208 hits, scored 112 runs and struck out only 10 times in 617 at-bats. He also led the league with 48 stolen bases and was the league's top fielding second baseman.

Behind the Flash's inspirational play, the Cardinals won three more games than the Hornsby-led 1926 champions. The season belonged to Pittsburgh, however, and the Pirates won the pennant by 1½ games over the Cards.

"The greatest player I ever saw in any one season was Frankie Frisch in 1927," noted Bob O'Farrell, who replaced Hornsby as manager that year. "Frank did everything that season. Really an amazing ballplayer."[19]

The gamble had certainly paid off for Breadon. Although Jimmy Ring turned out to be a bust and finished 0–4 in his only season with the Cardinals, Frisch's play more than made up for it. The ballclub even set a record for attendance, proving that the fans had survived the loss of Hornsby.

"After the season of 1927, I never again was afraid to dispose of a player, regardless of his ability or popularity," Breadon said several years later. "I knew after that year that what the fans want is a winner, and that a popular player is quickly forgotten by one who is equally popular."[20]

For three of the next four seasons, Frisch and the Cardinals won the pennant. And each time, McGraw's Giants were left close behind in the standings. In those three World Series, the Cardinals lost to the Yankees in 1928 and then split with the Athletics in 1930 and 1931. Frisch batted at least .300 during each of these championship seasons and won the MVP award in 1931, when he batted .311, led the league in stolen bases, and played his usual top-notch defense.

Perhaps Frisch's most memorable season in St. Louis came in 1934, when he was part of—and in charge of—the Gas House Gang. It was a team that featured such rowdy characters as Pepper Martin, Leo Durocher, Joe Medwick, Rip Collins and, of couse, Dizzy and Paul Dean. They fought hard every game, and even fought among themselves. Along the way, they captured the imagination of a country trying to struggle through the Great Depression. Frisch, who had taken over as manager in the middle of the 1933 season, was able to bring out the best in his wild boys by using a tough approach of his own.

Before the 1934 season started, Frisch laid down the law: "Listen you guys, we're going to win the pennant. I don't mind a bit of horseplay, but I want an honest day's work and beardown baseball from you. If any of you humpty-dumpties don't think we can win, turn in your jock straps now, and [traveling secretary] Clarence Lloyd will get you your train ticket back to the coal mines or farm, or wherever else you can starve these days. Mr. Breadon feeds you buzzards pretty damned good. So, take your choice: Play to win, or get your rear ends out of here and into the bread lines. Now, let's go!"[21]

Durocher noted in his autobiography that "Frisch was rough and tough, and the team took its personality from him. ... We may not have been the best, but there were 25 players on that team who thought we were, and that's half the battle."[22]

Frisch also led by example in 1934. He hit .305 in what was his last big season with the bat.

Everything fell into place for the Cardinals that September as they put on a late charge to overtake the fast-fading Giants and win the pennant by two games. The Gang then beat the Tigers in the World Series four games to three, with the Dean brothers winning two games each. Dizzy Dean, who finished the regular season with a 30–7 record, was named the league's MVP.

"With due respect to the powerful Yankees of the Babe Ruth era, the most colorful, picturesque club of modern baseball was the Gas House Gang of St. Louis," longtime sportswriter Fred Lieb noted in 1944. "The main cogs on the Gas House Gang were frolicsome, exuberant spirits, with boundless energy. They got right down in the dirt and played hard, winning ball."[23]

Branch Rickey, then the Cardinals general manager, added: "It was a high class team, with nine heavy drinkers.... They were the best team I ever had."[24]

After the 1934 triumph, Frisch started to cut down on his playing time and then retired as a player in 1937. He had been in eight World Series with the Giants and Cardinals, compiling stats that rank in the top 10 in such World Series categories as hits, doubles, triples and stolen bases. When he was let go as Cardinals manager near the end of the 1938 season, it marked the end of his 12-year relationship with the ballclub. The Flash was gone, but not forgotten.

Notes

1. Bob Broeg, "Tops in superswaps: Hornsby for Frisch," *Trade Him!*, edited by Jim Enright (Chicago: Follett, 1976).

2. *New York Times*, 23 August 1926.

3. Peter Williams, *When the Giants Were Giants: Bill Terry and the Golden Age of New York Baseball* (Chapel Hill, N.C.: Algonquin, 1994) .

4. *New York Sun*, 23 August 1926.

5. *New York Sun*, 30 August 1926.

6. *New York Sun*, 23 August 1926.

7. Mrs. John J. McGraw, with Arthur Mann, *The Real McGraw* (New York: David McKay, 1953).

8. Rogers Hornsby, with J. Roy Stockton, *My Kind of Baseball* (New York: David McKay, 1953).

9. Eugene Murdock, *Baseball Players and Their Times: Oral Histories of the Game, 1920–1940* (Westport, Conn.: Meckler, 1991).

10. Arthur Mann, *Branch Rickey: American in Action* (Boston: Houghton Mifflin, 1957).

11. Rogers Hornsby, *My Kind of Baseball.*

12. *St. Louis Post-Dispatch*, 22 December 1926.

13. *St. Louis Post-Dispatch*, 21 December 1926.

14. *New York Times*, 22 December 1926.

15. *St. Louis Post-Dispatch*, 24 December 1926.

16. *New York Sun*, 21 December 1926.

17. *New York Times*, 11 January 1928.

18. Rogers Hornsby, *My Kind of Baseball.*

19. Lawrence S. Ritter, *The Glory of Their Times* (New York: William Morrow and Company Inc., 1984).

20. Frederick G. Lieb, *The St. Louis Cardinals* (New York: G.P. Putnam's Sons, 1944).

21. Bob Broeg, *The Pilot Light and the Gas House Gang* (St. Louis: The Bethany Press, 1980).

22. Leo Durocher, with Ed Linn, *Nice Guys Finish Last* (New York: Simon and Schuster, 1975).

23. Frederick G. Lieb, *The St. Louis Cardinals.*

24. Murray Polner, *Branch Rickey* (New York: Athenium, 1982).

A Difference of Opinion

November 28, 1927:
The Pittsburgh Pirates trade
Kiki Cuyler to the Chicago Cubs
for Sparky Adams and Pete Scott

In Pittsburgh, it was called simply The Cuyler Case. It involved a stubborn ballplayer named Hazen "Kiki" Cuyler, a future Hall of Famer who was not willing to accept changes implemented by his manager. And it involved a stubborn manager in Donie Bush, who was willing to bench a star of Cuyler's stature for a good part of the 1927 season and then hold him out of the ensuing World Series as a matter of principle.

It was a bitter dispute that enraged many Pirate fans who didn't understand why one of their favorites was suddenly pulled out of action. Although Cuyler and Bush both eventually told their sides of the story to the newspapers, neither pinpointed exactly how or when their feud actually started. Cuyler himself was known to call it an unsolved mystery. The matter was not settled until November 28, 1927, when the Pirates finally unloaded the 28-year-old Cuyler by trading him to the Chicago Cubs for veteran second baseman Sparky Adams and utility outfielder Pete Scott.

The big winner in the whole affair turned out to be the Cubs, who had Cuyler in the lineup for the following 7½ seasons. He teamed up with such standouts as Hack Wilson, Gabby Hartnett, Riggs Stephenson and Billy Herman to keep the Cubs among the NL's front-runners and help them win pennants in 1929 and 1932. Cuyler batted better than .300 during five of his seasons with the Cubs—including .360 in 1929 and .355 in 1930—and he led the league in stolen bases three times.

The Pirates, on the other hand, always came up short after Cuyler's departure. It is not to say that Cuyler would have made a difference, but the Bucs' best finish during that period was second in 1929, 1932 and 1933—and in two of those years, they trailed only Cuyler's Cubs.

Although there was an aura of secrecy surrounding Cuyler's falling out with the Pittsburgh organization, one thing cannot be denied: Before any problems set in, Cuyler put in three standout seasons with the Pirates.

Cuyler broke into the Pittsburgh lineup in a big way in 1924, batting .354 in his first full season. In 1925 he batted .357 and led the league in triples with 26 and runs scored with 144 as he helped the Pirates win their first pennant since 1909, when Honus Wagner was king of the town. In the 1925 World Series against Washington, Cuyler had the key hit—a bases-loaded double off Walter Johnson in the eighth inning of game seven that gave the Pirates a 9–7 victory and the championship. Cuyler got off to another fast start in 1926, and despite slumping late in the season, he still finished with a .321 average and led the league in runs scored and stolen bases.

Bill McKechnie was the Pirates' manager during those three seasons. When McKechnie was fired after the 1926 season, Donie Bush was brought in by owner Barney Dreyfuss. For Cuyler, things were never the same.

The popular story is that Cuyler got into trouble with Bush for not sliding into second base one afternoon. Well, that is only part of it.

Cuyler and Bush apparently were at odds right out of the box. A newspaper story reported that Cuyler had questioned Bush's managing ability during spring training camp in 1927 and referred to him as a "busher."[1] Neither Cuyler nor Bush publicly acknowledged that tale. But early in the season, Bush told a Pittsburgh reporter that "Cuyler is not my style of ballplayer. He wants to do what he wants to do, not what he is told."[2]

Bush then started to tinker with his lineup, and it directly affected Cuyler. In May, Bush moved Cuyler from his customary number three spot in the lineup to number two. This bothered Cuyler because he didn't think he had the bunting skills usually required of a number two hitter. Cuyler was later dropped down to the number five slot, and then put back at number two at the beginning of August.

Cuyler was also shuffled around on defense. Beginning in late June, he was periodically moved from his regular center field spot because Bush believed newcomer Lloyd Waner was better in that position. Cuyler played some games in right field, and in late July was moved to left. This move was especially annoying for Cuyler because he said the sun bothered his eyes when he played left field in Forbes Field. After a week of starting assignments in left, Cuyler was shifted back to center.

Each time Bush made a change that did not agree with Cuyler, the disenchanted Cuyler told him about the problems it presented. But Bush wasn't about to change his mind, and their relationship began to rapidly deteriorate.

Bush, in an interview many years later, recalled how things started to get ugly:

"One day in early August, in a close game, the opposing club had runners on first and third, with one out. The batter flied to Cuyler. He threw toward the plate, too high for a cutoff, and the runner on first advanced to second. From there he scored on a single. That run beat us.

"When Cuyler came in to the bench, I said to him, 'Won't you ever learn to throw the ball low?'

"He said, 'If you don't like the way I play, get somebody else.'"[3]

The situation came to a head on Saturday, August 6, when the New York Giants beat the Pirates 9–2 in Forbes Field. Cuyler made two base-running errors that helped kill Pirate rallies. The most noteworthy mistake came in the fourth inning, after Cuyler reached on a walk. Paul Waner followed with an infield grounder, and first baseman Bill Terry threw to second to start a double play. The fleet Cuyler went into second base standing up and beat the throw, but then was tagged out when his momentum dragged him off the base. Bush, contending that Cuyler should have slid into second base, fined Cuyler $50 for failing to run the bases properly.

As it turned out, the blunder virtually ended Cuyler's career in Pittsburgh. He played in only a handful of games the rest of the season, mostly as a pinch hitter. The Pirates went on to win the NL pennant by 1½ games over the St. Louis Cardinals, and the offensive stars were the Waner brothers—Paul batted a league-leading .380 and was named NL Most Valuable Player; Lloyd batted .355. Cuyler finished the regular season with a .309 mark, appearing in only 85 of the Pirates' 154 games.

Cuyler's status didn't change during the World Series against the powerhouse New York Yankees led by Babe Ruth and Lou Gehrig. The fans chanted "We want Cuyler" and put up banners to support him, but Cuyler was never called off the bench. The Pirates lost the Series in four straight games, and considering the competition, Cuyler's absence probably was not a factor. It was not until the World Series was under way that Bush finally told his reasons for the benching.

The national wire services reported Bush's comments:

> Cuyler was mumbling to himself and acting dissatisfied early in the season. I never could understand his actions, and apparently he didn't care to understand mine. Then came that incident when he failed to slide into second base and I fined him $50. Naturally, I benched him at the time.
>
> Later, I went to Kiki and told him the incident was closed and that he could return to the game and forget about the past. I told him I wanted him to play left field and bat in second place. He said he couldn't do either, as the positions weren't natural to him.
>
> I told him he'd have to do as I said. I explained to him that Lloyd Waner was too good to be removed from center field and that Paul Waner was hitting so well in third place I couldn't change him. "If that's the way you feel about it, I'd just as soon not play at all," Cuyler replied very sharply. So I told him I'd keep him on the bench until I was ready to put him in the lineup.
>
> With that, this case ended.[4]

The day after the World Series finished, it was Cuyler's turn to give his side of the story as he agreed to a lengthy interview with a sportswriter in New York. "It has been stated often that the Cuyler Case began with my being

A run-in with the manager put an early end to Kiki Cuyler's career in Pittsburgh as the Pirates traded him to the Chicago Cubs in 1927 (George Brace photograph).

fined for not sliding into second base," he began. "It may have begun there, but I think it began a long time before that." Cuyler then discussed his decision not to slide in that ill-fated game in August, claiming it was only an effort to break up the double play: "In my judgment, it was the proper thing to do." Next, he criticized Bush for an incident that supposedly took place shortly after he was fined the $50: "Bush coached me far off third in a game. I protested that it was dangerous, but obeyed. The ball was snapped to third and I was caught. Then Bush berated me for being caught. I said I was willing to take blame for my own lapses, which every player has, but not those of others."

Cuyler went on to talk about the midseason lineup changes that caused such a flap: "I made the mistake of speaking about these things, I realize now. I should have batted second and played left field without saying anything, but I wanted to help and felt I could be of more help in center and batting in any other position than second."[5]

When those comments hit the newspapers, Bush snapped back: "Cuyler's own statement convicts him."[6] Barney Dreyfuss, the Pirates' owner, backed up his manager.

If there was any question about Cuyler's future with the Pirates beforehand, that settled it. The bidding then began for Cuyler, and Dreyfuss reportedly received offers from the Cincinnati Reds, St. Louis Cardinals, Brooklyn Robins, Boston Braves, Philadelphia Phillies and the Cubs.

When the trade was finalized with the Cubs on November 28, the Pirates made the usual upbeat comments about acquiring Sparky Adams. Adams had batted .292 for the Cubs that season, and the Pittsburgh management believed he would solidify the infield and help make up for Cuyler's loss. But Adams, who was 33 at the time of the trade, played only two years with the Pirates before they sold him to the St. Louis Cardinals.

Cuyler, meanwhile, moved to Wrigley Field and gave the Cubs an outfield that stacked up with the best of them. In center was the great Hack Wilson, who led the NL in home runs four times and averaged 141 runs batted in from 1926 to 1930. In left was Riggs Stephenson, who batted at least .319 in 12 of his 14 seasons and retired with a .336 lifetime average. And in right was Cuyler, a line-drive hitter who also had the ability to steal bases.

In 1929, Cuyler, Wilson and Stephenson each collected more than 100 RBIs, one of only three outfield trios to accomplish the feat this century (the others were the 1921 Detroit Tigers and the 1984 Boston Red Sox). That season, Cuyler batted .360 with 102 RBIs and a league-leading 43 stolen bases, as the Cubs won the pennant by 10½ games over the second-place Pirates.

In 1930, Cuyler's .355 season—and everybody else's season for that matter—was overshadowed by Wilson's unforgettable performance. Wilson set a National League record with 56 home runs and a major league mark with an incredible 190 RBIs. Cuyler took advantage of Wilson's hitting to score a career-high 155 runs.

After the 1930 season, Wilson, Cuyler, Gabby Hartnett and Cliff Heathcote gave the fans a special treat by putting on a vaudeville-style show at various Chicago theaters. Actually, it was not such a treat at all. The four were hired to talk about baseball and sing a bit, but they were not really qualified to do the latter. A few years later, Cuyler recalled this story about the act:

"The show people seemed a little shocked when they learned that Heathcote was the only one who could read music or play a ukulele. I eased them up a little by saying I could carry the lead of a quartet if I heard the song several times and had a chance to study the words. Then they turned to Wilson and Hartnett. They admitted that they didn't even mumble 'The Star-Spangled Banner' when caught at community sings.

"There are hundreds of theater-goers and fans in Chicago who think that Gabby Harnett has a rich, deep bass voice and Hack Wilson has a ringing baritone. It hurts me to reveal that during four weeks of our engagement, neither Gabby nor Hack sang a note, just stood there and moved their lips while two professionals, screened behind them, sang with Cliff and me. And even though they didn't have to sing, they said they'd never worked so hard for their money in all their lives."[7]

Cuyler batted .330, .291, .317 and .338 during the next four seasons with the Cubs. But he apparently never was a favorite of manager Charlie Grimm, who took over in 1932. Therefore, it was no surprise when Cuyler was released midway through the 1935 season. Cuyler was 35 at the time, and as Grimm explained, "I decided that Cuyler has outlived his usefulness to us."[8]

Cuyler hung on for three more seasons before retiring with a .321 career average. In 1968, 18 years after his death, Kiki Cuyler was elected to the Hall of Fame by a unanimous vote of the veterans' committee.

As for Donie Bush, he maintained for the rest of his life that he did the right thing by making his stand against Cuyler back in 1927. "I had great respect for Cuyler as a player," Bush said. "His only trouble was his bullheadedness. If he would have apologized to me, I would have put him back in the lineup."[9]

Notes

1. *Chicago Tribune*, 21 September 1932.
2. *Pittsburgh Post-Gazette*, 10 October 1927.
3. Fred Russell, "Why Kiki Cuyler Was Benched," *Baseball Digest* (May 1968).
4. United Press International, 11 October 1927.
5. Associated Press, 9 October 1927.
6. *Pittsburgh Press*, 10 October 1927.
7. *Chicago Tribune*, 2 June 1935.
8. *Chicago Tribune*, 4 July 1935.
9. Russell, "Why Kiki Cuyler Was Benched."

Triple Crown Trade Bait

*November 21, 1933: The Philadelphia Phillies
trade Chuck Klein to the Chicago Cubs
for Ted Kleinhans, Mark Koenig,
Harvey Hendrick and $65,000*

Some players were born to play in a particular ballpark. Babe Ruth and Lou Gehrig were right at home at Yankee Stadium. Mel Ott's swing was tailor-made for the Polo Grounds. In recent times, Ken Griffey, Jr., has been helped along by playing in that bandbox in Seattle known as the Kingdome. And in Philadelphia, the perfect match was Chuck Klein and Baker Bowl.

Klein, a former foundry worker from Indianapolis, had muscles on his muscles which helped him develop into a good hitter with good power. But when Klein played in the Phillies' Baker Bowl, he was a great hitter with great power.

Baker Bowl, now long gone and pretty much forgotten, was one of those old, quirky ballparks built to fit within the restraints of a city block. One of the unique aspects of the park was its abbreviated right field. It was only 280 feet down the first base line and about 320 feet in the right field power alley. A 40-foot-high tin wall and screen was built in right to keep some balls from leaving the park, reminiscent of the Green Monster at Boston's Fenway Park. "There were dents and holes all over the wall," recalled catcher Bob O'Farrell, who spent many an afternoon in Baker Bowl during his 21-year career. "It sounded like a drum beat when a ball hit it. It's true that certain hitters benefited from the short distance to get a lot of home runs."[1]

Klein, who batted from the left side, was one of those hitters. When he joined the Phillies midway through the 1928 season, he immediately set his sights on that inviting tin wall that seemed close enough to spit over. In 64 games that year, he batted .360 and hit 11 home runs.

For the next five seasons, Klein was a regular in the Phillies' outfield and piled up statistics at the plate that made him the National League's top slugger. He batted .356, .386, .337, .348 and .368 and became one of a very select group of players who collected at least 200 base hits in each of their first five full seasons. Even Phillies' owner William Baker's decision to raise the right field wall from 40 feet to 60 feet in 1929 had little effect on Klein. He slammed a league-record 43 homers in 1929 and followed that with totals of 40, 31, 38 and 28. The only time he didn't get at least a share of the league lead in homers during this five-year span was 1930, when Hack Wilson had his memorable season with 56.

Klein was named the NL Most Valuable Player in 1932, and in 1933 he became one of only 12 players this century to win the Triple Crown as he collected 120 runs batted in to go along with his .368 average and 28 homers. Considering all the impressive numbers Klein was putting up, Phillies teammate Dick Bartell described him as "the ultimate in Baker Bowl hitters."[2]

If this were a perfect world, Klein would have been able to spend his entire career playing for the Phillies at cozy Baker Bowl. But it was not to be. On November 21, 1933, he was traded to the Chicago Cubs for three marginal players and a tidy sum of cash. It was a history-making transaction, marking the only time a player has been traded during the off-season after winning the Triple Crown. The trade was also noteworthy for the effect it had on Klein.

As soon as Klein packed in his Phillies uniform, it was like Cinderella's coach turning into a pumpkin. Well, that's somewhat of an exaggeration. But it's true that as far as Klein's career was concerned, things started to go downhill after that day.

"He was supposed to be the great star and all, but he wasn't with the Cubs," said Woody English, a Cubs infielder from 1927 to 1936. "He'd been with the Phillies too long with that short right-field fence there."

Before the trade, the Cubs had been pursuing Klein for several years in hopes of adding some left-handed power to their predominantly righty lineup. The Cubs reportedly offered as much as $250,000 at one time, but the Phillies refused all propositions.

In 1933, though, the Phillies had to reconsider their options as the organization was running into serious financial problems. Attendance was down everywhere due to the Great Depression, and the Phillies drew just 268,914 fans in 1932 and 156,421 in 1933. The situation was very similar to what was happening just a few blocks away, where the Athletics' Connie Mack was also reaching a financial crisis due to a lack of fan support. "Sometimes there were more people on the field than in the stands," noted the Phillies' Dick Bartell.[3]

In desperate need for money, the Phillies appeared ready to sell Klein to the Cubs in May 1933. That deal fell through, only to be revived at the end of the season. There were rumors as early as September that Klein had already been dealt to the Cubs, but official word did not come until November that Klein was heading west.

In return for Klein, the Phillies received minor league pitcher Ted Klein-hans, utility players Mark Koenig and Harvey Hendrick, plus $65,000. The three players never amounted to anything with the Phillies, but the money sure came in handy. Besides the financial situation, there was another reason the Phillies were willing to part with their hitting star: In Klein's six seasons with the ballclub, the Phillies had only one winning season and never finished higher than fourth.

As noted in the *Philadelphia Inquirer* the day after the trade, "Klein without doubt is the greatest ballplayer in the National League. Yet, the all-powerful fact remains that the Phillies with Klein did not draw cash customers through the gate and did not finish anywhere in the National League race. A baseball fan, despite all his talk, will come to the ballpark only to see a winner. Klein, notwithstanding his individual prowess, did not possess the 'color' to pull them through the turnstyles."[4]

In Chicago, the fans did not care that Klein lacked "color." All they knew was that he averaged 36 home runs a season, had a .359 career batting average up to that point, and was coming off a Triple Crown season. And he was only 29 years old.

As one Chicago reporter wrote, "Before he gets through, his fans predict he'll chase Hans Wagner, Rogers Hornsby and several other of the greatest greats right out of the record books."[5]

The Cubs management also had high hopes that Klein would join such standouts as Gabby Harnett, Billy Herman, Charlie Grimm and Kiki Cuyler to get the ballclub back on top. The Cubs had won the pennant in 1932, but they were swept by the Yankees in the World Series. The excitement seemed to be missing in 1933 as they slipped to third place, and that is why they made such a determined effort to get Klein. Before the Cubs and their fans started whooping it up, however, they should have taken a close look at Klein's statistics. Raymond J. Kumpf did.

Kumpf was a baseball fan from Colorado Springs, but he was more than just a casual observer. He followed Klein's every action with the Phillies, and the figures he compiled were quite revealing.

As indicated by Kumpf's calculations, which were authenticated and printed in the *Inquirer* two days after the trade, Klein was a sensation at Baker Bowl and an average player away from it. In 1933, for example, Klein batted .467 at home and just .280 on the road. In 1932, he hit .411 at home and .267 on the road. And of the 66 home runs he hit in those two seasons, only 17 were hit away from Philadelphia.

This is how Klein fared in 1932 and 1933 at the eight National League ballparks:

City	1932	1933
Philadelphia	.411	.467
St. Louis	.391	.378
Chicago	.227	.341
Brooklyn	.316	.311
Pittsburgh	.277	.289
Cincinnati	.156	.260
Boston	.250	.239
New York	.256	.152
Total	.348	.368

When word reached Chicago of those Jekyll-and-Hyde tendencies, local sportswriters tried to downplay the figures. But sure enough, Klein never did get comfortable playing with the Cubs or in Wrigley Field. There was the new stadium, of course, plus the new teammates. But the biggest change was the new kind of pressure he faced. Klein came from a ballclub which never contended for anything, and all of a sudden he was a key figure on a team with great expectations.

Even Klein admitted that nobody had ever paid much attention to whether or not he hit with the Phillies, and that it was a different story with the Cubs. "Here, they watch you on every pitch," he said.[6]

After Klein got off to a fast start in 1934—he was batting .347 with 12 home runs in mid–May—he started his nosedive. By midseason, when he was selected to play in the All-Star Game, his average was down to .318. Then came the nagging charley horses which periodically kept him out of the lineup. He also started having trouble hitting against lefties, something which never happened during his days with the Phillies. If that was not bad enough, he had a difficult time adjusting defensively to his new home field. With all the problems, Klein played in only 115 games in 1934, batting .301 with 20 home runs. Those are pretty fair numbers, but certainly not up to his old standards. The Cubs, by the way, ended up third again.

The following season things were no better. Still plagued by charley horses and a less-than-thunderous bat, Klein started as the regular right fielder and finished the season on the bench. During September, when the Cubs were in a heated pennant race with the Cardinals, Klein was not a factor. He lost his starting assignment after an 0-for-18 slump and did not even play in 18 of the 21 straight victories that wrapped up the NL championship.

Although Klein salvaged some pride by hitting a home run against the Tigers in the World Series, the Cubs were beaten four games to two. It was a disappointing finish to another disappointing season for Klein, who ended up with a .293 average and 21 homers. Again, decent numbers for anyone but Chuck Klein.

Chuck Klein won the Triple Crown in 1933, but his career went straight downhill when the Philadelphia Phillies traded him to the Chicago Cubs (George Brace photograph).

During those two seasons with the Cubs, Woody English says Klein never talked much about the good old days in Philadelphia. "But sometimes we wished he had stayed there," English added with a chuckle. "He didn't help us one bit."

The Cubs management must have been equally unimpressed with Klein, because he was traded back to the Phillies early in the 1936 season. At the time, the Cubs were interested in acquiring pitcher Curt Davis, and Phillies president Gerry Nugent said he would agree to a deal only if Klein were to be included.

The Cubs quickly gave the o.k. and on May 21 sent Klein and pitcher Fabian Kowalik to Philadelphia for Davis and outfielder Ethan Allen. The Cubs reportedly also included $50,000 cash, meaning they paid to acquire Klein and then paid again when they got rid of him. When informed of the trade, Klein said hopefully, "I feel I will take up where I left off as a Philly."[7]

The return to Philadelphia did seem to give Klein a second wind, and he had the greatest game of his career on July 10, 1936, when he hit four home runs in a game against Pittsburgh. Interestingly enough, the show of power came in Forbes Field instead of Baker Bowl.

However, Klein was on his way down by then. He was 31 years old and his after-hours habits—he had a reputation for being a serious drinker—began to take their toll. He finished the 1936 season with a .306 average and 25 home runs, and then had one more decent year with a .325 average and 15 homers in 1937. He hung on for several more seasons, and was used mostly as a pinch hitter during the war years.

It was a fitting coincidence that as Klein was winding down, so was Baker Bowl. In June 1938, the Phillies left the old ballpark for good.

Notes

1. Eugene Murdock, *Baseball Players and Their Times: Oral Histories of the Game, 1920–1940* (Westport, Conn.: Meckler, 1991).

2. Dick Bartell, with Norman L. Macht, *Rowdy Richard* (Berkeley, Calif.: North Atlantic Books, 1987).

3. Ibid.

4. *Philadelphia Inquirer*, 22 November 1933.

5. *Chicago Tribune*, 25 November 1933.

6. Warren Brown, *Chicago Cubs* (New York: G.P. Putnam's Sons, 1946).

7. *Philadelphia Inquirer*, 23 May 1936.

Score One for Mr. Rickey

*December 8, 1947: The Pittsburgh Pirates
trade Billy Cox, Preacher Roe and Gene Mauch
to the Brooklyn Dodgers for Dixie Walker,
Vic Lombardi and Hal Gregg*

It started out looking like a real clunker of a trade for Branch Rickey and the Brooklyn Dodgers. They were just coming off their pennant-winning season of 1947, and Rickey was trying to tinker with his roster to get ready for another title run in 1948. When the legendary general manager found the players he wanted and made the deal, it did not exactly excite the folks in Brooklyn. "What was Rickey getting? An infielder who had been shook real bad during the war and a skinny pitcher with a busted head," asked Elwin "Preacher" Roe, and was not exaggerating. After all, he was the guy with the busted head. And the shook-up infielder was Billy Cox.[1]

When Roe and Cox arrived in Brooklyn for the 1948 season, they might have seemed like a damaged set of china. But the two roommates ended up fitting in exactly where Rickey needed them most. During their seven seasons with the Dodgers, they teamed up with such standouts as Pee Wee Reese, Jackie Robinson, Duke Snider, Roy Campanella, Gil Hodges, Don Newcombe and Carl Furillo to form a powerhouse ballclub that won three pennants and barely missed out on two more. Considering the way things turned out, the transaction that netted Roe and Cox is generally regarded as one of Rickey's greatest trades. And that says quite a bit.

As far as Rickey was concerned, the key player in the whole affair was Cox. The Dodgers finished first in 1947 with rookie Spider Jorgensen at third base, and Rickey was looking to upgrade his lineup at that position.

Cox had been the Pirates' shortstop since he got out of the service and joined the club in 1946. He batted .290 and .274 in his two full seasons in Pittsburgh, but his defense was disappointing and he never really caught on with the Bucs. Cox was quiet and moody to begin with, and he apparently had had some tough experiences in the war which did not help matters. As one Pittsburgh sportswriter noted, Cox "failed to live up to expectations."[2]

Still, Rickey saw something special in Cox. "He was the player we were really after, way back toward the close of the 1946 season," Rickey acknowledged.[3]

By autumn of 1947, Rickey knew that if he wanted to finally get his hands on Cox, he would have to give up a pitcher or two. The Pirates' pitching was a disaster in 1947, when the ballclub finished in last place and had the worst team earned run average in the majors.

The Pirates were interested in two young Dodger pitchers who had done fairly well in limited roles: 25-year-old lefty Vic Lombardi, who was 35–32 between 1945 and 1947, and 26-year-old righty Hal Gregg, who was 28–22 over the same period. To get them, Pirates president Frank McKinney finally agreed to give up Cox.

When the trade was completed on December 8, 1947, it was also announced that the Pirates would receive 37-year-old Dixie Walker, the popular Dodger outfielder known as "The People's Cherce." Although Walker was a lifetime .306 hitter, it was no surprise that he was leaving Brooklyn because he had earlier requested a trade when the Dodgers broke the major league color barrier by bringing up Jackie Robinson. There had been rumors that Walker was going to Pittsburgh as much as six months beforehand.

In return for the three players, the Dodgers received the enigmatic Cox plus two other players: left-handed pitcher Preacher Roe and little-used infielder Gene Mauch. Considering Roe was almost 33 years old and had compiled a 34–47 record in his four seasons with the club, the Pittsburgh sportswriters did not think their Pirates had given up too much to acquire two potential frontline pitchers. "I believe they got the better of it in the trade," wrote *Pittsburgh Post-Gazette* sports editor Al Abrams.[4]

As Abrams and the Pirates ultimately found out, they did not get the better of it. In fact, few teams ever got the better of it when dealing with the crafty Rickey, who seemed to have a sixth sense when it came to baseball matters.

Lombardi pitched well for Pittsburgh in 1948 and finished 10–9, but he won only five more games over the next two seasons and that was the end of his major league career. Gregg also stayed with the Pirates for three seasons and contributed just three wins. Walker was the most productive performer of the three, batting .316 as the regular right fielder in 1948 and .282 as a part-timer in 1949. That is more than the Pirates could have expected, because they knew Walker was near the end of the line when they got him. When Walker retired after the 1949 season at age 39, he left a Pirate team that was destined to stay in last place through much of the early 1950s.

In Brooklyn, meanwhile, Rickey's trade started paying off that first season as Cox and Roe stepped right in. Cox moved into the starting lineup in 1948 when incumbent third baseman Jorgensen hurt his arm. Cox still was not impressing anyone, but the Dodgers quite honestly had nobody better.

In 1949, however, Cox finally put his game together like the Pirates

After struggling with the Pittsburgh Pirates, Elwin "Preacher" Roe suddenly turned into a big winner when he was traded to the Brooklyn Dodgers in 1947 (George Brace photograph).

management had expected years before. At the age of 29, he blossomed into one of the game's top-fielding third basemen.

Cox held down the regular third base spot through the 1953 season, adding the perfect touch to what has to be considered one of baseball's greatest infields. At first was Gil Hodges, the quiet slugger who showed little emotion but ended up hitting 370 home runs. At second was the multitalented Jackie Robinson, who put up with seemingly unbearable racial insults to carve out a Hall of Fame career. At shortstop was Pee Wee Reese, the unchallenged team leader whose all-around excellence earned him a spot in the Hall of Fame as well. And at third was Cox, who was regarded as baseball's slickest-fielding third baseman until Brooks Robinson came along.

Cox never hit for a real high average (his career-high was .291 in 1953), but he did contribute his share of clutch hits and managed a .302 batting average in his three World Series. Still, the reason he was in the lineup was his glove, and he led the league's third basemen in fielding in 1950 and 1952. As author Roger Kahn noted, Cox's fielding once caused Yankee manager Casey Stengel to grumble, "That ain't a third baseman. That's a fucking acrobat."[5]

Although Cox turned out to be quite a success in Brooklyn, the story involving Preacher Roe was even more remarkable. Roe, a string bean of a pitcher who stood 6 feet 2 inches and weighed only 170 pounds, had made his major league debut a decade earlier and was still waiting to make it big when he came to the Dodgers. Roe pitched in just one game in 1938 after Branch Rickey's brother Frank originally signed him with the Cardinals. He then spent the next five seasons in the minors. He made it back to the big leagues with the Pirates in 1944 and had his best season in 1945, when he was 14–13 and led the league in strikeouts.

The following winter, he got into a fight while coaching a high school basketball game and ended up with a fractured skull. Although he pitched regularly for the Pirates for the next two seasons, he had to fight off dizzy spells as well as opposing batters. Victories were few and far between as he posted records of 3–8 and 4–15.

"Why, sometimes I couldn't even see the batter up there at the plate," Roe recalled in a 1951 article in the *Saturday Evening Post*. "And most of the time I couldn't catch the catcher's signals."[6]

When Roe was picked up by the Dodgers, things changed dramatically. To begin with, he had recently paid a visit to the Mayo Clinic and was in a good frame of mind. And secondly, he was about to alter his style of pitching.

Early in his career, Roe had been a fire-ballin' fastball pitcher. But in Pittsburgh, he began to slow things down and rely more on control. When he started toiling for the Dodgers, he added one final pitch to his repertoire: the illegal spitter.

In a controversial 1955 *Sports Illustrated* article, published after his retirement, Roe talked about his reasons for using the wet one:

"I was about through when I decided to get me the pitch. 'If I get caught,' I told myself, 'they'll kick me out. If I don't, I'm through anyway, so how can I lose?' Some people say Mr. Rickey made the deal [with Pittsburgh] with a gun because it turned out so lopsided. But I think even Mr. Rickey doesn't know that it wouldn't have been such a good deal if I hadn't decided that winter to use my spitter.

"I threw spitballs the whole time I was with the Dodgers. Seven years in all…. My spitter was my 'money pitch.'"[7]

Perhaps the spitter was the big difference. Or perhaps it was just Roe's time to finally grab the spotlight. Whatever the reason, Preacher certainly broke in with the Dodgers in a big way in 1948. After being used sparingly at first, he notched two straight complete game victories in late May to get rolling. He finished the season 12–8 and led the staff with a 2.63 ERA. At an age when many pitchers are thinking about hanging up their spikes, Roe was just getting warmed up.

In 1949, Roe finished 15–6 and led the league in winning percentage. Next up was a 19–11 season in 1950, and then a spectacular 22–3 mark in 1951. He followed that with 11–2 and 11–3 seasons. During those glory years, between 1949 and 1953, Roe was the most consistent winner on a formidable staff that included standouts Don Newcombe and Carl Erskine. To show how far he had come from his dog days in Pittsburgh, Roe was named to the All-Star team for four straight years beginning in 1949.

Roe also played a big role in helping the Dodgers win pennants in 1949, 1952 and 1953, and perhaps his greatest single-game performance came in the 1949 World Series. In game two against the Yankees, Preacher pitched a six-hitter and won 1–0 despite playing in considerable pain after suffering a broken finger on his glove hand, the result of fielding a hot smash in the fourth inning. He labored through 136 pitches and allowed only one baserunner to get as far as third base.

"To tell you the truth, my right index finger gave me almost as much trouble as the Yankees," Roe said after the game. "My finger started to hurt so badly that the trainer had to drill a hole through my nail to let the blood flow out."[8]

After that performance, a joyous Branch Rickey sought out Roe as he emerged from the shower and gave him a dripping-wet hug. "That boy is an artist—a supreme artist," Rickey gushed.[9]

In Roe's three World Series, he compiled a 2–1 record with a 2.54 ERA. Each of those World Series, incidentally, finished with the Dodgers losing to the all-conquering Yankees.

During Roe's rise to stardom, he also became known for being one of the biggest characters on the Dodgers' roster. Making the most of his country charm, the chatty Arkansas native entertained everyone in the clubhouse with an endless array of stories about baseball, his family and life in general. Some of the stories, quite naturally, stretched the truth a bit. He also gained a small measure of fame when he refused to fly in airplanes after a couple of bad incidents in 1948.

"People may remember Preacher more for his colorful personality than his exceptional pitching skills," Duke Snider noted in his autobiography. [10]

Unfortunately for Roe, his two winningest seasons ended up in major disappointments for the Dodgers. In 1950, Brooklyn put on a late rush in September and went into the final game of the season needing a victory over the first place Phillies to force a playoff. The Philadelphia Whiz Kids won that one 4–1 in 10 innings on Dick Sisler's three-run home run.

Roe was just about unbeatable in 1951 and his record was 15–2 in mid–August when Brooklyn held a commanding 13-game lead. That is when the Giants started to get hot. Heading into the final week of the season, the lead was down to three games and Roe was sitting at 22–2 with a 10-game winning streak.

Things really went sour for Brooklyn during the final few days of September. Even Roe suffered one of his rare losses on September 27 when the Boston Braves beat the Dodgers 4–3 on a disputed run. The following day, the Dodgers lost another game and the Giants finally pulled even in the standings. Then, in the final game of the season on September 30, Roe was knocked out after just two innings and Newcombe had to come to the rescue in relief as the Dodgers scrambled to beat the Phillies 9–8 in 14 innings. Roe had missed 10 days in August with arm problems, and now his arm was bothering him again. Of greater importance, the Dodgers and Giants finished in a tie for first place to force a three game playoff to determine the National League champion.

The teams split the first two games, setting up perhaps the most electrifying moment in baseball history. When Bobby Thomson's ninth inning, three-run homer gave the Giants an improbable 5–4 victory in game three, the Dodgers were left shattered in their clubhouse.

"Outside, it was bedlam," recalled the Dodgers' Carl Erskine. "But inside our clubhouse, it was like a tomb."[11]

Roe, despite his magnificent season, did not get a chance to pitch in the playoffs. He watched the action from the bullpen, waiting for his sore arm to come around.

Roe went on to pitch through the 1954 season, when he finally tailed off with a 3–4 record and appeared in just 15 games. When he retired after that season at age 39, he had compiled a 93–37 mark in seven seasons with the Dodgers. Besides giving credit to his spitter for his impressive stretch run in Brooklyn, he also seemed to take special delight in the fact that he was able to outsmart hitters rather than overpower them.

"A fellow like that can go on winning for 20 years," he said in 1951. "It'll be that long before someone catches on that he isn't pitching with his arm anymore, but only with his brain."[12]

Interestingly enough, Branch Rickey did not stick around Brooklyn long enough to reap all the benefits from his acquisition of Cox and Roe. Rickey left the Dodgers after the 1950 season and took over as GM of the Pirates. It was quite a change. While the team he assembled back in Brooklyn battled for one pennant after another, Rickey spent five years in Pittsburgh trying to get his new team out of the cellar.

And where did Walker really fit into the trade? The popular Dodger outfielder known as "The People's Cherce" was apparently involved in the deal in name only.

According to Arthur Mann, who was an aide to Branch Rickey and later wrote a biography about him, Walker actually went to the Pirates on waivers before the trade was even made. And he cost the Pittsburgh ballclub only $1. Walker's name was later included in the Pirate-Dodger trade, Mann explained, so Rickey would not have to tell the public that one of their favorites was "traded for a dollar."

The Walker deal culminated a nine-month ordeal that started in spring training of 1947 when it became obvious that the Dodgers were about to put Jackie Robinson on the roster. A number of Brooklyn players—mostly Southerners like Walker, who was from Alabama—reportedly made it known they did not want to play alongside black players. Walker even sent a letter to Rickey on March 26 stating that "a change of ballclubs would benefit both the Brooklyn Baseball Club and myself. Therefore I would like to be traded as soon as a deal can be arranged."[13]

Rickey understood Walker's personal dilemma and tried to trade Walker to the Pirates in June, but the deal fell through at the last moment. Walker went on to bat .306 and help the Dodgers win the National League pennant.

Walker also seemed to accept—at least to some degree—the idea of playing with Robinson. During the season, Walker even asked if Rickey would return the letter in which he requested a trade. Walker later spoke glowingly of Robinson after he won the NL Rookie of the Year award.

After the season, Rickey offered the 37-year-old Walker the manager's job for the Dodgers' minor league team in St. Paul. When Walker declined the offer, saying he preferred to continue as an active player where he could make more money, Rickey said he would arrange a trade with Pittsburgh.

According to Mann, Rickey then set up the token $1 waiver arrangement with Pittsburgh. This enabled the Pirates to take the money they normally would have used to acquire Walker and add it to his contract. So, in the end, Walker made the kind of money he was hoping for in 1948 and 1949.

When it was announced that Walker was on his way out of Brooklyn, it ended a special 8½-year relationship between the player and his fans. He batted at least .300 seven times with the Dodgers, including a league-leading .357 in 1944. Throughout these years, Dodger fans whooped it up for Walker more than for any other player.

When "The People's Cherce" exited Brooklyn, *New York Times* columnist Arthur Daley wrote: "The bland Mr. Walker has been a baseball phenomenon, the most idolized player of his generation. ... Things just won't be the same at Ebbets Field any more."[14]

Notes

1. Peter Golenbock, *Bums: An oral history of the Brooklyn Dodgers* (New York: G.P. Putnam's Sons, 1984).

2. *Pittsburgh Post-Gazette*, 10 December 1947.

3. *Chicago Tribune/wire service report*, 11 April 1948.

4. *Pittsburgh Post-Gazette*, 10 December 1947.

5. Roger Kahn, *The Boys of Summer* (New York: Harper & Row, 1971).

6. Harold Rosenthal, "The Dodgers' Oddest Star," *The Saturday Evening Post* (February 3, 1951).

7. Dick Young, "The Outlawed Spitball Was My Money Pitch," *Sports Illustrated* (July 4, 1955).

8. *New York Times*, 7 October 1949.

9. Ibid.

10. Duke Snider, with Bill Gilbert, *The Duke of Flatbush* (New York: Kensington, 1988).

11. Peter Golenbock, *Bums*.

12. Rosenthal, "The Dodgers' Oddest Star."

13. Arthur Mann, *Branch Rickey: American in Action* (Boston: Houghton Mifflin, 1957).

14. *New York Times*, 10 December 1947.

Home Run King Is Exiled

*June 4, 1953: The Pittsburgh Pirates
trade Ralph Kiner, Joe Garagiola,
Howie Pollet and Catfish Metkovich
to the Chicago Cubs for Preston Ward,
Bob Schultz, Toby Atwell, Gene Hermanski,
Bob Addis, George Freese and $150,000*

When the Pittsburgh Pirates and Chicago Cubs came out for pregame warmups on June 4, 1953, nobody suspected it would be anything more than just a lazy, midseason contest between two of the National League's weaker teams. But it was just the beginning of an afternoon that baseball fans in Pittsburgh will likely never forget.

After loosening up, the players took batting practice as usual. Ralph Kiner, the Pirates' slugger and future Hall of Famer, hit a couple over the left field wall in typical fashion. Everyone then headed for the clubhouse in Forbes Field. That's when the news broke: A whopping 10-player trade had been worked out as Kiner and three teammates were going to the Cubs for six players and $150,000. As Kiner recalled, "The clubhouses were right next to each other at Forbes Field, so I just went into the other clubhouse and put on a Cubs uniform."

"We were shocked the way the trade was done," said Pirates pitcher Bob Friend. "Everybody traded uniforms. It was really unique. The way the thing was done was unheard of."

If the players were shocked, the fans in attendance were absolutely thunderstruck. Although there had been rumors for some time that Kiner was on the trading block, nobody quite expected it to happen like this. Here was their hero, Kiner, leaving the field as a Pirate and emerging minutes later as a Cub.

"There was a lot of booing and stuff," Friend added. "Obviously, the fans didn't like it."

It was probably the most unpopular trade in Pirates history, and for good reason. Kiner was more than just the team's hitting star. He was a crowd-pleasing home run champion. He was the reason fans came to the ballpark in record numbers. He was the Pittsburgh Pirates.

Before that afternoon when he switched uniforms and allegiances, Kiner spent 7½ seasons with the Pirates. After leaving the military, he became the Pirates' regular left fielder in 1946 and had an eye-opening rookie season with 23 home runs. He was 23 years old, and it was the first of seven straight seasons in which he would win or share the National League home run title.

His first monster season was 1947, when he batted a career-high .313 and connected for 51 home runs to tie the Giants' Johnny Mize for the league lead. They were the first NL players since Hack Wilson in 1930 to hit more than 50 home runs.

Over the next five seasons, Kiner piled up home run totals of 40, 54, 47, 42 and 37. He was the first National League player to hit 50 home runs more than once, and one of a handful of players to hit more than 100 home runs in his first three seasons. Every year, in fact, the question was raised whether Kiner would match Babe Ruth's magic number of 60 home runs.

In addition to his talent for hitting the long ball, Kiner batted over .300 three times and played just about every game of every season. And although he was slow afoot, he nonetheless did an adequate job patrolling whatever ground he could in left field.

Kiner's home run production was no doubt aided a bit by playing his home games in Forbes Field, where a wire fence had been installed in 1947 that shortened the home run distance in left field by some 30 feet down the line. The fence was put in to make the ballpark more of a home run haven for veteran slugger Hank Greenberg, who had come over from the Tigers and finished his career with the Pirates in 1947. The extra space behind the barrier was used to accommodate the bullpens and was immediately dubbed Greenberg Gardens.

Although Kiner did have the advantage of the so-called Greenberg Gardens, this did not diminish the fact that he was one of baseball's most feared hitters of his era.

"The way we played against him, we got everybody on the left-hand side of the field," said Cubs third baseman Randy Jackson. "And he could still hit the ball between us. Even if we were 10 feet apart, he could hit it between us. Playing third, I didn't like to see him come up because he hit the ball so darn hard."

While opponents feared Kiner, the fans in Pittsburgh came to idolize him. In 1947, the Pirates attracted a million fans for the first time in franchise history. They drew more than 1 million in each of the next three seasons, including a high of 1,517,021 in 1948. Considering the Pirates never finished higher than fourth place during Kiner's stay, it is obvious why the fans showed up in record numbers.

"I packed 'em in, there was no doubt about that," Kiner said. "And I made that organization a lot of money."

Still, Kiner was destined to finish his career elsewhere. The reason was

Branch Rickey, who became the Pirates' general manager after the 1950 season.

The legendary Rickey had already had his glory years in St. Louis, where he transformed the Cardinals into a powerhouse that won five pennants between 1926 and 1934. He had already had his glory years in Brooklyn, where he helped build a dynasty that would rule the National League in the late 1940s and early 1950s. Along the way, he had invented the minor-league farm system, started the practice of holding huge tryout camps to uncover fresh talent, and finally broken baseball's long-standing color barrier.

Rickey had molded his teams into winners by scouting young prospects, making shrewd trades and sometimes dealing veteran ballplayers with high salaries. His well-known philosophy was that it is better to trade a player one year too early than one year too late.

By the time Rickey arrived in Pittsburgh, he had done it all. Now he was making the last significant stop of his storied career, and he was determined to turn around the Pirates' fortunes.

Rickey figured there was only one way to do it: Get money to bring in some young prospects. And that brings us back to Kiner, who was the team's only marketable player and was being paid quite handsomely by a ballclub that was consistently finishing in the second division.

"I admired Rickey; he was a brilliant man," Kiner said. "But the guy was so mercenary. He believed that nobody should be making any money … that's one of the faults he had. And I was making a lot of money.

"His whole philosophy was to get a lot of ballplayers, and maybe one of them would be good. That's the way he operated. So I knew I was going to be gone in a matter of time."

Soon after taking the Pirates job, Rickey reportedly started a campaign to convince team president John Galbreath that Kiner was not the kind of player who could help win a championship. Rickey even sent Galbreath a letter in spring training of 1952 listing 20 reasons why Kiner should be traded. "He is one of the nicest boys I ever met," Rickey noted, "but Ralph satisfies my requirements in only one respect—as a home run hitter. To me that isn't enough."[1]

When the Pirates finished seventh in 1951 and then dropped to eighth in 1952—with a 42–112 record!—attendance plummeted to less than 700,000. That's when Galbreath announced that the ballclub would consider all offers for Kiner, and Rickey started preparing to get rid of his high-priced slugger.

The Cubs wasted no time jumping into the bidding for Kiner, offering a reported $200,000 in January 1953. Rickey did not bite because he was not interested in just cash—he wanted some players. Soon the Cincinnati Reds and Boston Braves were also involved in trade discussions. However, nothing could be hammered out between Rickey and the interested clubs.

Things then got real interesting when Kiner and Rickey went head-to-head in a much-publicized spring training dispute. It started when Rickey flew out to California in February to talk to Kiner about a new contract. Kiner had made $90,000 in 1952—reported to be the highest salary in the National League—and Rickey wanted to reduce his pay by the maximum-allowed 25 percent.

Here is Kiner's account of what followed:

> We met at Gilmore Stadium, which is a minor-league ballpark for the Pacific Coast League where the Hollywood Stars play. When we finally did agree to terms [including the pay cut], he agreed to allow me to miss the first two weeks of spring training in Cuba. I was living in Palm Springs and I didn't really look forward to going to Cuba, with the amount of time we were going to have down there. I told him I'd get in shape in Palm Springs and be there for the first exhibition game.
>
> He agreed to that, and he went back to Pittsburgh. Then he reneged on the deal that he had made with me verbally. He sent me a wire that said the deal was off. And I wired him back and said if that's the case, then I'm not going to show up.

The two then kept in touch through the mail as Kiner stayed at home in Palm Springs and Rickey went to Havana with the ballclub. During this period, Rickey complained openly that negotiations were going poorly because Kiner wanted his contract to include special privileges. According to Rickey, Kiner wanted to sit out some exhibition games and he wanted assurances that Greenberg Gardens would remain intact as long as he stayed with the Pirates.

"He told a whole bunch of lies," Kiner says. "Those things were never discussed. He made it look like I was the one causing all the problems."

As Kiner also recalled, he was given Rickey's famous ultimatum: "We finished last with you, and we can finish last without you."

About a month after the sparring began, Kiner ended the holdout and signed his contract. According to Kiner, the terms of the contract were the same as those he had verbally accepted in that original meeting in California. He then showed up in Havana after missing two weeks of spring training.

Once the season started, the trade rumors continued to swirl as Cubs personnel chief Wid Matthews kept coming back to Rickey with new offers for Kiner. The Cubs were in last place and it was believed that they wanted to add a gate attraction such as Kiner to make the fans in Chicago forget the team's problems. The Cubs were also hoping Kiner would take some of the burden off outfielder Hank Sauer, who had won the 1952 Most Valuable Player award after leading the majors with 121 runs batted in and tying Kiner for the major league home run title with 37.

"With Ralph, they thought they'd have somebody to back me up or me back him up," Sauer said. "We had problems with the people who hit behind me, so pitchers would walk me or make me swing at bad pitches. When you have sombody to back you up, they're going to pitch more to you."

So Matthews and Rickey kept talking. Finally, on June 4, just about an hour before game time, the details were finalized on the 10-player deal.

Kiner's wife, Nancy, was caught off-guard by the timing of the trade. "She came to the ballpark after the game had started," Kiner said, "and she couldn't understand why I was in a Cub uniform."

Nancy Kiner was not the only fan taken by surprise. Roy McHugh, a sportswriter with the *Pittsburgh Press* at the time, tells this story about a co-worker: "He was driving to work and had the game tuned to the radio, and he heard the announcer talk about Ralph Kiner being at bat for the Cubs. He said he thought Rosey Rowswell, the announcer, must be drunk or had lost his mind."

The Pirates beat the Cubs that afternoon 6–1, and Kiner had a double in four at-bats for his new ballclub. But the action on the field was almost like an afterthought.

The following day, Pittsburgh columnist Al Abrams tried to assess the trade: "On paper, it would appear the Cubs' Matthews outsmarted Rickey. … The trade would rate as the most daring gamble in Rickey's long, and prior to his arrival in Pittsburgh, illustrious career. Upon it will rest part of the future of the Pirates and his own."[2]

Another local columnist, Jack Hernon, wrote: "It is like losing a close friend to see Mr. Slug move out of town."[3]

Considering the number of players involved, it is remarkable that in the end, the trade made no significant impact on either club. On the day of the deal, the Pirates were in sixth place and the Cubs were in eighth. They would remain also-rans for seasons to come.

Here are the players who went from the Cubs to the Pirates:

• Preston Ward. The first baseman/outfielder was the key acquisition for the Bucs. As the Cubs' Matthews said to reporters, "I'm bleeding at every pore. I did not want to part with Ward."[4] Ward's big chance with the Pirates came in 1954 and he hit .269. But his average dropped to .212 in 1955 and he was traded early in 1956 to Cleveland for journeyman catcher Hank Foiles. The once-promising Ward finished with a .253 career average, playing for five teams in nine years.

• Bob Schultz. The little-used left-handed pitcher was 0–2 with the Pirates in 1953 and was then sold to Detroit.

• Toby Atwell. He shared catching duties in 1954 (when he batted .289) and 1955, but was released during the 1956 season.

• Gene Hermanski. The veteran outfielder was at the end of a nine-year career and played only part-time for the Pirates in 1953, batting .177.

• Bob Addis. The backup outfielder played in only four games for the Pirates in 1953, and that closed out his major league career.

• George Freese. The infielder was pretty much a career minor-leaguer who played a bit for the Pirates in 1955 and batted .257.

Here are the players who went from the Pirates to the Cubs:

• Joe Garagiola. The catcher lasted 1½ seasons with the Cubs and was then sold to the Giants in September 1954. He was a lifetime .257 hitter who gained a lot more fame as a television broadcaster after his baseball career ended.

• Howie Pollet. The left-handed starting pitcher stayed with the Cubs through 1955 and was 17–19 in 2½ seasons. He was then released.

• Catfish Metkovich. The reserve outfielder batted .234 in 61 games with the Cubs in 1953. He was then sold to Milwaukee.

And then there is Kiner, who the Cubs were hoping would team up with Sauer to form a one-two punch second to none. Kiner did add considerable power to the Cubs' lineup in 1953, batting .283 with 28 home runs in his 117 games with Chicago. Overall, he finished the season with 35 homers, but his home run title streak was snapped by the Braves' Eddie Mathews, who hit 47.

As far as forming that dynamic duo with Sauer, it never materialized. Sauer was sidelined for a good deal of the 1953 season with three separate hand fractures and managed only 19 home runs, the first time he hit fewer than 30 since he became a regular in 1948. Sauer was healthy again in 1954 and rebounded with 41 homers, but this time Kiner tailed off and finished with just 22. And defensively, with the slow-footed Kiner in left field and the equally slow-footed Sauer in right, it was not exactly a match made in heaven.

"We had Kiner, [Frankie] Baumholtz and Sauer in the outfield, and that was 'ball drop in time'," the Cubs' Randy Jackson remembered with a laugh. "The ball would drop in consistently out there 'cause nobody covered any ground. I think Baumholtz got old in one year playing between those guys."

Despite the addition of Kiner, the Cubs finished the 1953 season in seventh place with a 65–89 record. They were seventh again in 1954, with a nearly-identical 64–90 mark. The only NL team with a worse record each season was the Pirates.

As far as the Pirates were concerned, perhaps the best thing that came out of the Kiner trade in 1953 was that it gave them a chance to look at a promising young player named Frank Thomas. He replaced Kiner in left field and finished with 30 home runs and 102 RBIs to get rolling on a distinguished, 16-year major league career. "It was a blessing in disguise for me," Thomas said about the trade.

Kiner, meanwhile, lasted only 1½ seasons with the Cubs. Believing that the big slugger was not the answer to their woes after all, the Cubs traded him to the Cleveland Indians in November 1954. In return, the Cubs got pitcher Sam Jones, reserve outfielder Gale Wade, plus some cash to make up for the original trade.

Like a meteor, Kiner's career then flamed out in 1955 when his bad legs and bad back made it too difficult to perform every day. He played in a career-low

113 games and hit a career-low 18 home runs. He was only 32 years old when he called it quits after the season. He retired with 369 home runs and a 7.1 percent home run ratio that is second only to Babe Ruth.

"I threw out the ligaments in my back while I was still playing for Pittsburgh," Kiner said. "It bothered me off and on for a year and a half, but not to the point where I couldn't play. Then it really affected me in 1955."

Sauer, an old golfing partner of Kiner's back in California, was not surprised that Kiner's career lasted only 10 years.

"I knew he was hurting and was playing hurt," Sauer said. "His legs were always taped up. When you're in the big leagues, you're supposed to be top dog. And when you're hurting as bad as he was hurting...."

Coincidentally, while Kiner was bowing out in Cleveland, Rickey was resigning his front-office post in Pittsburgh. Rickey's five-year plan had failed to produce a winner, and instead the Pirates had finished last for four straight seasons. Although Rickey and his scouting system had probably laid the groundwork for the Pirates' championship that would come in 1960, he stepped aside on a disappointing note after the 1955 season.

Kiner and Rickey were reunited, in a sense, a few years down the road. Both were eventually elected into the Hall of Fame, with Rickey receiving the honor in 1967 and Kiner joining him in 1975. Kiner received another special honor in 1987, when the Pittsburgh Pirates retired his number 4 uniform.

Notes

1. Arthur Mann, *Branch Rickey: American in Action* (Boston: Houghton Mifflin, 1957).

2. *Pittsburgh Post-Gazette*, 5 June 1953.

3. Ibid.

4. *Chicago Tribune*, 5 June 1953.

61 in '61

*December 11, 1959: The Kansas City Athletics
trade Roger Maris, Joe DeMaestri and Kent Hadley
to the New York Yankees for Hank Bauer,
Don Larsen, Norm Siebern and Marv Throneberry*

It was a big trade, but no one quite realized how big at the time.

The New York Yankees, continuing their recent string of transactions with the Kansas City Athletics, obtained outfielder Roger Maris in a trade involving seven players. The most famous name was Yankee pitcher Don Larsen, who along with outfielders Hank Bauer and Norm Siebern and first baseman Marv Throneberry, was traded on December 11, 1959, to Kansas City for Maris, shortstop Joe DeMaestri and first baseman Kent Hadley.

Larsen, 30, had pitched the only perfect game in the World Series when he blitzed the Brooklyn Dodgers in the fifth game of the 1956 classic. But he had fallen on hard times because of arm trouble, so the 25-year-old Maris loomed as the pivotal player in the trade. Maris batted .273 with 16 homers and 72 runs batted in as the Athletics' right fielder in 1959. Maris had shown his vast potential the previous year when he blasted 28 homers playing for Kansas City and the Cleveland Indians.

The trade marked the 15th transaction between the Yankees and Kansas City. The dealing, which started shortly after the A's moved west from Philadelphia in 1955 to former Yankee farm territory, involved 59 players. "We have tried unsuccessfully to trade with other clubs in both leagues," said Yankee general manager George Weiss. "The Yanks and Kansas City have faith in each other."[1]

Of course, it was easy for Weiss to exude confidence in trading with the A's. New York invariably enjoyed the upper hand in those transactions. One particularly memorable trade between the teams occurred in February 1957, when a whopping 12-player deal was consummated. It turned out the three most productive players were third baseman Clete Boyer and pitchers Bobby Shantz and Art Ditmar, all players who were traded to the Yankees. Those three combined to play in 10 World Series with New York.

After being traded to the Yankees, Maris was immediately listed by manager Casey Stengel as one of the Yankees' starting outfielders, along with the venerable Mickey Mantle and Hector Lopez—another player the Yankees had recently pried away from Kansas City in trade. It wasn't too much longer before Stengel was calling Maris "the best man I ever got in a deal."[2]

Maris, in his fourth full season, earned the raves with an excellent start to the 1960 season. He was batting .436 with four homers and 14 RBIs through May 7, even though he did not hit his first homer until his 11th game of the season. Maris was even overshadowing Mantle, who was batting .325 with one homer and seven RBIs. Maris' strong start was tempered though by the fact that he had also displayed a magical bat through mid–May in 1959, but returned to earth with a thud after coming down with appendicitis.

After hitting for average the first month, the new Yankees' right fielder put on a power burst in a manner reminiscent of another Yankee right fielder, the legendary Babe Ruth. That would be a name that would come up again and again in Maris' life.

On June 30, Maris smashed his 14th homer of the month and 25th of the season when he connected against his old Kansas City teammates. That homer off of Bob Trowbridge gave him nine more than his entire output from the previous season. It also put him five games ahead of Ruth's record-setting pace of 1927.

Maris, however, wanted no part of talk about the record. "Who's kidding who. No one's ever going to beat his record—certainly not me," said Maris, who was leading the majors in homers, leading the American League in RBIs with 64 and batting a solid .326. "Home runs aren't the only thing in my life."[3]

Although Maris was quick to downplay his accomplishments, others had no qualms. Stengel said Maris "has certainly been everything we hoped for when we dealt for him with Kansas City last winter. Never saw anything like it. The pitchers all look alike to him. He looks like a million bucks."[4]

Uneasy over the tribute, the left-handed-hitting Maris responded: "I only hope Stengel feels the same way about me at the end of the season as he does now."[5]

Fresh in Maris' mind was his 1959 season. His season was respectable, but somewhat disappointing because he tailed off so greatly from his sizzling start. In Maris' eyes, the time to start disseminating praise came after the season—and not until then.

"I'll be happy if I have a good year," Maris said. "Last year (with Kansas City), I got off to the best start I ever had. People were predicting I'd lead the league in hitting. Then I had to have an operation for appendicitis. I was out for about a month and when I started to play again, I never did get going again."[6]

Maris' concerns panned out during the 1960 season. After June 30, Maris totaled only 14 more homers to finish with a still-impressive 39, but hardly a threat to Ruth's 60-homer benchmark. Maris, in fact, was not even the Yankees'

In his second season after being traded from the Kansas City Athletics to the New York Yankees, Roger Maris became forever linked with Babe Ruth (George Brace photograph).

homer leader, as Mantle clouted 40. Still Maris finished second in the league in homers, led the league with 112 RBIs, slugging percentage at .581, and batted a nifty .283 in 136 games. Maris also was named the league's Most Valuable Player.

Maris' strong season helped the Yankees run away with the American League pennant. He then blasted two more homers in the World Series, although the Pittsburgh Pirates held off New York to win in seven games.

So after four seasons that ranged from decent to superb, what would 1961 hold for Maris? The Yankees entered the season—in which the American League had expanded from eight to 10 teams and the schedule had increased from 154 to 162 games—with a sizable group of players capable of big power numbers. First baseman Bill Skowron, third baseman Clete Boyer, catchers Elston Howard and Johnny Blanchard, left fielder Yogi Berra (who was being shifted from catcher), the magnificent Mantle in center field and Maris gave the Yankees a powerful line-up.

Maris started slowly in 1961, hitting his first homer off the Detroit Tigers Paul Foytack in New York's 11th game. He hit only two more by May 16. But then Maris got red-hot and the homers came in bunches. He belted 15 during the first three weeks of June and entered July with 27 homers, triggering comparisons again with Ruth's record pace. Ruth had not hit his 27th homer in 1927 until July 8, in game number 78. Through June, the Yankees of 1961 had played only 71 games and would play eight more games than the Yankees played during Ruth's 60-homer season.

Maris fielded questions easily on June 30, showing no signs of any impending tenseness at the comparisons to Ruth. He talked easily and grinned a lot. He said he basically was doing everything the same way he did in 1960. But there was one difference. "The homers are just coming more often," Maris acknowledged. "I don't know why."[7]

Perhaps the bats were different? "Bats don't have anything to do with it," Maris said. "I don't even use my own bat all the time. I try different ones now and then. I've hit about four of my homers using Bob Cerv's bat, which is an inch longer and a couple of ounces heavier than my usual stick."[8]

Maris was confident and comfortable. Facing left-handers did not bother him, he said. Nor did it matter if he played day or night games. "Under the lights, you can't see as much of the ball," Maris said. "On the other hand, most of the parks have bad backgrounds for day games. So, it about evens up."[9]

Maris remained hot in July, so hot that on July 17, commissioner Ford Frick—anticipating that Maris might threaten Ruth's record—made a major announcement. Frick, who had covered and adored Ruth when he was a baseball writer, said Maris could tie or break Ruth's record only if he achieved the feat in 154 games, the traditional length of a season before the expansion in 1961. Frick said an asterisk would be placed next to Maris' name if he required more than 154 games to tie or break the mark.

Frick was among a vocal segment who cherished Ruth and deplored the challenge to the greatest player in baseball history. This faction pointed out that Maris was hitting far below Ruth's high standard in 1927 and that he was making his run at the record with the aid of expansion, which had diluted the pitching talent. However, young fans and most of Maris' fellow players rooted for him to break Ruth's record. And on July 17, Maris appeared that he was on course, having hit 35 homers. He was three weeks ahead of Ruth's pace.

As Maris moved closer to challenging Ruth's record, the pressure increased as well. Mantle also was enjoying a career year and he too had a shot at eclipsing Ruth's record. So Maris was not only trying to eclipse the much-revered Ruth's record, but he was trying to outshine Mantle, who had climbed out of the shadow of former Yankee great Joe DiMaggio to become the darling of Yankee fans. Maris now had two legends to contend with.

But Maris seemed immune to pressure. He hit 13 homers in July, giving him 40 for the season. He had four in one day when the Yankees played a doubleheader against the Chicago White Sox at Yankee Stadium.

Maris' homer total kept growing and reached 48 in the team's 119th game. It was three homers more than Mantle and 15 games ahead of Ruth's 1927 pace. The nation's focus had descended on the Yankee pair and Maris was feeling the heat. In mid–August, Maris admitted he was not coping exceptionally well. "I was born surly," Maris said, "and I'm going to stay that way. Everything is tough in life."[10]

Basically a loner, Maris was being besieged by daily requests for interviews by the media. It was an ordeal Maris disliked. "You fellows (reporters) are tougher than some of those pitchers," he said.

"Where do you think up these silly questions? How the heck do I know whether I'll break Babe Ruth's record? Besides, you're the only guys thinking about it. I don't. All I'm interested in is having a good season and winning the pennant. I'd rather have the dough than the record. And if I have a real good season, I'm going to ask for real dough next year, too."[11]

Maris was earning $32,500 in 1961, far less than Mantle's $75,000 salary. Most experts believed Mantle, despite being behind Maris' homer total, had the edge over his teammate in the chase to overtake Ruth's mark. Part of the reasoning was that the switch-hitting Mantle could handle right-handers and left-handers alike, but Maris had sporadic problems against left-handers. Maris, however, claimed left-handers were not particularly bothersome.

"I was always able to hit left-handed pitching, that is until last year," Maris said. "That was because I didn't see enough of that kind of pitching. Now that they're using more southpaws against us, I'm getting used to it."[12]

Maris hit only one of his first 22 homers off left-handers, but revved up to blast 9 of his next 26 against lefties. Maris hit his 50th homer on August 22, and some people wondered if he might shatter the record with perhaps as many as 65 or 70 homers. On September 2, Maris hit two more to give him 53. Maris' inexorable push hit 55 on September 7. Maris belted number 56 on September 9, which allowed the M&M boys, Maris and Mantle, to set the one-season homer record for teammates, eclipsing the mark of 107 set by Ruth (60) and Lou Gehrig (47) in 1927. Mantle, plagued by an abscessed hip in September, had hit his 52nd the day before but would fall by the wayside in the Ruth chase.

Maris hit his 58th in game 152, a game-winning shot at Detroit on September 17. Three days later, it was the acclaimed game 154 against the host Baltimore Orioles and Maris still had 58 homers. This was the game through which he needed to officially tie or break the record, at least according to Frick's artificial deadline. Maris gave it a very game try. On his first at-bat, he nearly homered. On his second at-bat, he reached the stands off right-hander Milt Pappas to draw within one of Ruth's mark. Maris had three more dramatic tries at number 60, but the closest he came was a long drive that went foul by 15 feet in his next-to-last at-bat.

Eight games now remained and Maris' 60th appeared a cinch. But it did not come so easily. Maris remained stuck on 59 for six days until September 26 when he tagged Baltimore Oriole right-hander Jack Fisher for the historic number 60 in the third inning. The homer came in New York's 158th game of the season. Maris, who had been struggling and pressing to blast his 60th, singled in his first at-bat before whacking a 375-foot shot into the upper-right-field tier of Yankee Stadium.

Maris had fouled off the first two pitches before taking two balls to run the count to 2-and-2. He then fouled one into the dirt before connecting, helping the Yankees score a 3–2 victory. "I knew it was gone the moment I hit it," Maris said. "All I was interested in was whether it would go fair or foul."[13]

After he returned to the dugout amid thunderous applause by the crowd of 19,401 fans, Maris' teammates insisted he go out and take a bow. Maris then moved to the top dugout step and the crowd roared when he doffed his cap and beamed.

"I didn't want to do it," Maris said. "I didn't know whether it would be the right thing to do or not, but they shoved me out."[14]

The Orioles' Fisher seemed to be building a reputation as a pitcher who allowed historic homers. He had also given up Ted Williams' 521st and final homer. Williams retired on the spot after he hit it at Boston in 1960.

Fisher, though, seemed to take Maris' homer in stride, saying that losing the game was what really bothered him. "I don't care who hits home runs as long as I win," Fisher said. "It was a curveball. I got it too high. I knew it was number 60 the minute he hit it."[15]

Maris seemed to have a premonition that the Yankees' 158th game would turn out to be the record-tying day. In previous days, Maris typically put off reporters before each game by saying, "I guarantee you I won't do it today."[16] But it was different on the record-tying night.

"I feel real good," he said quietly but confidently before practice. "I have a hunch this might be the night. I kind of feel it."[17]

Maris, obviously relieved, said he had no quarrel with Frick's pronouncement. "In a way, it's just as well I didn't break it in 154 games," said Maris, sitting on 60 homers, six more than Mantle. "It's a little hard to explain but I have my reasons. I'd like to get one more. Even if I don't, though, I'm happy and fortunate to have gotten as many as I did."[18]

Four games remained on the Yankees' schedule. Could Maris now break the record in 162 games? If he was gunning for it, it certainly did not show in the Yankees' next game against the Orioles, New York's 159th game. Maris took the day off, leaving him with three games against the Boston Red Sox at Yankee Stadium to produce one more homer.

"I'm just bushed," said Maris, explaining why he sacrificed a game from his record pursuit. "I think it's for my best interest and for the club's best interests for me to take a rest. Right now we have got to think of the World Series."[19]

After failing to homer in the Yankees' 160th and 161st games, it came down to game number 162, on October 1, and a shot at immortality for the 27-year-old Maris, who had notched 10 homers in September. The Yankees' opposing pitcher was Boston right-hander Tracy Stallard, who was struggling through a lackluster 2–6 season. Stallard barely contained Maris in his first at-bat as the Yankee slugger hit an opposite-field drive that left fielder Carl Yastrzemski hauled down with a one-handed catch, perhaps saving an inside-the park homer.

After three shutout innings and locked in a 0–0 tie, Stallard faced Maris again in the fourth inning. This time Maris took two balls before he rocketed a fastball into the right-field stands. Once Maris teed off on the pitch, there was no doubt it was homer number 61. A wildly appreciative crowd of 23,154 forced Maris to make two curtain calls to pay tribute to the 6-foot, 197-pound right fielder for doing something that not even the fabled Ruth could accomplish.

It turned out to be the only run in the Yankees' 1–0 victory. After the game, Stallard tried to shake off the significance of allowing the record-breaking homer—a feat that would forever mark his name as the answer to one of the most often-asked trivia questions.

"It was a damned good pitch," Stallard said. "I didn't want to walk him, and if he'd taken the pitch, it would have been a strike. It doesn't bother me in the slightest that Maris hit number 61 off me. He hit 60 off a lot of other guys. In fact, it was his first hit off me this year."[20]

Maris finished the night by striking out and popping out, but he ended the regular season by owning one of the most cherished records in baseball.

Thirty-one of his homers came on the road, 49 off right-handers and 36 in the daytime.

Some comparisons between Maris and Ruth during their record years:

• Maris hit 61 homers in 590 official at-bats, playing in 161 games and averaging a homer every 9.7 at-bats. Ruth hit 60 homers in 540 official at-bats playing in 151 games, averaging a homer every 9.0 at-bats.

• Maris had 16 doubles, four triples, 132 RBIs, 142 runs scored, and a .269 batting average. Ruth had 29 doubles, eight triples, 164 RBIs, 158 runs scored, and a .356 average.

• Maris walked 94 times and struck out 67 times. Ruth walked 138 times and struck out 89 times.

• Maris and Ruth both had teammates who finished second to them in the league homer race. Mantle was runner-up to Maris with 54 homers, while first baseman Lou Gehrig was second to Ruth with a distant 47 homers.

• Maris hit his 60th homer in his 158th game; Ruth hit his 60th in his 151st.

Maris' banner season earned him the league's Most Valuable Player award for the second straight year, and he became one of the most well-known sports figures ever. It was a season in which the Yankees ran away with the pennant, outdistancing the second-place Detroit Tigers by eight games. Six Yankees hit at least 20 homers, including Bill Skowron (28), Yogi Berra (22), Elston Howard (21) and Johnny Blanchard (21). Whitey Ford led the pitching staff with a league-high 25 victories.

Maris, though, was the leading player of all. His star was skyrocketing, but not all was well. Fans did not take kindly to Maris' overtaking Ruth's record, and Maris received an avalanche of nasty letters, crank calls and media insults. It was even reported that he was feuding with Mantle, although Mantle in his book, *The Mick*, refuted claims of a rift and wrote that Maris never cracked and broke the record like a true champion. But the heavy pressure took its toll on Maris, who began to lose his hair and could not understand the storm of negativism during his season of glory.

The World Series marked a turning point in Maris' career. Unable to maintain his torrid regular-season pace, Maris managed only two hits, including one homer, in nineteen at-bats. But the Yankees sported a superior cast and with Ford winning two games and Blanchard blasting two homers, New York defeated the Cincinnati Reds, four games to one.

When the season was all over, Maris wrote in a magazine story, "As a ballplayer, I'd be delighted to do it again. But as an individual, I doubt I could go through it again."[21]

Maris still had plenty of suppporters. New York manager Ralph Houk, for one, pointed out that Maris' all-around contributions were frequently overlooked during the record chase. In fact, several times in the final weeks when he was battling Ruth's pace, Maris gave himself up by bunting to improve his team's chances for a victory. "He was a team man all the way," said Houk, who took over for Stengel as Yankee manager beginning the 1961 season.[22]

The Yankees rewarded Maris with a one-year contract worth $72,000 for the 1962 season. It was nearly a one hundred percent increase over his previous year's salary. "They called me the lousiest hitter ever to win the home run title," said Maris, showing that some of the criticism had not been forgotten. "Well, I wish I could be the lousiest hitter in baseball this year and still hit 61 home runs. As long as I can be good in all the other departments, I'll sacrifice one, my batting average."[23]

Maris, the last Yankee to agree to terms for 1962, became the fourth highest paid Yankee in history. Joe DiMaggio earned $100,000 in his last two seasons. Ruth earned $80,000 one year and Mantle had signed a contract for $82,000.

Everything appeared to be turning to gold for Maris, but the honeymoon was screeching to a halt. In March of 1962, Maris abruptly said he would grant no more interviews. Too many stories were putting him in a bad light, Maris said, and enough was enough.

> I think Ted Williams had the right idea. You go your way and let the writers go theirs. They are going to write what they want about you anyway.... I'm not going to give out any more interviews. I went out of my way last year to give interviews to everybody. Sometimes I spent as much as an hour and a half in the dressing room after a game talking to writers.
>
> And what happened? They wrote a lot of stuff about me that wasn't true. Now every time I come out of the dugout, the fans are on me.... They had a story in the Miami paper saying I wouldn't sign autographs and that the few I did sign I signed with X's. That just isn't true. I signed for everybody who asked me.
>
> After reading stuff like that, it's no wonder the people boo me. I'm going to be friendly and pleasant this year but I'm just not going to give out interviews. Why should I waste all that time when they are going to write about me the way they did last year? They gave everybody the idea I'm a redneck ballplayer and once the people get that impression, you can't change it no matter what you say.
>
> Sure, there are a lot of good writers and those guys treated me fairly but if 20 writers come in to interview me, I can't give out a story to the five good guys without giving it to the others.
>
> You should have seen some of the letters I got during the winter. People got all over me for things I didn't say or do.[24]

The best way to overcome the distractions would have been to continue his torrid hitting, but Maris found that harder to do in 1962. He got into a wretched four-week slump and was benched for the first time in his career in late June. Maris picked up the pace again and finished the year with strong numbers, hitting 33 homers and 100 RBIs despite a lackluster .256 average. They were good numbers but not nearly in the class of his record 1961 year.

The following year the decline continued as Maris managed only 23 homers and 53 RBIs. Maris was plagued by as many as 10 injuries and collected only 312 at-bats. In 1964, he regained his health, played a full season and blasted 26 homers, but the record-breaking 61-homer season seemed to be in the distant past.

Injuries took a toll on Maris again in 1965, limiting him to 46 games. He batted .239 with eight homers. In 1966, Maris played 119 games but hit only 13 homers and drove in a paltry 37 runs. Maris' fall from prominence was not because of lack of effort. He played 46 games after suffering a bone chip in his hand. Unquestionably, this outstanding slugger—plagued by bruised kneecaps in 1966—was declining markedly and perhaps needed a change of scenery. So it was no surprise that in December 1966 Maris was traded to the St. Louis Cardinals for journeyman third baseman Charley Smith. After the trade, Maris admitted that life was difficult since he broke Ruth's record, calling it "six years of misery." [25]

"My last happy spring was 1961," Maris said. "From then on, it was just a drag and I had no peace."[26]

Maris expected things would be different in St. Louis. The reporters would leave him alone, Maris said. "It was an unhappy situation for me in New York and I definitely was glad to get away from there. There was a lotta knifing behind my back. It was the writers who did the damage. Not all, but some. They know who they are."[27]

What caused this problem with the media?

"I don't think it was the home runs," Maris said. "I think if I had ended just short of the record, it would've turned out the same way. But there was no point in staying where you're not liked. The writers said it was my bad attitude and I said it was their bad attitude."[28]

Maris, definitely a troubled man, brought to St. Louis a reputation as a difficult guy to get along with. He had been the target of a lot of boos in New York, but he took advantage of his fresh start and helped St. Louis win the pennant and World Series in 1967. He didn't regain his magic home run touch but batted a respectable .261, with nine homers and 64 RBIs during the regular season.

What's more, he collected 10 hits, including one homer, and batted .385 to help the Cardinals defeat the Boston Red Sox in seven games in the World Series. St. Louis fans welcomed this new addition and Maris reveled in the St. Louis surroundings.

In December 1967 Maris disclosed he was suffering from Bell's palsy, which was affecting the nerves and muscles on the right side of his face. A few months later during spring training, Maris, 33, said he had recovered and was primed for the 1968 season. Maris then played his final season, appearing in only 100 games and batting .255 with five homers and 45 RBIs.

It wasn't a robust ending to a career that was marked by some scintillating highs, but Maris did help the Cardinals reach the World Series again in 1968. Maris, though, collected only three hits—no homers—in 19 at-bats, as the Cardinals lost the World Series in seven games to the Detroit Tigers.

Maris finished his 12-year career with a .260 average, 275 homers and 851 RBIs. He appeared in seven World Series. Although many believed he deserved to be elected into the Hall of Fame because of his record setting 61-homer year and back-to-back MVP seasons, Maris failed to gain the necessary votes. But he did earn a reputation as one of the game's best all-around players.

The trade that sent Maris to New York from Kansas City turned out to be one-sided, but the A's did receive one quality player: Norm Siebern. The first baseman-outfielder enjoyed four strong seasons for the A's and batted .308, with 25 homers and 117 RBIs in 1962, his biggest year. Unfortunately for Kansas City, the A's finished no higher than eighth those four years, while the Yankees—with Maris—advanced to the World Series each season.

As for the other men the Yankees traded to Kansas City: Outfielder Hank Bauer ended a productive career with two unproductive seasons with the A's; first baseman Marv Throneberry had minimal sucess with the A's in two seasons, although he did receive recognition for playing—albeit abysmally—for the laughable first-year New York Mets team of 1962; and pitcher Don Larsen plunged to a 1–10 record in his first season with Kansas City and was traded the following year. Besides Maris, the A's-turned-Yankees included infielder Joe DeMaestri, a light-hitting reserve who batted only 76 times in two seasons for New York, and first baseman Kent Hadley, who played sparingly in his one season on New York.

Maris in 1982—21 years after breaking Ruth's hallowed record and long retired—took another shot at the snipers who bedeviled him during his record run.

> My going after the record started off as such a dream, I was living a fairy tale for a while. I never thought I'd ever get a chance to break such a record. Too bad it ended so badly. It would've been a helluva lot more fun if I had never hit those 61 homers. All it brought me was headaches.
>
> I was so happy when the season ended. I never had a chance to look forward to the World Series, and God, was I miserable in it. I was so tired of the fanfare. I don't want to sound bitter; I love baseball. But I was never liked in Yankee Stadium. I had so many people on my tail. People hated me for breaking Ruth's record, the press especially. They made me into a machine.
>
> The Yankees, too, played a part. Let's not kid anybody. They wanted Mantle to break the record, not me. They did everything to assure that. They wanted to reduce my chances at it. Even today I don't get the right credit for it.[29]

In November 1983 Maris learned that he was suffering from lymphona, a form of cancer that attacks the lymph glands. A doctor at the time told

Maris that it had gone undetected for five years. On December 4, 1985, Maris died of cancer at age 51.

Six years later, commissioner Fay Vincent eliminated the so-called asterisk from baseball's official records, allowing Maris to become the undisputed holder of baseball's single-season home run record. Actually, there was no asterisk to remove. The *Baseball Record Book* had simply listed Maris as the record-holder for 162 games and Ruth the leader for 154 games.

Notes

1. Associated Press, 12 December 1959.
2. United Press International, 2 July 1960.
3. United Press International, 2 July 1960.
4. Ibid.
5. Ibid.
6. Associated Press, 3 July 1960.
7. *Los Angeles Times*, 1 July 1961.
8. Ibid.
9. Ibid.
10. Associated Press, 18 August 1961.
11. Ibid.
12. Ibid.
13. United Press International, 27 September 1961.
14. Ibid.
15. Associated Press, 28 September 1961.
16. United Press International, 27 September 1961.
17. Ibid.
18. Ibid.
19. Associated Press, 28 September 1961.
20. Ibid.
21. *Los Angeles Times*, 15 December.
22. United Press International, 9 October 1961.
23. Associated Press, 27 February 1962.
24. Associated Press, 17 March 1962.
25. United Press International, 11 March 1967.
26. Ibid.
27. Ibid.
28. Ibid.
29. *Los Angeles Times*, 15 July 1982.

"I Swapped a Hamburger for a Steak"

April 17, 1960: The Cleveland Indians
trade Rocky Colavito to the Detroit Tigers
for Harvey Kuenn

42 HOME RUNS FOR 140 SINGLES!

That was the headline that screamed out to readers of the *Detroit Free Press* on April 18, 1960, the day after Rocky Colavito was traded from the Cleveland Indians to the Detroit Tigers for Harvey Kuenn. For those who deal strictly in statistics, that headline reduced the trade to its simplest terms. Colavito indeed had hit 42 home runs for the Indians in 1959 when he shared the American League home run crown with Washington's Harmon Killebrew. And Kuenn had collected 140 singles among his league-leading 198 hits for the Tigers in 1959 when he won the AL batting title with a .353 average. It was, in fact, the only time a batting champ has been traded for a home run champ before either had a chance to defend his title.

Statistics, however, do not begin to tell the story of this blockbuster deal. It was not a trade based solely on the players' on-field performances. Instead, it was a transaction rooted firmly in the personalities of those involved.

The most domineering personality in this sometimes ugly little saga was Frank Lane, the legendary trade master who was the Indians' general manager at the time. On one hand, Lane did not like Colavito. On the other, he coveted Kuenn. In the end, that is all that mattered. But before dealing with the events of April 1960, it is important to look back at Colavito's and Kuenn's careers before the trade. They surely were two of the American League's brightest stars.

Rocco Domenico Colavito signed with the Indians in 1951 after rejecting offers by the Yankees and Phillies. A native of New York, he came to copy Joe DiMaggio's batting stance and at times had similar results.

After tearing up the minor leagues for five seasons, his breakthrough season in Cleveland was 1956. He was on the Indians' Opening Day roster,

Few trades attracted as much publicity as the 1960 deal which sent home-run champion Rocky Colavito (right) from the Cleveland Indians to the Detroit Tigers for batting champion Harvey Kuenn (left). Photographs courtesy of the Detroit Tigers.

but was sent back to the minors before the season really got rolling. He played a little more than a month of Triple-A ball before rejoining the Indians for good. He finished that season with 21 home runs and 65 runs batted in.

In his next three seasons with Cleveland, he developed into one of the league's most feared long-ball threats, as he posted home run totals of 25, 41 and 42. He did not have a consistently high batting average, but that was not why he was in the lineup. When he went on a home run binge, nobody was safe.

His most awesome display came in June 1959, when he tied a major league record by slamming four home runs in four consecutive at-bats in a game against the Orioles. When he shared the home run title that season, he was just 26 years old. Considering he was a family man who took good care of himself off the field, his best years seemed ahead of him.

Perhaps more significant than his home run totals was the fact that Colavito was very popular with the Indian fans. Actually, he was more than just very popular. He was an idol, especially to the young fans who admired both his ruggedly handsome looks and his long home runs.

"Anybody's going to like a slugger," said pitcher Cal McLish, who played with Colavito for four years in Cleveland. "But it was also his personality. When he came out on the field, he acknowledged it when people were yelling at him before the game, before batting practice, after batting practice. He was always talking or signing autographs, waving to the people."

"He was a pious boy, and I think he impressed the fans just as much that way as with his ability on the field," added George Strickland, another of Colavito's teammates in Cleveland. "I think he might have dropped a four-letter word now and then—not a bad one—but only in a situation where he popped one up 2 miles instead of hittin' it out 2 miles. I don't think it took anything away from his morals in any way. He was just a clean-cut young man."

Kuenn was also a crowd favorite in Detroit, where legions of Tiger fans turned out to watch him spray line drives around Briggs Stadium. In fact, the area of center field where many of his base hits landed became known as Kuenn's Alley.

The stocky, tobacco-chewing shortstop signed with the Tigers after making a name for himself at the University of Wisconsin. He spent only 63 games in the minors before joining the Tigers at the tail end of the 1952 season.

He became an immediate star in 1953, batting .308 and leading the league with 209 hits en route to being named Rookie of the Year. In 1954, he was named Sophomore of the Year by sportswriters and sportscasters when he batted .306.

In Kuenn's seven full seasons with the Tigers, only once did he he finish with a batting average below .300. He was an acknowledged team leader and was named to the All-Star team each year. Although he was basically a singles hitter (his career high for home runs was 12), he teamed up with a young Al Kaline to give the Tigers a menacing one-two punch known as the KK Boys.

When Kuenn was shifted to the outfield in 1958 because of his limited range, his hitting did not skip a beat. His high-water mark was 1959, when he won his only batting title at age 28.

"Harvey Kuenn hit more line drives than I've ever seen in my life," said Frank Bolling, the Tigers second baseman who played with Kuenn for five seasons. "Even when he made outs, most of them were line drives somewhere. I think Harvey was the type of player that if the ballclub told him to hit 30 home runs a year and hit .250, he probably could adjust and do that. But he knew that his ability was to hit line drives, and hitting .330 or .340 would help the club more. That's where he was the best."

"My stance and style of hitting were geared for singles and doubles," Kuenn said after his playing days were over. "Only a few times did I go for the homer, and generally it was a mistake."[1]

And that brings us to Frank Lane, the third and most controversial figure of the Colavito-Kuenn trade.

Lane was a longtime general manager who acquired the nicknames Trader Lane and Frantic Frank for the rapid-fire transactions he made while running various clubs. Over the years, Lane's detractors charged that he was a publicity hound who advocated change for change sake. His supporters claimed that he was a baseball man, pure and simple, who made his many trades only in an attempt to improve his ballclub.

Regardless of his motives, a few things should be known about Trader Lane:

1. He had a genuine nose for talent. This ability was perhaps best displayed in Chicago, where he turned the White Sox into regular contenders by acquiring such players as Billy Pierce, Nellie Fox, Minnie Minoso and Luis Aparicio during the late 1940s and early 1950s.

2. He had his favorite ballplayers. Lane thought the world of Minoso, for example, and even referred to him as "my son." As a result of this admiration, Lane traded for Minoso twice: as GM of the White Sox in 1951 and as GM of the Indians in 1957.

3. There were no sacred cows. For a good example of this, go back to Lane's brief stint as GM of the St. Louis Cardinals in the mid–1950s. He traded away fan favorite Red Schoendienst and even had the gall to talk about trading the great Stan Musial. That, by the way, reportedly led to his departure from St. Louis.

4. Lane was known to have tunnel vision. Once he got a particular trade in mind, he would latch onto it like a pit bull. Bing Devine, who worked with him in St. Louis, noted that when Lane "wanted to make a deal, he looked for reasons to make it and he ignored reasons not to make it."

Lane came to Cleveland as GM in November 1957. By spring training of 1960, only a handful of the players he had inherited were still with the club. Also by spring training of 1960, he was ready to unload Colavito.

Why? Lane simply did not get along with the young slugger.

Sure, Lane complained that Colavito struck out too often and his batting average was not high enough. Lane also might have viewed Colavito with disdain for being what he often referred to as a "chocolate-soda type." Colavito, remember, was the family man who supposedly did not smoke or drink, while Lane preferred the tobacco-chewers of the world. Some observers even think Lane might have been jealous of Colavito's popularity. But at the bottom of it all was the problem Lane had signing Colavito to new contracts.

In the book *The Curse of Rocky Colavito*, Colavito recalls some of his nasty negotiations with Lane:

> It began when Frank was hired right after the 1957 season. I had to talk contract with him. I had hit 25 home runs and had 84 RBI in 134 games, and all Lane did was tell me how lousy I was. I wanted a $3,000 raise. He offered me $1,500. I told him that I wouldn't sign for a rotten raise like that. We went back and forth, and finally he said, "Take the $1,500 now. I'll give you the other $1,500 if you play well during the season. Don't worry. I'll take care of you." I didn't know Frank Lane, but I will take a man at his word until I find out that he can't be trusted. In early September 1958, I hit my 35th home run. I had 102 RBI. I had been waiting for a month or so for Lane to give me

the $1,500 he promised me. I made an appointment to talk to Lane, and I said, "I've got 35 home runs and 102 RBI. I've earned the other $1,500." He acted like he had no idea what I was talking about. He said he never promised me the other $1,500. I called him a "no-good liar." He lied to me and he knew it, and I lost all respect for him at that moment."[2]

Pitcher Gary Bell, Colavito's teammate, knew what Rocky was going through. "All the general managers in those days were tough on young kids. Here you have a guy in his early 20s trying to talk contract with a guy who'd been in baseball 30, 40 years. I'll tell you, if you didn't have some brass balls, they'd just beat up on you. They'd threaten you, intimidate you and pretty much say, 'Sign the contract or don't play.' That's the way it was then. With the reserve clause, they knew if you didn't play for them, you didn't play for anybody."

Colavito and Lane went to war over money before every season. Colavito even held out in 1960 before signing a contract in early March that was especially noteworthy in that it promised Colavito an extra $1,000 if he cut down on his home runs in favor of a higher batting average.

Bob Kennedy, who was on Lane's staff at the time, was well aware of the Lane-Colavito confrontations: "I can remember Frank arguing with him during the fall, trying to sign Rocky. And Frank would be hollering and swearing on the phone … hollering like blue blazes, and you could hear him out in the office. And I know that all Rocky was saying on the other end was, 'No.' He wouldn't argue with Frank. He'd just say no, and I think that made Frank 10 times madder."

The fans, of course, sided with Colavito in these battles. Their rallying cry became "Don't knock the Rock."

Determined to get rid of his source of irritation, Lane started talking about a trade while preparing for the 1960 season. Lane even joked to reporters about trading Colavito for Mickey Mantle.

In reality, he was pursuing Kuenn, whom he looked upon as a Nellie Fox-type of ballplayer who could do lots of things to help his team win. The Indians had come close in 1959—finishing just five games behind the first-place White Sox—and they were still trying to recapture the magic of the 1954 Indian team that won 111 games.

"Hoot Evers [the Indians' farm director] and I were in spring training and Frank came up to us and said he wanted to trade Colavito for Harvey Kuenn," Kennedy noted. "And we said, 'Frank, you're going to get killed if you do this.' But he wanted [Kuenn] as a leader. He was always on base. He was a steady .300 hitter no matter who pitched. Frank thought he would be better for our club."

The Tigers were willing to listen to Lane's proposals because, despite Kuenn's success, they had never been a contender during his stay. Besides that, new team president Bill DeWitt and his assistant Rick Ferrell were trying to change the look of the lineup.

"We needed some more power on our ballclub," said Jim Campbell, who was the Tigers' farm director at the time and later became the ballclub's general manager and president. "Harvey was a great hitter, but not a long-ball hitter. Rocky could give you that power."

Another reason the Tigers might have been willing to deal away the popular Kuenn was his off-the-field actions. At least that is the view of Billy Hoeft, Kuenn's roommate with the Tigers and one of his closest friends.

"Harvey was a good, fun-loving guy," Hoeft said, referring to Kuenn's widely acknowledged drinking habits. "Harvey was a rowdy guy, and I think there were times when the ballcub got a little down on him. I think they just thought, 'Hey, enough is enough … if we can get a guy who's going to knock in some runs for us, let's do it.'

"People also say Harvey was hard-headed. He spoke his terms. You knew exactly where he was coming from … no bullshit. There was no gray areas with Harvey. His opinion was black and white, and sometimes [the management] didn't appreciate that. You know, in the old terminology, you've got to kiss somebody's ass, and Harvey wasn't that kind of guy. They wanted him to be more of a politician, but he couldn't back down. That's the way he was.

"I think Harvey sort of played out his welcome in Detroit."

At first, the Colavito-Kuenn talks reached a stalemate. In mid–March, Lane and DeWitt held a news conference to publicly squash the trade rumors. But Lane was not about to let the deal die.

On April 12, almost as a warmup to the main attraction, the Indians sent promising young slugger Norm Cash to the Tigers for Steve Demeter. Considering how their careers panned out, the Tigers really snookered Lane on that one.

Lane then got back to business with Colavito and Kuenn. Bob Kennedy recalls the events of Saturday, April 16, the night before the trade:

"We had dinner that night and Hoot and I were still pretty much against the trade. Frank was giving us all the pros and cons, the good parts and so forth. He finally said, 'You guys sleep on it and let me know tomorrow.'

"So we didn't do much sleeping. We talked half the night. There was no doubt about Harvey Kuenn's ability to play and also to hit. But the power problem and, of course, the fan appeal was not the same as Rocky in Cleveland. I think the thing that I was against mostly was the age factor. That was a problem for Hoot also. If Harvey was the same age as Rocky, I don't think I would have had much doubt. But there was considerable difference. Rocky still was a young player … a very fine moral boy who took really good care of himself. He was going to last a long time.

"Finally, we just said, 'Well, Frank's going to do it anyway, so it won't make any difference.' So Hoot and I went to the ballpark. We gave him our reasons for not doing it, but said, 'If you think it's that important to you, and if you really want to go ahead, just go ahead and do it.'"

That Easter Sunday, April 17, was the last day of spring training, and Colavito and Kuenn turned in typical performances. Colavito ripped his eighth home run of the exhibition season as the Indians played the White Sox in Memphis. Kuenn had two hits against the the Kansas City A's in Lakeland, Florida, to raise his spring average to .418.

Then the news came.

Colavito learned of the trade when he was removed from the game after grounding into a forceout in the fourth inning. As he left the field, Lane matter-of-factly announced in the press box: "Well, that's the last time Rocky will bat for the Indians."[3]

Colavito immediately searched out his best friend, pitcher Herb Score. "Rocky walked down the right-field line, where I was sitting in the bullpen, and told me about it,"recalled Score, who was traded himself the following day. "Rocky was always a very calm individual ... very professional. He just said, 'I've been traded.'"

Later that day, Colavito told reporters: "Lane's certainly hard to figure. And you can never be sure what he'll do. I really was surprised this happened. If he did hold our disagreement against me, it certainly isn't right. It's the American way to fight for what you think you deserve."[4]

Colavito flew back to Cleveland with the Indians that night. And if the day was not memorable enough already, the players were able to look down on Memphis as they left and saw Russwood Park, where they had just played hours before, engulfed in flames. The old ballpark burned to the ground that night.

Kuenn learned of the swap in the same manner as Colavito, after being pulled out after six innings of his exhibition game. "I don't think anybody could believe it," said Tigers teammate Charlie Maxwell. "We thought he was kidding when he told us. A lot of guys didn't believe it 'til we saw Colavito."

At the time, Kuenn accepted the trade as being just a part of baseball. "He had heard the rumors," Billy Hoeft said. "His thinking was basically, 'Hell, if they don't want me, there's no sense in being here.'"

Shortly after his retirement seven years later, however, Kuenn talked about that fateful Easter Sunday in more poignant terms: "It was the most disappointing day I had in 14 years in the major leagues."[5]

The trade was immediately the talk of the town in both Detroit and Cleveland, as fans learned about losing their respective heroes. Stunned Indian fans took the news the hardest, and Gary Bell even remembers some hardcore Colavito supporters hanging Lane in effigy and carrying a coffin with Lane's name on it.

"We knew there was going to be an explosion, no doubt about it," Kennedy said. "But Frank didn't care."

"We thought Harvey Kuenn would be a permanent fixture in Detroit,"

Frank Bolling added. "Probably the same thing with Rocky Colavito in Cleveland. You had two guys who were so popular, it was almost like the teams were trying to confuse people."

The following day, the Lane-Colavito feud flared up again as Lane tried to sell the public on the trade. "They say I'm out of my mind," Lane told reporters. "But I say I swapped a hamburger for a steak. We'll see who's right.

"Rocky hit a homer every 14th time at bat last year. But what did he do the other 13 times? Nothing, that's what. It's a home run or nothing with him ... and there was plenty of nothing. Look at their strikeouts. Kuenn fanned 36 times ... 50 less than Rocky. And he made 47 more base hits. That means we eliminated 50 strikeouts and picked up that many more hits.

"I just think Kuenn will help us more than Colavito. Maybe Rocky will hit 50 homers, maybe more, for Detroit. But Kuenn will give us 200 hits, he's faster on the bases, he has more balance, and is much more consistent. That's what we wanted. That's why we traded."[6]

In a glorious bit of irony, the Tigers opened the season two days after the trade at Cleveland's Municipal Stadium. More than 52,000 fans turned out for the opener and, as expected, the Indian rooters gave the management an eyeful. According to newspaper reports, one banner in right field said "Lost—Rocky and the pennant." There were also a few banners directed at Lane, stating simply, "So long, Frankie."

The game itself was one for the record books. The Tigers won 4–2 in a 15-inning, 4-hour-54-minute marathon that was the longest Opening Day game in American League history. The action, however, was overshadowed by all the pregame hoopla surrounding Colavito and Kuenn.

Kuenn was 2 for 7 in the opener, but he was not really a factor. Colavito, admittedly pressing to show up his former bosses, went 0 for 6 and struck out four times. "If the fans were suffering, how about me?" Colavito told reporters after the game. "They only had to sit and watch. I was out there making a fool of myself."[7] Adding insult to injury, Lane announced he would buy his pitcher a new hat for each time he struck out Colavito. By the time the game was over, the fans had pretty much settled down and started to accept the new order. Colavito even received his share of boos from the huge crowd.

Kuenn, incidentally, pulled a leg muscle running out a grounder late in the opener. He was out of the starting lineup for about a week, kicking off an injury-plagued season that saw him sit out 28 games and miss the final few weeks with a fractured ankle. Naturally, he still hit over .300—.308 to be exact.

Colavito rebounded from his disastrous opener to hit three home runs during the first week of action. He then slumped horribly in May and was benched for a while by manager Jimmie Dykes. Still, he bounced back to finish with some impressive numbers: 35 home runs, 87 RBIs and a .249 average.

"It probably took Rocky that one year in 1960 to live through [the trade]," said Billy Hitchcock, the Tigers' third-base coach. "He was a very emotional type of fellow. It really shook him up."

In the end, neither Kuenn nor Colavito provided the immediate ticket to a championship that their new teams had hoped for. The Indians finished the 1960 season in fourth place with a 76–78 record. The Tigers were sixth at 71–83.

Lane, if nothing else, did gain some peace of mind during that season. Not only had he rid himself of one of his chief antagonists, but in Kuenn he acquired someone he could really relate to.

"Well, I know they [Lane and Kuenn] went out and I think they had a few after ballgames," Billy Hoeft revealed. "They even had dinner and had a few drinks before the trade came off. They were like the same."

The Lane-Kuenn partnership did not last long, however. As the Indians struggled through that 1960 season and attendance slipped, the ownership began to sour on Lane. The colorful GM even tried an unprecedented move by swapping managers with the Tigers at midseason—getting Jimmie Dykes while arranging for Joe Gordon to end up in Detroit. But that did not reverse the team's fortunes.

When the season ended, it was the same old Frantic Frank. Kuenn was no doubt a Lane favorite, but Lane unexpectedly traded him to the San Francisco Giants on December 3 for veteran pitcher Johnny Antonelli and young outfielder Willie Kirkland. It is interesting to note that Dykes said the Indians sought Kirkland to make up for the lack of power resulting from Colavito's departure.

Although some consider Kuenn's trade to the Giants as Lane's way of admitting he made a mistake in the first place, those close to Kuenn offer another view. They claim Lane sent Kuenn to the Giants so he could finish his career with a contending ballclub—sort of a unique way of showing respect to Kuenn for being his kind of player. Lane never publicly acknowledged this scenario, but Bob Kennedy said that "knowing Frank, he would do that. He was a lot better man than a lot of people thought."

As it turned out, Lane did not have much use for Kuenn in Cleveland anyway. A month after trading away Kuenn, Lane resigned his position with the Indians to work for the Kansas City A's. He lasted less than a season there before being fired by Charlie Finley.

Kuenn stayed in San Francisco for four seasons. His career was starting to decline then, as he batted .300 only once, but he finally had a chance to play in the World Series with the Giants in 1962. He retired after the 1966 season with a .303 career average and 2,092 hits. When he got a job as coach for the Milwaukee Brewers in 1971, it was none other than Frank Lane who hired him. It was a job that eventually led to Kuenn being named Manager of the Year in 1982 when he led the Brewer team known as "Harvey's Wallbangers" to the American League pennant.

While Kuenn did not have much of a chance to leave his mark on Cleveland, Colavito's stay in Detroit was somewhat longer and considerably more productive. In four seasons, he averaged 35 home runs and 107 RBIs. As always, there was nobody better than Colavito when he was on a hot streak.

He had his greatest season in 1961 when, by his own admission, the shock of the trade had finally worn off. He helped the Tigers finish second with a 101–61 record by batting .290 with 45 home runs and 140 RBIs. Those are MVP numbers to be sure, but that happened to be the season that Roger Maris hit 61 homers to win the award.

"For what we needed, I think we made a hell of a trade," said Jim Campbell, who became the Tigers' GM in 1962.

Colavito's talent for hitting home runs was not the only thing that carried over from his days in Cleveland. He discovered in Detroit that even though Frank Lane was out of his hair, there were still contract skirmishes to be fought.

"I had one a couple years after he arrived," said Campbell. "Rocky wanted a little more than I was offering. He held out for about three days. He was the first player I ever had hold out and miss the opening of spring training. And finally he came into the office one day, madder than hell. And I had the contract right in my desk because I wasn't going to budge off it. He said, 'Where is it? Where is it?' I said, 'You want the contract?' He said, 'You're not going to change it, are you?' 'Nope,' I said. He said, 'Give it to me.' He took it and signed it. He threw it down on the desk and started out the door. As he was going out the door, he said, 'You're at the top of the totem pole!' He went out and he slammed the door. I thought the building would come down. But it wasn't done shaking when the door flies open again. And Rocky said, 'I want to add something to what I told you. Frank Lane is still number one, but you're number two.' I used to tell that to Frank, and he'd laugh like hell."

Colavito was traded to Kansas City for the 1964 season and then returned to Cleveland the following year in a much-ballyhooed eight-player deal involving the Indians, White Sox and A's. To regain Colavito, the Indians paid dearly: Johnny Romano plus two future stars, Tommy John and Tommie Agee.

Cleveland general manager Gabe Paul had been trying to bring Colavito back to Cleveland since he took over for Lane in 1961, and now he was hoping Rocky would revive the Indians' slumping attendance. Colavito did rekindle some fan interest as he hit 26 home runs in 1965 and added 30 more in 1966. But the magic did not last. Colavito once again started feuding with the Indians management, and he was traded to the White Sox midway through the 1967 season. He split time in 1968 between the Dodgers and Yankees and then retired with 374 home runs and a .266 career average.

Rocky Colavito spent only six full seasons with the Indians, but in 1975 was voted by Cleveland fans as the most memorable personality in Indians history.

Notes

1. *Chicago Tribune*, 4 March 1967.
2. Terry Pluto, *The Curse of Rocky Colavito: A loving look at a 30-year slump*, (New York: Simon & Schuster, 1994).
3. *Detroit Free Press*, 18 April 1960.
4. *Cleveland Press*, 18 April 1960.
5. *Chicago Tribune*, 20 February 1967.
6. *Detroit Free Press*, 19 April 1960.
7. *Cleveland Press*, 20 April 1960.

Trade Managers?
Why Not?

August 3, 1960: The Cleveland Indians
trade Joe Gordon to the Detroit Tigers
for Jimmie Dykes

As baseball executives, Bill DeWitt and Frank Lane could be very different. DeWitt took more of a businessman's approach to running a ball-club, while Lane was a genuine fan who would sit up in the stands and live or die with each pitch.

There were times, however, when DeWitt and Lane could be remarkably alike. Some of these moments came when they took on the role of big-time gamblers, shuffling personnel with the hopes of hitting the jackpot.

The 1960 season was one such time. DeWitt was in his first season as president of the Detroit Tigers, and he was more than willing to make roster moves to put his own imprint on the team. And Lane, who was in his third year as general manager of the Cleveland Indians, was always looking for someone who was willing to talk trade.

It certainly was a wild time when they started making regular phone calls to each other. "They always had little things going," recalled Jim Campbell, the longtime Tigers executive.

Lane and DeWitt got things started in early April, when the Indians traded Norm Cash to the Tigers for Steve Demeter. That was quickly followed by the much-publicized trade in which the Indians sent 1959 AL home run champ Rocky Colavito to Detroit for 1959 AL batting champ Harvey Kuenn. In late July, a third and somewhat minor trade was made as the Indians sent Hank Foiles to the Tigers for Rocky Bridges and Red Wilson. Those deals set the stage for what happened in early August, when Lane and DeWitt made one of the strangest deals in baseball history.

As DeWitt told reporters at the time: "I was discussing possible player deals with Lane and said, 'Frank, we're getting nowhere on this, so let's trade managers.' I meant it to be facetious."[1]

Lane added: "I thought he was kidding, but he pressed the point."[2]

As a result of those offbeat conversations, Cleveland manager Joe Gordon and Detroit manager Jimmie Dykes exchanged jobs on August 3, 1960. It was a one-of-a kind deal, the only time managers have ever been traded for each other.

Actually, it was not even a trade in the normal sense. Because the managers' contracts basically were not tradeable, Gordon and Dykes both had to be released with the understanding that the other team would hire them. Both accepted the proposition, but when you think about it, what else could they do? They no doubt were in trouble and were probably going to be fired, and at least this way they ended up still wearing a manager's cap.

"At that time, we couldn't believe it," recalled Tigers second baseman Frank Bolling. "It was comical when you got down to trading managers."

Comical, perhaps. But in reality, it was simply a marriage of convenience. After all, here were two teams that had entered the season with high expectations but instead were spinning their wheels. At the time of the managerial switcheroo, the Indians were 49–46, in fourth place and sinking fast. They were near the end of a horrible road trip and had lost 9 of their last 12 games. The Tigers, despite a fast start in April, were 44–52 and floundering in sixth place. They, too, were near the end of a horrible road trip and had lost 10 of their last 13 games.

The Tigers' problems were widespread. Al Kaline, the young superstar, had been bothered by injury and illness and was batting around .230. Rocky Colavito had been erratic, and other players were having subpar seasons as the team batting average was a paltry .229. When asked about the Tigers' troubles at the end of July, veteran outfielder Charlie Maxwell said kiddingly, "Maybe too many of us are in the wrong business."[3]

The Indians were also having problems scoring runs. Harvey Kuenn, who had batted .353 with the Tigers the year before, was struggling a little below the .300 mark and was hardly making the fans forget the popular Colavito. Two other newcomers—second baseman Johnny Temple and third baseman Bubba Phillips—also were not contributing like management had hoped. Lane admitted to reporters that "the team appears to be disorganized."[4]

In cases like this, the managers are generally the first to go. And it just so happened, in this case there was an acceptable replacement just down the road.

As Bill DeWitt, Jr., noted, "I remember my father saying that Frank Lane was being critical of his manager, Joe Gordon, and he said to me, 'I think Joe Gordon is a pretty good manager.'" By the same token, Lane had always liked Dykes.

After DeWitt and Lane hammered out the details, Dykes and Gordon were informed about the impending trade and asked if they were willing to go along with the unique arrangement. They agreed. As expected, it was front-page news in Cleveland and Detroit and made big headlines elsewhere around the country.

Most of the players were not even aware that their managers were on the hot seat. Even the coaches were caught off-guard. Bob Kennedy, Lane's assistant, admitted that "we thought there might be a change, but not 'til after the end of the year."

In announcing the deal, DeWitt told the press: "In Gordon we are getting an aggressive man, something the Tigers can use. Dykes is more calm, and I think that'll help Cleveland, too."[5]

Lane also had his say: "I am not critical of Joe. Neither is DeWitt critical of Dykes. But we are not getting the results we think we should have and neither is Detroit. There are too many good players on each club to be down where they are."[6]

DeWitt's and Lane's comments simply covered the superficial reasons for the Gordon-Dykes deal. Beyond the unfulfilled promise and disappointing records of the two teams was a scenario which featured two iron-willed front-office generals who did not get along with their field managers.

Dykes, who had been a star infielder for the Philadelphia Athletics in the 1920s and 1930s, was in the twilight of a 21-year managerial career. By the time he arrived in Detroit, he had mellowed into a more thoughtful skipper who did not make much of a fuss unless things were going poorly or his authority was questioned. "Mr. Dykes just let you alone and let you play," the Tigers' Frank Bolling said. The wise-cracking, cigar-chomping Dykes took control of the last-place Tigers in May 1959, and then received the lion's share of the credit as he led the club to a 74–63 record the rest of the season. Despite the impressive finish in 1959, Dykes knew he was in trouble when Bill DeWitt was named president of the Tigers after the season ended.

In Dykes' autobiography, *You Can't Steal First Base*, he explained how his problems with DeWitt dated back to 1939, when Dykes was manager of the White Sox and DeWitt was running the St. Louis Browns. While the teams were negotiating a trade, a newspaper reporter wrote that Dykes was trying to pull a fast one on DeWitt. The following year, DeWitt confronted Dykes and questioned his integrity.

The long-simmering feud was never resolved, so it was no surprise that DeWitt and Dykes were at odds as soon as they were united in Detroit. There were run-ins during spring training in 1960 over the use of personnel, and the two then disagreed over the Kuenn-Colavito trade: Dykes wanted to keep Kuenn while DeWitt wanted the trade. Before the season even started, DeWitt had to publicly disclaim rumors that he was ready to fire Dykes.

"It was sort of general knowledge that Dykes and DeWitt apparently didn't get along," said Billy Hitchcock, Dykes' third base coach in Detroit. "It wasn't something you talked about, but it was known. There was a feeling that DeWitt was going to clean house."

The problems continued during the regular season as the losses mounted. According to Dykes, DeWitt constantly told him which players to use, even sending him telegrams on the road.

With this unhealthy situation in mind, here is how Dykes, in his book, described his actual response to the proposed manager trade: "My first thought was to tell Bill DeWitt to go jump into Lake Michigan. My second was to wonder if this was not one way out of the maze I was in.... Two little words from me would rid me of Bill DeWitt for life. I said them: 'I'll go.'"[7]

In Cleveland, Gordon had also been embroiled in a long-standing tempestuous relationship with Lane. Their problem—unlike the Dykes-DeWitt feud—was a clash of personalities.

Gordon was a fiery, emotional ballplayer when he was a star second baseman for the Yankees and Indians in the late 1930s and 1940s. He carried over those traits when Lane picked him to manage the Indians midway through the 1958 season. Lane, of course, was equally fiery and emotional, and apparently there was room for only one headstrong individual in massive Municipal Stadium.

"I would say it was a somewhat rocky relationship," said Indians infielder George Strickland. "I don't think it was an ideal marriage, so to speak."

"It was like mixing oil and water," added Indians pitcher Herb Score.

The Gordon-Lane controversy exploded in soap opera fashion in September 1959, as it became obvious that the Indians would not catch the White Sox in the American League pennant race. Lane openly criticized Gordon's managing style, in part for not taking a more conservative approach.

"You know, I'm not against gambling to win ballgames if the gambling is done right, but I'm really a percentage guy," Lane told reporters at the time. "Joe's a gambler. If you keep gambling and lose, then you're gambling too much. Gordon has been playing that kind of ball all year. To my mind, the hit and run is the worst play in baseball—unless you have specialists working it, like Nellie Fox and Luis Aparicio."[8] "Joe was a hunch player, no question," Score acknowledged. "He wasn't an Al Lopez-type who went by the percentages. Joe would say, 'You look like you're gonna get a hit. Go up there and pinch hit.' But Frank was a little bit of a hunch player himself. In many ways, they were alike."

Fed up with Lane's criticisms, Gordon announced he would resign as manager after the 1959 season. Not to be outdone, Lane fired Gordon on September 22. Then, at a press conference the following day, Lane announced that "we couldn't think of anyone better to succeed Gordon than Gordon himself," and he gave Gordon a new two-year contract. It was one of those bizarre episodes only Frank Lane could dream up.[9]

By August 1960, however, things had soured again between the two. And when his rollercoaster ride with the Indians ended, Gordon accepted his fate passively.

"If I can do anything to help an unpleasant situation, I will do it," Gordon said upon leaving Cleveland. "I tried everything I know and nothing has worked."[10]

Gordon might have had reason to publicly bash Lane, but he didn't.

"Joe was the type who didn't complain a lot," said Mel Harder, Gordon's pitching coach in Cleveland. "He didn't complain to the players. He just bid 'em all goodbye. And then he told me there's a good fella coming in, Jimmie Dykes."

If this were a Hollywood script, the ending would have been obvious: Gordon and Dykes would have magically turned around their teams' fortunes and they would have fought it out for the pennant. But that was not the case. In the end, the results of the Dykes-Gordon deal did not come close to living up to the fanfare that it first created.

Shortly after switching uniforms, Dykes and Gordon each arranged for his second-in-command to make a similar move. Jo Jo White moved from Cleveland to join Gordon, and Luke Appling moved from Detroit to join Dykes in what might be viewed as an equally rare "trade" of coaches.

But all the changes did not translate into victories. During the last two months of the season, Dykes was 26–32 with the Indians as they finished in fourth place, 21 games behind the champion Yankees. Gordon was 26–31 with the Tigers, as they finished in sixth place and 26 games out.

Although there was no big turnabout in the standings, at least there was considerably more peace under the new regimes. Gordon did add some of the enthusiasm DeWitt had hoped for. And Dykes' calming influence with the Indians was noticeable, particularly in his handling of the temperamental Jimmy Piersall, whose problems with Gordon were widely publicized.

"I wanted to send [Lane] some orchids when he traded Gordon," acknowledged Piersall.

However, the peace lasted for only a short time for both teams. Just after the 1960 season, Gordon resigned his position in Detroit to become manager of the Kansas City Athletics. The fates then played a cruel joke on him when the A's named a new general manager three months later. It was none other than Frank Lane, who had run into some trouble himself with Indians' ownership over their disappointing season and resigned under fire.

When Gordon and Lane were reunited in Kansas City, they went to great lengths to assure the public that they indeed could work together. But two months into the 1961 season, Lane fired Gordon one final time. Gordon managed only once more—with the 1969 A's—and he ended up with a career record of 305–308 in five seasons.

DeWitt also left the Tigers after the turbulent 1960 season. His actions were not what the ownership apparently wanted, and he also resigned under fire less than a month after Gordon's departure. He immediately went to the Cincinnati Reds as general manager, and his wheeling and dealing helped lead them to the 1961 National League pennant. In March 1962, he bought the ballclub.

Dykes was the only key figure of the manager trade to stay with the same team in 1961, but even he did not make it through the entire year. The day before the season ended, he was fired by new Indians general manager Gabe Paul as the team was heading toward another disappointing fifth-place finish. That was the end of the line for Dykes' managerial career, which featured 1,406 wins, 1,541 losses and not a single finish higher than third place.

Notes

1. *Detroit News*, 3 August 1960.
2. *Cleveland Press*, 3 August 1960.
3. *Detroit News*, 31 July 1960.
4. *Cleveland Press*, 2 August 1960.
5. *Detroit Free Press*, 3 August 1960.
6. *Cleveland Press*, 3 August 1960.
7. Jimmie Dykes, with Charles O. Dexter, *You Can't Steal First Base*, (Philadelphia: Lippincott, 1967).
8. *Chicago Tribune*, 22 September 1959.
9. United Press International, 24 September 1959.
10. UPI, 3 August 1960.

What a Steal!

*June 15, 1964: The St. Louis Cardinals
trade Ernie Broglio, Bobby Shantz
and Doug Clemens to the Chicago Cubs
for Lou Brock, Jack Spring and Paul Toth*

Every organization has made a trade that did not turn out exactly as it had planned. For the Chicago Cubs, and especially their fans, the bad dream that will not go away is the Lou Brock-for-Ernie Broglio deal. Sure, other players were involved in the transaction—it was actually a six-player exchange—but those others were just bit players in this production. The principals were indeed Brock and Broglio.

When the trade went through on June 15, 1964, the Cubs thought they had picked the Cardinals' pockets. Broglio had been an 18-game winner the season before, and the Cubs front office believed he would be the last link in forging a legitimate pennant contender.

When things finally settled out, however, it was the Cubs who were crying robbery. Broglio wound up with a bum arm and won only seven games for the Cubs before drifting out of major league baseball in 1966. And as for becoming an instant pennant contender, the Cubs had to wait until 1984 before finally reaching the playoffs.

Brock, meanwhile, became a star the instant he arrived in St. Louis and went on to a Hall of Fame career as one of the most acclaimed leadoff men and base-stealers of all time. Besides stealing 938 bases—a record later broken by Rickey Henderson—he finished with 3,023 hits and a lifetime .293 batting average. He also made the World Series his personal stage after helping the Cardinals win three National League pennants.

Brock's biggest contribution, however, went beyond mere numbers. He helped raise the art of base-running to a new level by showing that a stolen base could be almost as potent a weapon as a home run. Brock was very good at what he did, and he knew it.

"I don't steal bases. I take them," he once told a reporter. "I'm an artist and this is my masterpiece."[1]

Bing Devine, the Cardinals general manager who orchestrated the Brock trade, admitted he did not realize at the time that he was negotiating for a virtuoso.

"Did we know he'd go into the Hall of Fame? Absolutely not," Devine said. "Nobody's all that smart. All you do is take the best of the knowledge of the people surrounding you, and then you make a decision and hope that it's right. In Brock's case, it was.

"If a player is in the big leagues, then he has some talent. Sometimes it takes a change of scenery to bring it out."

Was that the case with Brock?

"Probably so."

It is not surprising that the Cubs were willing to give up so early on Brock, who still had not turned 25 when the trade was made. In a little more than two seasons on Chicago's North Side, he had done little to indicate he would someday have his name mentioned in the same breath as Ty Cobb.

Brock came up to the Cubs with great expectations in September 1961. In his only season of minor league ball, Brock led the Class C Northern League in hitting (.361), hits (181), runs (117) and doubles (33), in addition to stealing 38 bases. This prompted one Chicago sportswriter to describe Brock as baseball's next potential .400 hitter.

With the Cubs, however, he had two uninspired seasons in which he batted just .263 in 1962 and .258 in 1963. He combined for just 40 stolen bases during those seasons, and collected strikeouts at an alarming rate. If that was not enough, he impressed nobody with his fielding.

Oddly, his biggest moment with the Cubs was very un–Brock-like. On June 17, 1962, he hit a mammoth home run in New York's famed Polo Grounds—one of only a handful ever to reach the center-field bleachers there.

Despite his meager contributions with the Cubs, Brock had some big admirers down in St. Louis, where the Cardinals were looking for another outfielder to team up with Curt Flood.

"We actually had tried to acquire Brock almost a year before we did," Devine said. "We thought that we needed an outfielder, and several of our people were interested in him. I'm sure we had discussions about other outfielders with other clubs, too, but we liked Brock mostly because of his running speed, and the fact that to go with that, he had power."

Brock's unpolished defensive play was not a major concern to Devine or his manager, Johnny Keane. "The fact that he was a bad outfielder in Chicago was emphasized a lot by the nature of the field there, with the wind," Devine added. "We thought with a bigger outfield [in St. Louis], he could eliminate some of his shortcomings with his speed."

Devine soon discovered that if he wanted Brock so badly, the price would have to be a pitcher. Cubs General Manager John Holland was looking for a starter to complete the Cubs' starting rotation that included Dick Ellsworth, Larry Jackson and Bob Buhl. The Cardinals seemed to have more than enough pitching, with a staff that included Bob Gibson, Curt Simmons, Ray Sadecki and Ernie Broglio.

As Devine recalls, he talked to Holland and mentioned two or three pitchers who would be available for a deal involving Brock. On June 13, 1964, just two days before the trading deadline, Devine called Holland and found out the Cubs were indeed interested in making a deal. The pitcher Holland wanted was Broglio, a 28-year-old righty who had been 21–9, 9–12, 12–9 and 18–8 in four previous seasons in St. Louis.

Devine then caught up to Keane on the team's charter flight to Houston and asked if his manager would go along with the trade.

"What are we waiting for?" the enthusiastic Keane said.

The trade was announced two days later, with Brock and little-used pitchers Jack Spring and Paul Toth going to the Cards for Broglio, veteran reliever Bobby Shantz and outfielder Doug Clemens. The deal seemed made to order for both teams. The Cubs and Cardinals were flirting with the .500 mark and looked in desperate need of someone fresh to get their seasons back on track. At the time, both key players also seemed to be in need of a change: Brock was batting .251 with 10 stolen bases; Broglio was 3–5.

For the most part, the Cubs were ecstatic about the transaction. Third baseman Ron Santo said: "I've never had the feeling before that we could go all the way. With our pitching staff now, we can win the pennant."[2]

Cubs head coach Bob Kennedy publicly supported his general manager by telling reporters that "the deal puts us in a much better position to make a run for the flag."[3] In reality, Kennedy says it was a different story.

"The coaches—Fred Martin, Lou Klein and Rube Walker—and myself were deadset against it ... we told [Holland] we didn't want to make the trade," Kennedy recalled in 1994. "Brock was an everyday player, and he was just a young guy coming into his own. You didn't have to be any mental giant or genius of judgment to tell that.

"In fact, the day the trade was made was an off day. I told all the coaches to go hide someplace, and I told my wife that John Holland's gonna call ... they're gonna be lookin' for me cause this is the deadline on the trade. I said I'm gonna go play golf, and if anybody calls, you don't know where I am or what I'm doing. My wife lied all day, and finally it was going to cost me my job if she didn't tell him. So finally I had to come in, and I was the one who had to tell Brock he was traded.

"But that's the way it goes. If management wants to do it, they'll do it."

In St. Louis, Devine was widely criticized for the trade. As Cardinals first baseman Bill White recalled, "We thought we had given up too much. Brock was not a good fielder, he struck out a lot and didn't know how to run the bases."[4] Noted New York columnist Red Smith also questioned the trade when he wrote: "St. Louis has been desperate for outfielders with power, but at first thought, one has to wonder whether Brock is the guy to fill that need.

Or, to view it from a slightly different angle, did the Cardinals get full value for what they gave?"[5]

Even Devine had to wonder if he made the right call when Brock arrived for his first game and struck out as a pinch-hitter in his only at-bat against Houston.

"He didn't do much of anything that night, and the club played badly again and lost," Devine recalled. "An assistant of mine and I were sitting in the stands behind the Cardinal dugout and there were fans sitting around kind of making fun of the team and their performance. Their main chorus was kind of, 'Brock for Broglio, Brock for Broglio. Who could do that?' And my assistant and I walked down the steps leading under the stands after the ballgame, and I guess trying to be light-hearted about it, I said, 'The truth of the matter is, Who could do that?'"

Regardless of that inauspicious debut, Brock was thrilled to be in a Cardinals uniform. Or, more accurately, he was thrilled to be out of a Cubs uniform. The young outfielder had soured on the Cubs' system, which he claims had turned him into a player without focus.

When Brock arrived on the Cubs' scene, the team was experimenting with its so-called College of Coaches. Instead of having a manager and a staff of coaches to assist him, the Cubs gave the coaches more-or-less equal authority and rotated them in and out of the head position.

Brock had the physical talent to be a star, but he needed some direction. Under the College of Coaches, he got too much direction.

"It was like being in a prison yard with everyone waiting for you to do something wrong," Brock told reporters. "Trying to become acclimated to the big leagues, under that system, was the hardest thing for me in baseball. Manager? We didn't have one. Just 14 indians and 14 chiefs. And you couldn't believe the jealousy among the coaches. One would come to me and say, 'You're my man.' Then another would say, 'You'll just hit against right-handers because you can't hit left-handed pitching.' Then another would say, 'You're not gonna mess up my two weeks as head coach.'"[6]

In Brock's autobiography, *Stealing Is My Game*, he said that Cubs great Ernie Banks tried to boost his confidence by telling him to tune out the distractions and just rely on his God-given talent. It did not help.

Although the College of Coaches was put to rest before the 1963 season—when the Cubs settled on Bob Kennedy as head coach—the damage had been done. Brock was not a consistent long-ball threat, but he still fancied himself as a home run hitter. And although he had the speed to wreak havoc on the base paths, he kept his base-stealing attempts at a minimum rather than risk the wrath of the coach-of-the-day by failing.

In short, at the time he was peddled to the Cardinals, Brock was still a prospect struggling with his game both on the field and in his mind. At least that is how he described it in his autobiography: "I'm not sure I conquered

Lou Brock went from a struggling young prospect to a Hall of Famer after the Chicago Cubs made the infamous trade that sent him to the St. Louis Cardinals in 1964 (George Brace photograph).

any of my more glaring weaknesses, but I do know that I got unsteadier at the very things I could excel in. Little wonder they traded me."[7]

His arrival in St. Louis changed everything. Instead of being bombarded with instructions, he was basically told to go out and contribute. Nothing more.

"Among the first things I noticed with St. Louis was that the club was run on the principle of individual independence," Brock noted. "If you wanted to do something, you did it; you didn't have to fill out forms.

"Once—this was the major turning point in my experience—Johnny Keane said to me, 'Since you've got the speed for it, I guess you're going to want to try stealing bases.'

"'Hell yes, for sure,' I said.

"'Well, you're on. Go when it seems right to go.' That's all he said."[8]

Given the green light to steal on his own and develop his own batting style, Brock flourished. And he flourished faster than anyone could imagine.

Batting in the number two spot behind Curt Flood, Brock started rapping out hits by the bunch. There was that doubleheader against Philadelphia on June 28 when he went 2-for-4 and 3-for-5. And that doubleheader against Pittsburgh on July 13 when he was a combined 7-for-11. And that first series against his former teammates in late July when he went 6-for-16 and helped the Cards sweep the Cubs three straight.

By August 1, just a month-and-a-half after the trade, Brock's average was up to .301 and he had 25 stolen bases. Despite Brock's contributions, however, the Cardinals could not seem to make a run at the first-place Phillies. On August 17, with the Cards still in fifth place, owner Gus Busch fired Bing Devine.

In late August, the Cards went on a hot streak in which they won 13 of 16 games to get back into the race. Then they won eight in a row in late September. This allowed them to overtake the Phillies, who led St. Louis by 6½ games on September 21 but blew the lead in legendary fashion by losing 10 in a row.

Going into the final day of the season, the Cardinals and Cincinnati Reds were tied for first, with the Phillies a game back. When the Cardinals beat the Mets 11–5 and the Phillies beat the Reds 10–0, St. Louis was the National League champion. Following the Cardinals' victory, fans rushed onto the field and carried off Brock on their shoulders.

Cardinal third baseman Ken Boyer was named league MVP and Ray Sadecki finished 20–11 to lead the pitching staff, but Keane was quick to acknowledge that the team would not have reached the World Series without Brock, who batted .348 and stole 33 bases in his 103 games with St. Louis. He was especially productive against the Cubs, batting .418 while helping St. Louis win 9 of 12 games. For the season, Brock finished with a .315 average and 43 stolen bases.

In the World Series, the Cards beat the Yankees in seven games as Series MVP Bob Gibson picked up a pair of victories. Although Brock batted .300, he did not contribute the key hits. It was a rather low-key performance, but he would make up for that a few years later.

Bing Devine, who received some vindication after the season when he was named Executive of the Year by the general managers of major league baseball, gives Keane the credit for Brock's quick turnabout.

"Johnny Keane was probably the best manager I've ever worked with," Devine said. "He saw some things in Brock that would give him a chance to maximize his best ability. And this wasn't just with Brock, but with all ballplayers."

The 1964 Cubs, on the other hand, found out that Broglio was not the answer to their dreams. Although he was impressive in his debut—pitching seven shutout innings before losing 2–0 to the Pirates—it took a month and six more starts before he won his first game for his new team. The Cubs wound up in eighth place with a 76–86 record, and Broglio finished 7–12 and in need of elbow surgery during the off-season.

He would spend two more seasons with the Cubs, and win only three more games during his stay in Chicago. Broglio admitted in an interview in 1995 that he had hurt his arm before the deal was even made: "At the time, it wasn't very serious. It kept getting worse."[9]

Devine denies that he knowlingly delivered damaged goods to the Cubs. "I've heard that story, too," Devine said. "I don't think I've ever traded a ballplayer in my life that I had any suspicion was having a problem before we checked out the problem and ascertained for sure what was true. And that goes for Broglio."

While Broglio was fading out of the picture, things kept getting better and better for Brock. Although his chief benefactor, Keane, left St. Louis after the 1964 championship, new Cardinals manager Red Schoendienst allowed Brock to remain the point man of his attack. In fact, Schoendienst started using Brock in the leadoff position in 1965, and he was even more effective.

For the next 15 seasons, Brock's mission would never change: Get on base, steal another, and set up the batters behind him. In short, his job was to distract and torment pitchers around the National League.

Brock also started to build up the statistics that made him a four-time All-Star. Until his production started to tail off at age 38 in 1977, he never stole fewer than 50 bases in any season. He led the league in stolen bases eight times during this stretch. He was also consistent at the plate, batting .300 or better eight times. Although Brock was still considered a defensive liability and he never could completely shake the strikeout bugaboo, those failings were overshadowed by his feats on the base path.

"My approach to stealing bases was that I was in the league three years before I found my career was going in that direction," Brock said.[10]

The baseball world had a chance to see Brock at his best in 1967 and 1968. He had back-to-back World Series performances that set new standards for offensive production.

Against the Boston Red Sox in 1967, Brock batted .414, piled up 12 hits, stole seven bases and scored eight runs as the Cardinals won the Series in seven games. It was a quintessential Brock show, as he kept the Boston pitchers off-guard with his base-running bravado. During one sequence in game seven, for example, Brock singled, stole second, stole third and then scored on a sacrifice fly.

Against the Detroit Tigers in 1968, Brock's offensive contributions were even a notch higher. He batted .464, with a Series record-tying 13 hits and seven more stolen bases. The only downside was that the Cardinals lost this Series in seven games.

That was Brock's final fling in postseason play, but he left his mark in the record books. His 14 total stolen bases tied the record for World Series play, and his composite .391 batting average was second best.

Between then and his retirement in 1979, Brock would dominate the headlines three more times:

• In 1974, when he was 35, Brock shattered the single-season stolen base record when he swiped 118. Brock said it took 12 years of analyzing opposing pitchers before he could complete the "book" that allowed him to break Maury Wills' record of 104.

• On Monday, August 29, 1977, Brock became baseball's all-time stolen-base leader when he "took" a pair against San Diego to break Ty Cobb's career mark of 892.

• On Monday, August 13, 1979, Brock became the 14th player to reach 3,000 hits. Fittingly, the milestone base hit was a single against the Cubs.

In January, 1985, Brock became the 15th player elected to the Hall of Fame in his first year of eligibility.

"Changing the impact of the stolen base is my contribution to the game," Brock said. "Once upon a time, it was something you did only if you were two runs up or down. If you did it at other times, you'd get one in the ribs or get spiked or banged around. It took a few guys to take a pounding, to defy the whole theory. It took that kind of stance to change the attitude toward stolen bases. Now they are no longer an insult. I helped pioneer that area."[11]

Long-suffering Cubs fans, of course, wonder if Brock ever would have reached such heights if he had stayed in Chicago.

"Sure, he would have," Bob Kennedy said. "His potential was outstanding."

And then there is Ernie Broglio, whose place in baseball history is secure for all the wrong reasons. He simply had the misfortune to be traded for Lou Brock and never live up to everyone's expectations in Chicago. Many years after the trade, Broglio was invited to an old-timers' game in Chicago. The fans' reaction, as Broglio recalled with a laugh, was not unexpected: "I was probably the only player who got a standing boo."[12]

Notes

1. *Chicago Tribune,* 13 July 1979.
2. *Chicago Tribune,* 16 June 1964.
3. *Chicago Sun-Times,* 16 June 1964.
4. *Chicago Tribune,* 15 June 1989.
5. *Chicago Sun-Times,* 18 June 1964.
6. *Chicago Tribune,* 8 July 1977.
7. Lou Brock and Franz Schulze, *Stealing Is My Game* (Englewood Cliffs, N.J.: Prentice-Hall, 1976).
8. Ibid.
9. *Chicago Tribune,* 22 January 1995.
10. *Chicago Tribune,* 8 September 1974.
11. *Chicago Sun-Times,* 12 August 1979.
12. Associated Press, 7 June 1992.

New League, Same Story

December 9, 1965: Cincinnati Reds
trade Frank Robinson to
the Baltimore Orioles for Milt Pappas,
Jack Baldschun and Dick Simpson

"An old 30."[1]

That is how Cincinnati Reds owner and General Manager Bill DeWitt dismissed Frank Robinson after trading him to the Baltimore Orioles on December 9, 1965. It was a bold and calculated move by DeWitt, a fearless wheeler-dealer who had pulled off other blockbuster trades. But the trade of Robinson was still a gamble.

After all, the power-hitting Robinson had torn up the National League since he broke in with the Reds in 1956 and won Rookie of the Year honors by batting .290 with 38 home runs. For 10 years with the Reds, Robinson averaged 32 home runs and 101 runs batted in, including a Most Valuable Player season in 1961 when he batted .323, belted 37 homers and led the team to the National League pennant.

But DeWitt, who built the Reds' 1961 championship team with the aid of some shrewd trades, believed the team needed considerable improvement in 1966 to contend for another title. And his trade bait was Robinson. The slugging outfielder was a force in 1965 with a .296 batting average, 33 homers and 113 RBIs, but the bottom line for the Reds was their team finish—fourth place behind the champion Los Angeles Dodgers, San Francisco Giants and Pittsburgh Pirates. That did not cut it with DeWitt, who offered Robinson to a number of clubs, including the Houston Astros and New York Yankees.

The Orioles, with new general manager Harry Dalton, were more than willing to acquire Robinson and add some sock to an already potent lineup that included Brooks Robinson, Boog Powell and Curt Blefary. Baltimore was envisioning a modern-day "Murderers' Row" with the ferocious-playing Robinson.

So the interleague deal between the Orioles and Reds was consummated—Baltimore got Robinson and Cincinnati obtained pitchers Milt Pappas and Jack Baldschun and outfielder Dick Simpson. The Orioles had moved into position to deal with the Reds only days earlier by acquiring two players that Cincinnati also had pursued. Six days before the trade, Baltimore had obtained Simpson, a speedy rookie, from the California Angels in exchange for Norm Siebern. And three days before the trade, the Orioles had traded outfielder Jackie Brandt and pitcher Darold Knowles to the Philadelphia Phillies for Baldschun who was 5–8 with a 3.82 earned run average in 1965.

Dalton, the former director of the Oriole farm system who had been appointed to his new position only two days earlier, was ecstatic about obtaining Robinson. "I'm thrilled with the deal because it gives us that big established power hitter which we have sought for so long," Dalton said. "We've now got four cannons at the four corners—Frank Robinson in right, Curt Blefary in left, Brooks Robinson at third and Boog Powell at first."[2]

And Dalton's opinion was heartily endorsed by Hank Bauer, the Orioles' manager. "This is the guy we've been looking for," Bauer gushed. "I think he's a helluva ballplayer. At least he has been for 10 years. He drives in 100 runs a year and from the reports I have, he's a good man to have on the club, a team leader. I know we gave up a lot to get him, but any deal is a gamble."[3]

Robinson's reaction? It came from the perspective of a veteran who had played a decade in the majors. "It's the sort of thing you kind of come to expect in baseball," Robinson said.[4]

Robinson, bothered by chronic soreness in his right shoulder each spring, had contemplated quitting only three years earlier. The trade, however, put Robinson in a different frame of mind. Robinson said giving up the game "is now the farthest thought from my mind. I aim to keep going in the game just as long as I can, and I'm looking forward to playing in Baltimore. Now that I've kinda got myself together and thought it over, I like the deal."[5]

The Reds believed they got sufficient return for Robinson, a player they thought could be headed for an imminent decline. Cincinnati was subscribing to the belief that it was important to trade a marquee player before he underwent a noticeable slowdown that would greatly diminish his value.

The Reds thought the trade satisfied their biggest need—pitching. DeWitt believed in experienced pitching and he got it with the 26-year-old Pappas, one of the Orioles' most consistent pitchers in 1965 with a 13–9 record and 2.61 ERA. The right-handed Pappas had compiled a winning record each year for Baltimore since he went 15–9 in 1959. And the Reds expected the 29-year-old Baldschun to bolster their relief corps.

"Don't forget pitching is the name of the game," DeWitt said. "The lack of it, especially in the bullpen, beat us last season."[6]

That was the year in which the Reds were in pennant contention for most of the season but faded in the final weeks and finished fourth. The key player as far as Cincinnati was concerned was Pappas, who owned a 110–74 career record and had pitched more shutouts, complete games and innings and had made more starts than any other active or retired Oriole. And his statistics

No player has ever made a bigger impact following a trade than Frank Robinson (above). After Baltimore picked him up for the 1966 season, he won the Triple Crown and led the Orioles to the world championship. Milt Pappas, who went to the Reds in the deal, never lived up to their high expectations. Photograph courtesy of the Cincinnati Reds.

could have been more impressive had he not endured a series of injuries. "I'm going to a good club," said Pappas, "and the Orioles are getting a great hitter. I think both teams will be pennant contenders next year."[7]

The Orioles, who had finished third in the American League in 1965 with a 94–68 record, certainly were capable of a first-place finish if Robinson could produce a banner season. But there were several questions hovering over Robinson. Would his career—which by all appearances had Hall of Fame written all over it—continue to flourish in another league? DeWitt had thrown down the gauntlet. Was Robinson up for the challenge? And could Robinson adjust to American League pitchers?

The answers were not long in coming. Robinson, batting third ahead of Brooks Robinson, got off to a great start in 1966. The Orioles opened the season April 12 with a 5–4 victory over the Boston Red Sox at Fenway Park as Robinson made it known that at 30, he was far from over the hill, and in fact, might still be peaking. Robinson collected two hits, including a homer, and perhaps making a point or just acting frisky, also swiped a base. The next day Robinson continued his surge with another homer in the Orioles'

8–1 victory over the Red Sox. After two games, Robinson had two homers—and two stolen bases—and the Orioles were 2–0.

Baltimore lost its first game in its home opener against the New York Yankees, but once again Robinson provided a thrill. With one out in the ninth inning and the Orioles trailing 3–1, Robinson blasted a pitch by left-hander Fritz Peterson into the left-field bleachers to stir a crowd of 35,624 fans. Peterson got the next two batters to gain the victory, but Robinson did not disappoint the home folks, producing his third homer in three games.

Robinson's homer streak ended at three games, but he still contributed a run-scoring double in the Orioles' 7–2 victory over the Yankees that boosted Baltimore to a 3–1 record. Brooks Robinson cracked a three-run homer in that game—his third homer of the season—to put opponents on the alert that they had a double dose of Robinsons to worry about.

Two weeks into the season, Frank Robinson was bashing the ball at a team-high .444 clip, but there was one discouraging note. He admitted his right shoulder hurt "more than it has in 10 years" and he was forced to relay his throws from right field to the second baseman.[8] But the pain seemed to have little effect on his potent bat.

With Robinson leading the way, the Orioles maintained a furious early pace. The Orioles won 12 of their first 13 games. Even when the Orioles lost three of the next six games, they remained tied for first with the Cleveland Indians. By contrast, the Reds were spinning their wheels. Cincinnati was floundering in ninth place with a 7–14 record—a dismal .333 pace—and trailed the San Francisco Giants by a whopping nine games four weeks into the season.

What is more, Robinson was showing no signs of easing up. In the Orioles' 19th game of the season, Robinson became the first player to hit a fair ball out of Baltimore's Memorial Stadium. It came in the first inning of the second game of a doubleheader sweep over the Indians, as Robinson swatted a home run that cleared the left-field bleachers. It was Robinson's second homer of the day and his seventh of the young season. An admiring Brooks Robinson said of his teammate's mammoth shot: "It was measured at 451 feet on the fly and 540 feet overall. He really creamed it. He's a tremendous guy to be playing with and to hit behind. He gets on base so often, and he can steal and set up a run for us. Sure, that puts pressure on me, but I enjoy it."[9]

And Frank Robinson was enjoying his torrid start. Even when most of his teammates stopped hitting in May, he remained hot. Boog Powell, the Orioles' first baseman, endured a 1-for-40 streak. "In all the time I have been in baseball," said Manager Hank Bauer, "I have never seen a team go into a hitting slump like this. If we hadn't had Brooks and Frank, I don't know where we would be."[10]

With the spotlight on the Orioles' right fielder, the Reds' mastermind of the Robinson trade tried to explain his rationale for the move. DeWitt, who became general manager of the Reds in late 1960, was well-respected in baseball circles. He turned around a team that finished sixth the year before into a National League champion in his first year by trading two older players, pitcher Cal McLish and shortstop Roy McMillan, for pitcher Joey Jay and third baseman Gene Freese. But DeWitt was clearly on the defensive with the Robinson trade, although he maintained in June 1966 that it was the way to go in his bid "to balance the age" of the Reds.[11]

> We traded Robinson because we needed pitching. In the spring of 1965, we thought we had the best pitching staff in the league. It didn't turn out that way—it was one of the worst—and we felt that we couldn't go along with the pitching we had. Joey Jay had an ordinary year, Jim O'Toole a poor one and we didn't know if they'd come back.
>
> We had to shore up the pitching. We talked to Baltimore, the Giants, the Cubs, everybody. Baltimore kept saying, "We need an outfielder." We had tried to get Baldschun from Philadelphia, we had made half a dozen offers, but we couldn't get him. Then Baltimore got Baldschun and they got Simpson from California.
>
> They put the three of them together—Pappas, Baldschun and Simpson— and we made the trade. Last year we scored 200 more runs than the Dodgers and when you score runs like that and finish fourth, it means that scoring runs is not the whole answer to winning.
>
> We had Robinson here 10 years. We won one pennant with him. But to follow the [longtime baseball executive] Branch Rickey theory, we'd rather trade a player too soon than a year too late. And Pappas is winning for us now.[12]
>
> I learned from a guy named Rickey that you have to have a lot of speed on a ballclub. Speed can help you on offense and defense. We try to get speed all the time.
>
> The guy we got in the Frank Robinson trade, Dick Simpson, is one of the fastest in professional baseball. He runs the 100 in 9.5. Speed and youth. You try to keep your regular players young and your pitchers experienced.[13]

What DeWitt did not count on was Robinson playing with such reckless abandon. By mid–June, Robinson was leading the league in batting average at .349 and homers with 18. Robinson also won a game with his defense, leaping into the seats at Yankee Stadium to snare a potential game-winning three-run homer off the bat of Roy White with two out in the bottom of the ninth.

Was Robinson's stirring performances a surprise? Not to those who had seen Robinson play day in and day out in the National League. Gene Freese, the White Sox infielder who had played with Robinson on the Reds' team that won the pennant in 1961, was typical. "He is absolutely the best ballplayer I've ever played with," he said. "He's got more guts than anyone I've ever seen, bar none."[14]

Robinson always challenged pitchers to throw inside on him. He led the National League in being hit by pitches six of his ten seasons there. In the

American League, he continued to make things miserable for pitchers by daring them to throw near him. If he could reach base somehow to help his team, even by getting hit by a pitch, it was worth it.

"He's one of the greatest guys to play with that you could ever find," said Smoky Burgess, the Chicago White Sox pinch-hitting standout, "and there's just no backing him away from the plate. He'll just stand right there and let the ball hit him."[15]

No one appreciated Robinson's presence more than Brooks Robinson, winner of the American League's Most Valuable Player award two seasons earlier. "To me," Brooks Robinson said, "it's just like trying to keep up with the Joneses. With Frank in the lineup, I can count on having a man on base practically every time I come to bat.

"This has got to make it easier for me to drive in runs. I don't know whether it's because he's here or not but I'm off to the best start of my career."[16]

With his $60,000 annual salary, Frank Robinson came to the Orioles making considerable more than Brooks, despite the fact that the latter had made the all-star team the previous six years. But there was no envy, no jealousy. Brooks realized Frank Robinson's importance.

"You look at Frank's record," said Brooks, "and you've got to see right away why he's making big money. He's the best hitter the Orioles have had since they've been back in the league."[17]

Behind the two Robinsons, the Orioles extended their lead to 12 games over Detroit in late July. This was a sharp contrast to the woes of the Reds, who had lost 11 straight and had fired their manager, Don Heffner, and replaced him with 33-year-old Dave Bristol.

Although Brooks Robinson could not sustain his torrid pace in the second half, Frank Robinson did not let up and the Orioles were sailing toward the pennant. But there still were some unhappy moments for the Orioles. Brooks was peeved in August that he was quoted as saying his team already had locked up the pennant. "I never said it," he insisted.[18]

Frank Robinson, however, told Brooks not to worry. "You don't have to apologize for nothin'. We're ahead. Let 'em come catch us if they can."[19]

With Frank Robinson almost a lock to be named the league's Most Valuable Player, DeWitt still believed his trade might possibly look a little better the following year. But there was no denying the Orioles were thriving and the Reds were not. Cincinnati won 22 of its first 33 games under Bristol, but they were too far back by then to make a difference. The Orioles, meanwhile, seemed to shake off every mini-slump they encountered.

After Baltimore lost 10 of 15 games, Robinson picked up the sagging Orioles with another dramatic display. This time he slammed a two-run homer off Cleveland's Luis Tiant in the eighth inning to give the Orioles a 2–1 victory.

With a month to go in the season, an Orioles pennant appeared inevitable. But there still remained some suspense. Robinson had a shot at the Triple Crown. He was leading the league in homers, leading the league in batting and contending for the lead in RBIs. As for pressure? Robinson did not feel any.

He said his ability to stay loose was the prime force behind his remarkable season. "I don't try to be relaxed," he said simply. "I just am."[20]

Although the Orioles cooled off down the stretch, there were not many anxious moments. Baltimore finished in first place with a 97–63 record, easily beating out the Minnesota Twins, who finished nine games behind, and the Detroit Tigers, who wound up 10 games off the pace.

In the Orioles' 6–1 pennant-clinching victory over the Kansas City A's, Robinson knocked out three hits and drove in two runs. He ended the season as the Triple Crown winner, with a .316 batting average, 49 home runs and 122 RBIs. Robinson won the Triple Crown with ease, outdistancing runners-up Tony Oliva in batting by nine points, Harmon Killebrew in homers by 10 and Killebrew in RBIs by 12.

Baltimore's World Series opponent was the Los Angeles Dodgers, a team that had squeaked past the Pittsburgh Pirates and San Francisco Giants to claim the National League pennant. The Dodgers, who finished two games ahead of the Pirates and four ahead of the Giants with a 91–64 record, were favored over the Orioles primarily because of their awesome pitching. Twenty-seven game winner Sandy Koufax led a staff that also included Don Drysdale, Claude Osteen and Phil Regan. Furthermore, Baltimore, though its lead dipped below 10 games only in early September, had not been impressive down the stretch.

But Robinson was in no mood to be upstaged. He had come this far and did not want anything to mar his remarkable season.

In game one of the World Series, the Robinsons—Frank and Brooks—hit back-to-back homers in the first inning off Drysdale. Although Baltimore starter Dave McNally was ineffective, the Orioles hung on for a 5–2 victory. Robinson took a back seat to the Orioles' pitching in games two and three, with Jim Palmer and Wally Bunker throwing shutouts in 6–0 and 1–0 victories. But in game four, Robinson again delivered. He smoked a fourth-inning solo home run into the left-field stands off Drysdale that would be the only run of the game. With McNally hurling the shutout, the Orioles swept the Series by holding the Dodgers scoreless the final three games; Los Angeles did not score in the last 33 innings. For the series, Los Angeles scored only a run in the second and third innings of game one. Robinson was named the outstanding player of the fall classic.

There was no surprise when the American League Most Valuable Player ballots were tabulated: Frank Robinson had won and it was unanimous. He was the third unanimous American League Most Valuable Player selection, joining Mickey Mantle of the New York Yankees, honored in 1956, and Al

Rosen of the Cleveland Indians, honored in 1953. Robinson also became the first player to be selected Most Valuable Player in both leagues.

"The first one [MVP] is always a big thrill," Robinson said. "But this is even bigger than the first one because I'm the first player to do it in two leagues."[21]

In 1961, Robinson had fallen only one first-place ballot short of another unanimous Most Valuable Player selection when he was named the top choice on 15 of 16 ballots. Pitcher Joey Jay, Robinson's teammate in Cincinnati, had been named first on the other ballot.

Robinson's selection as Most Valuable Player demonstrated how one-sided his trade to Baltimore was. Pappas, who was traded to Atlanta in June 1968, labored to a 12–11 record and 4.29 earned run average for the Reds, who plunged from fourth to seventh place. Baldschun was battered in relief and finished with a 1–5 record and 5.49 ERA. Simpson, the speedy outfielder, was unimpressive in 84 at-bats, hitting .238 with 26 runs, 14 RBIs, four homers and no stolen bases.

Evaluating his stirring year with the Orioles the following February, Robinson said he did not even consider it his top season to date, nor did he believe his 1961 MVP season with the Reds was his best. Instead Robinson cited his 1962 season with the Reds when he batted .342, with 39 homers and 51 doubles among his 208 hits, and drove in 136 runs.

"From mid–May on, I carried the club," said Robinson about the 1962 season in which the Reds finished third. "I hit the ball consistently and hard, and nearly half of my hits went for extra bases. But I didn't come close to repeating as the MVP. Tommy Davis [of the Dodgers] batted .346, had 230 hits and drove in 153 runs. And if that wasn't enough to bury me, Maury Wills [of the Dodgers] won the MVP award by stealing 104 bases."[22]

Frank Robinson was not one to mince words. Outspokenness came easily to him—and sometimes controversy followed. Before the 1967 season, Robinson took considerable criticism after saying that the National League was stronger than his new league, prompting a stinging reaction from some American League players. Still, Robinson wouldn't back away from the heat.

"I did say the National League was stronger overall," Robinson said. "But what this story doesn't mention is that I also said if you took the top five teams from each league and threw them in together, they'd play about even.

"The National League has more established stars, like [Willie] Mays, [Hank] Aaron, [Roberto] Clemente and [Willie] McCovey. But the American League is building up."[23]

Throughout his career, Robinson demonstrated he was not content with success, that he continually resolved to improve. And such was the case after his top-notch 1966 season. Robinson said he could do better in 1967. "I honestly believe I can improve on my .316 average and knock in more than 122 runs. Topping 49 homers will be the toughest job," said Robinson, whose season catapulted him into the exclusive $100,000-a-year salary class.[24]

Robinson came up with another solid season in 1967, but he could not match his Triple Crown year. His home runs fell by 19 to 30. His RBIs dropped by 28 to 94. And his average slipped five points to .311. All in all, it was an outstanding season for Robinson but not for the Orioles, who finished 76–85 as only one pitcher, Tom Phoebus, won at least 10 games.

Then in 1968, Robinson suffered through a miserable season in which he batted .268 and mustered only 15 homers. But this did not mark the end of the road for this proud player. Far from it. He rebounded the next three years to carry the Orioles into the World Series each time. The Orioles lost to the New York Mets, four games to one, in 1969, and to the Pittsburgh Pirates, four games to three, in 1971, but they earned the world title in 1970 with a four-games-to-one mastery of the Cincinnati Reds.

During those three seasons, Robinson averaged 28 homers and 94 RBIs. Traded to the Dodgers for the 1972 season, Robinon blasted 19 homers. After one season with the Dodgers, Robinson was shipped to the California Angels in 1973 and few expected much of an improvement. He was 37. But he was obviously a young 37 because Robinson smacked 30 homers and drove in 97 runs in a rousing season in which he played 147 games.

One of the most memorable homers in Robinson's career came in 1975, a year in which he became the first black manager in major league baseball. Robinson, then the player-manager of the Cleveland Indians, stroked an electrifying homer in the Indians' home opener—in his first at-bat. Robinson, the designated hitter, blasted a 2-and-2 fastball from the Yankees' Doc Medich over the left-field wall in the first inning. The crowd of 56,204 went wild and the Indians proceeded to score a 5–3 victory.

Robinson was named to the Hall of Fame in 1982 after finishing his 21-year career with a whopping 586 homers, fourth on the all-time list. He hit an impressive 262 of them—or almost 45 percent of his career total—after he turned "an old 30."

Notes

1. *Los Angeles Times*, 12 June 1966.
2. *Baltimore Sun*, 10 December 1965.
3. United Press International, 10 December 1965.
4. *Baltimore Sun*, 10 December 1965.
5. Ibid.
6. Ibid.
7. Ibid.
8. *Sports Illustrated*, 25 April 1966.
9. *Sports Illustrated*, 30 May 1966.

10. Ibid.
11. Ibid.
12. *Sports Illustrated*, 13 June 1966.
13. Ibid.
14. *Los Angeles Times*, 12 June 1966.
15. Ibid.
16. Ibid.
17. Ibid.
18. *Sports Illustrated*, 22 August 1966.
19. Ibid.
20. *Sports Illustrated*, 12 September 1966.
21. UPI, 9 November 1966.
22. *Los Angeles Times*, 16 February 1967.
23. *Los Angeles Times*, 21 March 1967.
24. Ibid.

The Makings of an MVP

*May 8, 1966: The St. Louis Cardinals
trade Ray Sadecki to the San Francisco Giants
for Orlando Cepeda*

After driving in more than 100 runs in three seasons and blasting more than 30 homers in four of the previous five seasons, Orlando Cepeda of the San Francisco Giants began the 1966 season as a backup first baseman. It was not the kind of role the 28-year-old slugger had envisioned for himself. So Cepeda was naturally disenchanted and downcast the first month of the season as Willie McCovey, a slugger in his own right, got the call at first base for the Giants.

Cepeda had played only 33 games in 1965, when an ailing right knee limited him to 34 at-bats. But Cepeda deemed himself healthy in 1966 and wanted to play. And on May 8, 1966, Cepeda got his wish and became a regular again.

The Giants, searching to bolster their starting pitching and improve their already strong hand, obtained former 20-game winner Ray Sadecki from the St. Louis Cardinals in exchange for Cepeda. For the power-poor Cardinals, the acquisition of Cepeda was huge. St. Louis had been trying to obtain Cepeda since the early part of spring training.

"Cepeda was the player we wanted," recalled Bob Howsam, the Cardinals' general manager, in 1967. "Branch Rickey taught me one thing; you must have balance on your ballclub. We didn't have balance because we did not have a cleanup hitter.

"Cepeda was a cleanup hitter. We offered the Giants a choice of three players for Cepeda at various times. Then when the Giants came to St. Louis in May, [Giants general manager] Chub Feeney and I sat around at the ballpark and worked out the deal. Cepeda for Ray Sadecki. But we were not going to announce it until after the game the next day."[1]

As circumstances would have it, the Giants pounded the Cardinals the next afternoon, 10–5. And the Giants' offensive star of the game happened to be Orlando Cepeda, who got the start because McCovey was nursing an injury.

After the game, Giant ace Juan Marichal put his arm around Cepeda as they were walking down the runway and told him, "They won't trade you now."[2] But the trade already had been finalized and Cepeda was headed for his second team in his nine-year major league career.

Upon learning of the trade, Cepeda had mixed feelings. He got the regular job at first base that he desired. But Cepeda, who boasted a .308 lifetime batting average and won the National League home run and runs batted in titles in 1961 with 46 homers and 142 RBIs, still took umbrage on what he considered shabby treatment by Giant manager Herman Franks.

"He [Franks] thought I could play last year when my knee bothered me," Cepeda said. "There's no way a man could change toward another the way he did toward me. He wanted to trade me badly."[3]

Cepeda, the National League's Rookie of the Year in 1958 for the Giants, acknowledged that "one of us, McCovey or me, had to go…. I took [the trade] better than I expected. I'm ready now. I've forgotten why they traded me. They didn't want me."[4]

The Cardinals, on the other hand, made it plain they dearly wanted Cepeda and were ecstatic about obtaining him. St. Louis manager Red Schoendienst immediately told Cepeda, "You are going to play first base and you are going to bat fourth. That's all."[5]

Given this vote of confidence, Cepeda got off to a solid start with his new team. Not only did he hit, but he fit in well with his teammates, winning them over with his dedication to the game and his sense of humor.

Sadecki was not so lucky. He came to the Giants amid lofty expectations. The Giants were strong contenders for the National League title at the time of the trade and Sadecki was expected to provide that extra boost to carry them safely to the pennant.

In picking up Sadecki, the Giants lived up to their reputation as a team willing to take a gamble to procure that one extra ingredient that might catapult it to the top. Shortly before the 1959 season, for instance, San Francisco obtained veteran pitcher Sam Jones from St. Louis in exchange for Bill White, a young first baseman with tremendous potential. The Giants failed to win the pennant that year, finishing four games behind the Los Angeles Dodgers, but it was not the fault of the gritty Jones, who won 21 games.

Sadecki, who won 20 games in 1964 but dropped to 6–15 in 1965, understood the situation well. He was expected to help deliver the Giants, who finished two games behind the first-place Dodgers in 1965, to a pennant. San Francisco boasted plenty of punch in Willie Mays, McCovey and Jim Ray Hart, and now Sadecki was around to bolster the pitching. "There is pressure," said Sadecki, trying to take the trade in stride, "but I'm not much of a worrier."[6]

The Giants, however, became worried when Sadecki inexplicably failed to match Cepeda's hot start and was shelled four straight times. It was not the way to make a good first impression. San Francisco withstood Sadecki's struggles for a month but finally after 36 days in the lead, relinquished first place to the Dodgers. Nor was there to be a resurgence by Sadecki. By winning a game in mid–July, Sadecki served only to escape a possible demotion to the minors.

Meanwhile, Cepeda was providing the power the Cardinals needed, and he was hitting for average too. His importance was magnified when he was forced to sit out a game in June after being hit in the face with a line drive during batting practice. The resulting Cardinals lineup had a season total of only nine home runs.

Cepeda also exacted revenge on the Giants in midseason when he broke up a no-hit bid by San Francisco's Bob Bolin, who had gone seven innings without allowing a hit. In the eighth inning, Cepeda first hit a foul popup to third baseman Jim Ray Hart, whose catch was nullified by an umpire because he had stepped into the Giants' dugout. On his second opportunity, Cepeda singled to end Bolin's no-hitter.

The Cardinals, even with a sizzling Cepeda, still were not strong enough to become a big factor in the National League race. With Cepeda leading the way with a batting average in the .330s, the Cardinals won 12 of 13 games to close within five games of first-place Los Angeles in early August. But the Cardinals then lost five straight and their pennant hopes were summarily dashed. Still Cepeda finished with an excellent season in which he totaled 20 homers, 73 RBIs and batted .301. He batted .303 for St. Louis.

The Giants, even with an erratic Sadecki, remained in the thick of the pennant race to the very end with the Dodgers and Pittsburgh Pirates, riding the consistency of pitchers Marichal and Gaylord Perry. Although undependable, Sadecki provided one highlight for San Francisco, spinning a stunning three-hit shutout in a key victory over the Dodgers in September.

But Sadecki overall was a big disappointment for the Giants, as San Francisco finished 1½ games behind the champion Dodgers. Sadecki, who was 2–1 before being traded, finished the season with a 5–8 record and an unflattering 4.80 earned run average. Giant fans were left wondering what the season would have been like had San Francisco kept Cepeda. After all, the Giants often found themselves starved for runs despite the magnificent seasons of Mays (37 home runs and 103 runs batted in) and McCovey (36 homers, 96 RBIs).

When the 1967 season began, optimism ran high in St. Louis. Cepeda was starting the season with the Cardinals, who picked up additional sock when they obtained home run king Roger Maris from the New York Yankees for journeyman third baseman Charley Smith. Maris gave St. Louis three formidable left-handed hitters, including catcher Tim McCarver and outfielder Lou Brock.

Anticipating a possible glorious season for his Cardinals, Cepeda worked diligently on strengthening his injured knee by walking on the sandy beaches of Puerto Rico. The season certainly started the way Cardinal fans had hoped—with four straight victories, leaving St. Louis as the only major league team with an undefeated record.

The spotlight was suddenly glaring on the Cardinals. Although Cepeda was smoking, he did not have to do it alone. Brock powered five homers in his first four games. He had only 15 the entire 1966 season.

Maris, five seasons removed from his 61-homer year, and coming off a season in which he batted only .233, also contributed timely hits as the Cardinals raced to a 7–2 start. Key players abounded for St. Louis as they maintained a heady pace into July. Third baseman Mike Shannon was a hero one day, second baseman Julian Javier the next, and outfielder Curt Flood the next.

The Cincinnati Reds posed the biggest challenge to the Cardinals in June, but they soon fell back and the upstart Chicago Cubs took their place. As the weather turned hot in July, the Cubs turned cold under their fiery manager, Leo Durocher.

The Cardinals, however, faced a big challenge in July, as they suffered key disabling injuries to brilliant starting pitcher Bob Gibson and center fielder Curt Flood. Gibson and Flood were placed on the disabled list with a broken leg and sore shoulder, respectively. It was up to the Cardinals' offense to come to the fore and the St. Louis bats did exactly that, particularly those of Cepeda's and McCarver's.

At the time, the loss of Gibson appeared devastating. Gibson had averaged 20 victories a year for the previous three years. He was expected to be sidelined at least a month after the Pittsburgh Pirates' Roberto Clemente blistered a shot off his leg.

But the Cardinals were able to weather the loss of Gibson because of Nelson Briles, who filled in splendidly after registering a 4–5 record the previous year. That was the *modus operandi* for St. Louis all season. Challenges were continually popping up and the Cardinals were continually passing them.

For instance, on July 22, the Cardinals dropped a 13-inning game to the Atlanta Braves at St. Louis' Busch Stadium. But the Cardinals, reeling after the disheartening loss, rebounded with a doubleheader sweep of the Braves the next day to generate the momentum they needed to win 13 of their next 15 games.

In July, Cepeda had a particularly memorable hit. With the Cardinals holding a three-game lead, Cepeda requested a day of rest from Schoendienst, who kept his cleanup hitter out of the starting lineup against the Pirates. But the Cardinal manager had not forgotten about Cepeda when the Cardinals batted in the bottom of the seventh, trailing 1–0.

With runners at first and second and one out, it was time for Cepeda to get the call. Schoendienst looked around for Cepeda, but he was nowhere in sight. A clubhouse boy was dispatched to locate Cepeda and the Cardinal slugger was found in the dressing room talking long distance to a friend in Chicago. Alerted that he was needed, Cepeda ran to the dugout, grabbed a bat, quickly stretched his right knee and bounded up five steps onto the playing field where he was greeted with a thunderous ovation from the 25,668 fans in St. Louis.

Cepeda then produced the Cardinals' third hit of the game, rocketing a single to left to drive in Alex Johnson with the tying run and sending Julian Javier to third. Javier scored on an error and the Cardinals went on to claim a 2–1 victory. Afterward, Cepeda savored the Cardinals' win and the role he played in securing it.

"That was only my third pinch-hit in a couple of hundred tries," Cepeda said. "I got one off [Elroy] Face and I hit a home run off [Joe] Nuxhall in 1965. But today was payday, and I had to earn my money. You know when my father played ball back home in Puerto Rico and no get a hit on payday, we no eat for the whole weekend. Ah, mucho bueno. Mucho bueno."[7]

At the time Cepeda was leading the league in batting, base hits and RBIs. He was the one player the Cardinals could not afford to lose. "Without Cepeda, we are down with the Pirates and look where they are," said Cardinal third baseman Mike Shannon about sixth-place Pittsburgh.

"It's not just his statistics. It's also what happens in the clubhouse. It's intangible. I can't really explain. Orlando is a prestige player and we have him—the other clubs don't.

"Put it this way. I'm walking down the street and two tough guys coming the other way want to start a fight. Then this friend of mine—a big guy—comes around the corner and when the two tough guys see him, they disappear. Well, my friend the big guy is Cepeda—you can't take him away from me. So I'm going to beat you."[8]

Cepeda recognized that the big key in his success was his ability to stay healthy. After being hobbled the last several years, Cepeda was operating with his right knee at 95 percent efficiency. He injured his knee originally in 1952 when he was 14 years old. He had cartilage removed that year, but reinjured the knee in a 1961 home-plate collision with the Dodgers' Johnny Roseboro.

"The knee hurt me all the time [before this season]," Cepeda said, "and I always aggravate it when I slide or stretch or even hit. Some people think because we are Latins—because we did not have everything growing up—we are not supposed to get hurt. But my knee was hurt."[9]

But that was then. Now he was on a tear and everything felt better. His knee felt fine because of his 45 minutes of daily exercises in which Cepeda alternately took massages from trainer Bob Bauman and lifted weights. And his hitting was never better either.

"I have the ability to hit and I always have confidence that I can hit," Cepeda said. "I am not a scientific hitter. It don't matter how you stand. You remember Bob Speake. He used to be with the Giants. He had the best swing I've ever seen, but he always hit .200 or something. I don't know how to hit. It's just what you do when the ball is right here—right over the plate. I follow the pitcher's arm and wait for the ball and keep my head down—like all those golfers."[10]

In each at-bat, Schoendienst instructed Cepeda to "stay easy and relax."[11] Coach Dick Sisler advised Cepeda to "concentrate."[12]

"Then I tell myself I'm gonna hit this cat," Cepeda said, "and boom, boom, boom."[13]

With Cepeda's help and with key contributions from Brock and Flood, the Cardinals asserted themselves in August and moved to a season-high 8½-game lead. The Cubs, who weeks earlier had tied St. Louis for the lead, were faltering badly. Now it was the Atlanta Braves who were the Cardinals' closest pursuer.

St. Louis suffered a blow when Cepeda received a two-game suspension after a verbal assault on umpire Stan Landes. Although the Cardinals' rivals rejoiced, Cepeda returned with a vengeance, stroking two game-winning hits to help the Cardinals beat the San Francisco Giants in three straight one-run games.

St. Louis appeared at its best in close games. The Cardinals were 25–13 in one-run games, the mark of a champion. And St. Louis unmistakably had the look of a championship team. "The Cardinals are ready for a showdown all the time," Brock said. "There are a lot of players on this team who have responsibilities [a total of 62 children] and we've come too far down the road to turn back now."[14]

There were few showdowns in September. With a healthy Gibson back on the team, the Cardinals were making a shambles of the pennant race. And St. Louis was running away from the pack with a badly slumping Cepeda, who was struggling after carrying a league-leading .349 average late into August.

The Giants mounted a minor challenge to close within 10½ games, but St. Louis would not falter. The Cardinals wound up finishing 10½ games ahead of San Francisco, compiling a 101–60 record, and winning their 11th pennant in 42 seasons.

The Giants took second for the third year in a row. Although Mays had a substandard season, San Francisco got an unlikely shot in the arm from Ray Sadecki, the man for whom Cepeda was traded a year earlier. Sadecki won his last six games to finish with an admirable 12–6 record and a sparkling 2.78 earned run average.

The Cardinals, though, were more than satisfied with their acquisition in the Sadecki trade. St. Louis was headed for the World Series, and a big reason was the magnificent season of Orlando Cepeda.

St. Louis drew the American League champion Boston Red Sox, led by

Triple Crown winner Carl Yastrzemski and 22-game winner Jim Lonborg. The Boston right-hander logged his last victory on the final day of the season, as the Red Sox survived a wild four-team race to edge the Detroit Tigers and Minnesota Twins by one game and the Chicago White Sox by three games. It was the first pennant since 1946 for Boston, which finished 92–70.

It was a great Series matchup and the teams—loaded with stars—played like it. St. Louis took the first game of the Series, 2–1, as Gibson picked up the victory and Brock rapped out four hits. The Red Sox countered by winning the second game, 5–0, behind Lonborg's one-hit masterpiece. St. Louis then won the next two games, 5–2, and 6–0. Mike Shannon blasted a three-run homer in game three and Gibson pitched a shutout—his second victory—in game four. Before Gibson's gem, Maris sounded off: "One of the few things that sometimes bothers us is that people are in such a hurry to compare us with the Gas House Gang. We're 'El Birdos' because Cha-Cha [Cepeda] named us that and that is what we want to be called and remembered as. There were quite a few who said in the spring that St. Louis could not win because it had two troublemakers in Cepeda and myself. But one day Cha-Cha just pointed at me and said, 'Roger, you and me. You know what I mean?'"[15]

It may have been Cepeda's team, but it was not Cepeda's World Series. He remained in the persistent slump that had plagued him at the end of the season. Entering his final at-bat in game three, Cepeda had managed only one ball out of the infield in 10 tries. But on his 11th at-bat, he blasted a double off the right-field wall to drive in Maris.

His teammates consoled Cepeda during the Series with friendly needling. "Cha, Cha," they said, "we've been carrying you all year long. Now, you're getting heavy."[16]

Cepeda took the ribbing well. He knew he was accepted and that his teammates were pulling for him. While Cepeda was slumping, Brock and Maris were on fire.

And Gibson was proving to be unbeatable. When Boston forced game seven by winning games five (3–1) and six (8–4), Gibson was on center stage in the pivotal game. And he did not disappoint, pitching the Cardinals to a 7–2 victory. It was Gibson's third complete game and third victory in the Series. And it came only four weeks after his recovery from a broken leg. Cepeda wound up with only three hits—two doubles and a single—in 29 at-bats in the Series for an anemic batting average of .103.

When it came time to decide the National League's Most Valuable Player, however, there was no debate—Cepeda was the unanimous winner, becoming the first National League player to garner all the first-place votes. Cepeda, who batted .325 with 25 home runs and a league-leading 110 RBIs, was the first first baseman to win the MVP award since Stan Musial, the Cardinals' general manager, had won it in 1946.

Cepeda's career with the Cardinals, however, was not marked by longevity. He stayed with St. Louis only one more year. He batted only .248 with 16 homers and 73 RBIs in 1968, but St. Louis still won the pennant behind a marvelous pitching staff led by Gibson (21 wins) and Briles (19 wins). Cepeda batted .250 in the World Series against the Detroit Tigers, smacking a key three-run homer in game three. But the Tigers won the Series when Mickey Lolich outpitched Gibson in game seven, as Detroit prevailed 4–1. It was the third and final World Series appearance for Cepeda, who had also reached the fall classic in 1962 with the Giants.

Before the 1969 season, Cepeda was traded to the Atlanta Braves for top-notch catcher Joe Torre. Cepeda batted .257 with 22 homers and 88 RBIs to help the Braves win the West Division championship and then enjoyed his first dynamic postseason series, batting .455 in the three games of the National League Championship Series. Unfortunately the New York Mets won all three games in what proved to be Cepeda's last postseason appearance.

In 1970 at age 32, Cepeda returned to peak form. He enjoyed one of his top seasons, batting .305 with 34 homers, but the Braves finished second to last. Cepeda was involved in one more big-name trade when he was shuttled off to the Oakland A's in June 1972 for Denny McLain, a 31-game winner in 1968 but in the twilight of his career. Cepeda's last rousing season came in 1973 when he batted .289 with 20 homers and 86 RBIs for the Boston Red Sox. He finished his career with 379 homers and a lifetime average of .297 for his 17 years in the majors.

Those were strong credentials for Hall of Fame consideration, but Cepeda had trouble generating the necessary support. There was a belief—though difficult to prove—that Cepeda did not get the necessary votes because of a 1975 drug arrest. He was found guilty of smuggling marijuana into his native Puerto Rico and served 10 months in prison for the offense. But before his 15th—and final—year on the writers' ballot, Cepeda received national attention because of an intensive campaign by the San Francisco Giants and several Hispanic members of Congress to put him into the Hall of Fame.

Typical of the endorsements was one from Giants owner Peter Magowan, who stated in a letter to baseball writers in 1993: "Orlando has paid his debt 100 times over. He is doing more good under the banner of baseball than anyone I know. He's turned his misfortune into an opportunity to help others. He is deeply involved with many worthy causes, including anti-substance, inner-city schools, AIDS and the homeless."[17]

Cepeda needed 75 percent of the 455 votes cast—or 342 votes—to gain access to the Hall of Fame. But when the vote was announced in January 1994 he narrowly missed. He needed seven more votes, finishing at 73.6 percent. He had received only 59.6 percent of the votes the previous year, so the campaign apparently was a big help.

Cepeda said in 1994 it was heartbreaking to come so close without making the Hall of Fame, "like losing a 1–0 game." He added it was a victory in that so many people rallied behind him. "I believe I was as good as anybody who played," he said. "I know I belong (in the Hall) and we did everything we could to convince people."[18]

At the time of the vote, Cepeda was the only retired player with more than 300 homers and a lifetime batting average of more than .295 not to have been voted into the Hall of Fame. "I made a mistake 20 years ago," Cepeda said. "Since then, I've done so many wonderful things for the community and myself. Too many writers today are looking for things other than what a player does on the field. Too many writers today don't know what they are doing."[19]

Sadecki pitched for 18 seasons, winning 135 games and losing 131. His career ERA was 3.79. Despite those solid numbers, he will be remembered mainly as the man traded for Cepeda.

Notes

1. *Sports Illustrated*, 24 July 1967.
2. Ibid.
3. *Los Angeles Times*, 10 May 1966.
4. Ibid.
5. *Sports Illustrated*, 24 July 1967.
6. *Sports Illustrated*, 19, May 1966.
7. *Sports Illustrated*, 24 July 1967.
8. Ibid.
9. Ibid.
10. Ibid.
11. Ibid.
12. Ibid.
13. Ibid.
14. *Sports Illustrated*, 22 July 1967.
15. *Sports Illustrated*, 16 October 1967.
16. Ibid.
17. *Baseball Weekly*, 28 December 1993.
18. *Los Angeles Times*, 13 January 1994.
19. Ibid.

A Late Bloomer

*May 29, 1971: The San Francisco Giants
trade George Foster to the Cincinnati Reds
for Frank Duffy and Vern Geishert*

Born in Alabama, George Foster dreamed early in his childhood that one day he would play alongside his idol, another Alabaman by the name of Willie Mays. And like a fairy tale, Foster signed with the San Francisco Giants in 1967 and rose from the ranks to join Mays in the San Francisco outfield one year later.

With the tutelage he received from Mays on his hitting and fielding, a long and prosperous career with the Giants seemed to be in the offing for George Foster. But after failing to distinguish himself as anything more than the Giants' fourth outfielder behind Mays, budding star Bobby Bonds and Ken Henderson, Foster was dealt to the Cincinnati Reds on May 29, 1971, for light-hitting reserve shortstop Frank Duffy and Vern Geishert, an anonymous minor league pitcher.

The Reds were looking for Foster to become a backup center fielder to Bobby Tolan. "Bobby was a good athlete, but he wasn't a center fielder," said Reds president Bob Howsam in 1976. "This was a year before we got Cesar Geronimo. We checked around and found the Giants wanted a shortstop and were willing to give up either Charlie Williams or Foster."[1]

After watching Foster and Williams in a game, Howsam and superscout Ray Shore selected Foster. It was one of the smartest decisions the Reds ever made.

The trade was a devastating blow to Foster, who roomed with Bonds at the end of the 1969 season. "The biggest hurt was that Bobby Bonds and I had become close as brothers," Foster said.[2]

Five years in the Giants' organization apparently had not sold San Francisco on Foster. But Cincinnati was ecstatic the moment the trade was consummated. The Reds took one look at the 22-year-old right-handed-hitting Foster and proclaimed him a potential superstar. Great power. Great speed. Great throwing arm. A great pick-up, the Reds crowed.

The Reds were not alone with the superlatives for Foster. Los Angeles

Dodger manager Tommy Lasorda remembered scouting Foster when he was the manager of the Dodgers' minor league team in Spokane. The report Lasorda wrote to the Dodgers' organization on Foster in 1970 was an absolute endorsement.

"I had his potential down on paper … the speed, the power, the arm," recalled Lasorda in 1976. "I wrote that if he's available or we could sneak him into a deal, go after him. I don't think the Giants knew what they had. They gave him up for a steal. I said that to some people in [the Dodger organization] and they laughed at me."[3]

But if the Reds thought that Foster would tear up the league the moment they got him, they were quickly disappointed. In 1971, Foster batted only .234 for the Reds in 104 games, after hitting .267 in 36 games for the Giants. His combined average was .241 with 13 homers in 473 at-bats. Foster struck out a whopping 120 times, an average of about one for every four at-bats. Foster's start for his new team was inauspicious, but the Reds were not giving up so soon.

In 1972, Foster got another shot at fulfilling those sizable expectations. But again he failed to produce and Cincinnati shipped him to Indianapolis, the Reds' triple A team. Foster later said being optioned to the minors was a blessing. "The demotion really helped straighten me out," said Foster, who batted a meager .200 in 59 games for the Reds. "I realized I had to give it my all because it might be my last shot."[4]

Still, Foster had difficulty registering big-time numbers in the majors. The next two years were more unfulfilled expectations. If Foster was a future superstar, he was having a tough time showing it. Foster had a total of 315 at-bats in 1973 and 1974, popping 11 homers but hardly living up to the Reds' expectations when they obtained him. But Foster gave a hint of his talent and potential in 1974 when he batted .264 with 7 homers, 18 doubles and 41 RBIs in 276 at-bats. Not bad, but certainly nothing close to All-Star caliber.

Entering the 1975 season, Foster had played parts of six seasons in the majors without developing into the blue-chip player the Reds' organization had envisioned. What Foster needed was a breakthrough season, and he got it in 1975.

At 26, Foster demonstrated that he was just a late bloomer. Given the chance, Foster tried to show he could deliver in the Reds' star-studded lineup. And deliver he did—with a vengeance.

The Reds inserted Foster into the cleanup role, bumping All-Star catcher Johnny Bench. And Foster was placed in left field, bumping Pete Rose to third base. Rose said he agreed to the move partly because of Foster's potential. "I could have told them to go to hell when they asked me to do it," Rose said, "but I felt George would help the team."[5]

Playing regularly for the first time in the majors, Foster turned out to be the final cog in the Big Red Machine. By mid–July, Foster had belted 15 homers, most of them tremendous shots. Three months into the season, even Foster had to admit that 1975 "is my year."[6]

That Foster was having a big year and the Reds were jelling was no coincidence. The Reds won 41 of 50 games after Foster was designated for regular duty and became a regular contributor. "I am now trying to reach my potential," said Foster in mid–July. "I just pray I have the strength to do it."[7]

Potential. Whenever George Foster was discussed in the past, that word always was brought up. Now he was realizing his vast potential and suddenly Foster did not mind talking about the subject. Potential, said Foster, is a word cloaked in mystery.

"You don't know what your potential is, so you keep reaching out after it," Foster said. "That's why I don't set any long-range goals. Say you set 30 home runs and you reach it. You have the tendency to quit, to stop trying."[8]

So what turned it around for Foster? After reaching the majors at age 20 with the Giants, how did Foster find his mark six years later? Some said it was his hard work in the weight room that made him a chiseled, 6-foot-1, 195-pound terror. Others said it was his sessions with a hypnotist.

Foster said it was the work of God. But he gave an assist to his hypnotist for drawing on Foster's understanding of God and the Bible to show him how everything in life has a purpose.

"By homing in on my deep-seated belief in God," Foster said, "the hypnotist showed me how to erase my resentments and emphasize the positive. I believed in what he was telling me and I believed that God was speaking to me through the hypnotist.

"I made up my mind to stay ready, to work hard, to be prepared, to make the most of every opportunity, even if it was in a platoon role. I regained the aggressiveness I had lost sitting on the bench. I believe that if I had gone on sulking, I'd have never received the opportunity that I got last year."[9]

Foster had turned to a hypnotist in 1973 after the Reds optioned him to Indianapolis. "I was mad at myself, mad at [Cincinnati manager] Sparky [Anderson]," Foster said. "I was mixed up, period."[10]

But by 1975, Foster had straightened out and finished with a .300 average, 23 homers and 78 runs batted in. His 16-game hitting streak was the team's longest. Foster then helped Cincinnati win its first World Series since 1940 by batting .276 in the Reds' seven-game triumph over the Boston Red Sox. It was the start of something big for Foster.

"It was a combination of the physical, the mental and the spiritual all coming together," said Foster about the 1975 season. "That season went by so fast that I really didn't feel a part of everything. I was just trying to play instead of focusing on excelling."[11]

Foster went from good to better in 1976. Much better. By late June, Foster was being discussed as a Triple Crown candidate. On June 25, he led the league in RBIs with 61, and he was second in average at .341 and third in homers with 16.

As Foster continued to sting the ball, he drew more and more raves. On a team of superstars, such as Bench, Rose and Joe Morgan, Foster was called by Manager Sparky Anderson the strongest player on the team. Furthermore, Anderson said Foster was rapidly earning the label of superstar.

Foster reacted to all the praise with modesty. He knew it had taken him a long time to find his mark and he was still in search of consistency. Being a league leader was not on the top of his objectives. "I've been fortunate to be on a team of this type," he said, "because I am surrounded by good hitters whose advice has been of help. When I watch people like Pete Rose and Joe Morgan, I see how their pride keeps them driving despite their success and salary, and I'm that much more determined to go about it the same way. I believe in the saying about luck being the residue of hard work."[12]

In early September, Foster still entertained ideas of a Triple Crown bid but those hopes were dashed when his batting average could not keep up with his slugging and he fell into a 4-for-44 slump. Still, Foster finished the season with a league-leading 121 RBIs. He also belted 29 homers, batted .306, stole 17 bases and was the All-Star game's Most Valuable Player. He then batted .429 with four RBIs in the World Series as the Reds won their second straight world championship, sweeping the New York Yankees.

Foster finished a distant second behind teammate Joe Morgan for the league's Most Valuable Player award. Morgan won the award for the second straight year behind a monstrous season that included 27 homers, 111 RBIs, a .320 average and 60 stolen bases, but he was stumping MVP votes for Foster during the season. "As happy as I am for Joe Morgan," Morgan said, "I am sad for George. He had a tremendous year."[13]

Foster, who had earned an admirable reputation as one of those rare players who would not cuss, was not particularly pleased when he learned he had not won the MVP award. He suggested that voting for the award—the annual responsibility of the Baseball Writers Association of America—be turned over to the players. "No knock against Joe but I felt I had the credentials to win it," Foster said. "Writers have a tendency to be influenced by other writers. Players know more about what things should be considered and know more about the game."[14]

And Foster added: "Quite naturally I'm disappointed. I felt I was the catalyst of our team. My record speaks for itself. There have been a lot of people in the past who should have got the MVP that didn't."[15]

In 1977, Foster enjoyed a season that could only be described as remarkable. By contrast, the Reds were very unremarkable despite top-notch seasons by Rose, Morgan, Bench and pitcher Tom Seaver. Cincinnati, in last place in late April, was never in the race, although the Reds rallied to finish second.

Meanwhile, Foster was ablaze even though he did not start that way. Foster did not hit a homer until his team's eighth game and had only four home runs nearly one-quarter of the way through the season. Who could have predicted then that Foster would become the hottest player in the league?

Beginning May 25, he blasted seven homers in six games and drove in 30 runs during a 14-game stretch in June. He homered 12 times in both July and August. On August 3, he demonstrated his prodigious strength with a homer at Cincinnati's Riverfront Stadium that an engineer estimated might have traveled 720 feet from home plate had it not hit the stands.

By September, Foster showed he was going to challenge the 50-homer mark. But the long ball was not the sole part of his game. Late in the season, Foster enjoyed two consecutive four-hit games.

Even in a lively-ball season in which teams' hitting and scoring increased dramatically, Foster was enjoying a season for the ages. And his Hall-of-Fame-quality teammates were quick to acknowledge that fact.

"George is bleeping awesome," Rose said.

"He makes me feel inadequate," Bench said.

"I've never seen anything like this," Morgan said.

And Reds manager Sparky Anderson added: "Bench, Rose and Morgan are great players, but George has reached the point where he doesn't have to take a back seat to anyone. He's coming up to number one fast."[16]

Foster was doing just about everything right. But one of the few places where Foster was not leading the world was in publicity. Perhaps that was because he played on the same team as such high-profile players as Rose, Bench, Morgan and Seaver, all charismatic figures who generated considerable publicity. And perhaps that was due to his quiet style in which he spent much of his spare time reading the Bible.

In any event, Foster was having a great year. Still, Anderson judged there was room for improvement. Said Anderson: "George has reached the point where he needs to ask himself, 'How great do I want to be?' He's totally conquered the hitting part of baseball, but I want him to become a more complete player. If he wants to, he can become a well-rounded star like [Hank] Aaron, Mays and [Roberto] Clemente. And one of the things he's going to have to do is be more outgoing on the bases. He should be stealing 40 a year."[17]

Foster wound up stealing only six bases in 1977 but that was pretty much overshadowed by the fact that he led the league with a whopping 52 homers in 158 games, tying his idol, Mays, for the third-highest total in National League history behind Hack Wilson's 56 in 1930 and Ralph Kiner's 54 in 1949. Thirty-one of Foster's homers were hit on the road and 32 were hit off right-handers.

The 28-year-old Foster also led the league with an astonishing 149 RBIs, .631 slugging percentage, 388 total bases and 124 runs. His .320 average ranked fourth in the league.

This time when the MVP award was announced, Foster had no complaints. He picked up 15 of a possible 24 first-place votes to outdistance Greg Luzinski of the Philadelphia Phillies and become the sixth Red in eight years to pick up the award. Bench was duly honored in 1970 and 1972, Rose was named in 1973 and Morgan was selected in 1975 and 1976.

Notified he had been named the MVP, Foster credited his consistency for his superb season. "Consistency was the big thing I learned last year," Foster said. "One of the most pleasing things this year was that I was voted player of the month in August and it was August last year that I started a tailspin that probably cost me the MVP. I learned last year not to try to do something supernatural.... I felt if I didn't win it this year with my stats, I would never win it. I'm overpowered with delight and bubbling with enthusiasm."[18]

"Nineteen seventy-seven was the year I didn't want the season to end after 162 games," said Foster after his career ended. "I knew that nobody could get me out."[19]

George Foster was now in a groove and he maintained his blistering pace in 1978. He led the league again in homers with 40 and RBIs with 120—the third straight year he had won the RBI crown—although teams were trying to pitch around him. Recognition that he had earned a place in the superstardom category came in March 1979 when Foster signed a rich three-year contract extension with the Reds for an estimated $2.25 million.

"The contract recognizes Foster for what he is," said Reds' general manager Dick Wagner. "He's one of the premier hitters in baseball."[20]

The only disappointing part for Foster was that the Reds had finished second to the Dodgers in 1977 and 1978, thus sparking a shakeup of the awesome "Big Red Machine." Longtime catalysts Pete Rose and Tony Perez were gone and Manager Sparky Anderson was dismissed after the Reds fell short for the second straight season.

Foster enjoyed three more solid seasons with the Reds, but none could approach his breathtaking 52-homer season. In fact, as Foster was getting older, his homer total was shrinking, going from 30 in 1979 to 25 in 1980 to 22 in 1981. But the 22 homers were deceiving because it came during a strike-shortened season in which Foster played only 108 games. Foster drove in 90 runs that year, one short of tying Philadelphia Phillies' Mike Schmidt for the league's RBI crown, so his marketability remained high. And he soon found out just how high.

After the 1981 season, the 33-year-old Foster, in the option year of his contract, let it be known he was seeking a lucrative multiyear contract in excess of $1 million a year and a $1-million interest-free loan. Foster had the leverage to pursue such a deal after hitting at least 20 homers in seven straight seasons.

The rebuilding Reds, however, were not the ones who would pay all those millions. Instead, they traded their slugger to the New York Mets for catcher Alex Trevino and pitchers Jim Kern and Greg Harris. The Mets then signed Foster in February 1982 to a five-year, $10-million contract with several incentive bonuses. The contract made Foster the second-highest-paid player in baseball behind Dave Winfield of the New York Yankees.

Said Foster: "I'm not changing what I do or how I do it, just where it will be done."[21]

Foster, in moving to New York, was not expected to be the lone power source on the Mets. Dave Kingman and Ellis Valentine also were well-known deep threats so Foster would not have to shoulder the RBI burden alone. But not all believed that New York was the ideal place for Foster to put together more brilliant seasons. One outspoken voice belonged to hitting machine Pete Rose, who had left the Reds as a free agent after the 1978 season. Foster, said Rose, would experience a much tougher time driving in runs with the Mets than the Reds because he would miss his valuable Cincinnati teammates. And Rose added that while Foster was at the top of the list with Philadelphia Phillies third baseman Mike Schmidt for hitting homers, he needed to help his team in other ways.

Foster reacted to Rose's comments diplomatically. "I don't have any control over what others say," Foster said. "The best response to that is that they criticized Jesus Christ, and he's a better man than we are."[22]

The Mets entertained high hopes for Foster. In fact, manager George Bamberger said Foster and Kingman had the potential to blast 80 homers between them. Foster, for his part, realized the lucrative contract would bring great expectations. But he said he simply wanted to be consistent.

"I don't have anything to prove to people," Foster said. "I strive to do better and better. Each time I go out there, I try to keep on being consistent."[23]

But the man who hit 52 homers in 1977 proved to be a huge disappointment in his first season with the Mets. By April 18 Foster had three homers, but he did not hit another until May. In the next two months, he hit only four homers. The New York fans were displeased and they let Foster know it with their boos.

On September 12 Foster was struggling with a .252 average, 13 homers and 63 RBIs and not showing he was worth what his contract was paying. But Foster, who seemed to be able to tune out the catcalls and whistles from the home folk, remained hopeful. "I'm not giving up," said Foster, who had been slowed by the flu early in the year.

"As far as I'm concerned, I'm still striving to get on track. I know when I'm swinging the bat well, it'll be contagious. Any long-ball hitter that swings for average can get a ballclub going. I just have to be patient with myself. It won't happen automatically. I just can't quit on myself."[24]

Foster may not have quit, but he could not find the groove of his Big Red Machine days, finishing with a meager 13 homers, 70 RBIs and .247 average.

The biting New York media called him "George Flopster." But Foster made considerable inroads the following season when he belted 28 homers and drove in 90 runs, though he batted only .241.

Foster played three more seasons for the Mets, falling short of the Mets' expectations. In his five-year Met career, Foster averaged 20 homers and 73 RBIs, pretty good numbers for an outfielder but not for one who had received such a lucrative contract. He posted his highest average as a Met in 1984 at age 35, batting .269 in 146 games. His highest RBI total in New York came in 1982 and 1984 when he drove in 90.

"If I had to do it all over again, I still would have gone to the Mets," said Foster after his career was over. "The years in New York were tainted in the sense that I knew those were not the best stats I could put up. But I didn't have any help in the lineup, and I was trying to be the person everyone else wanted me to be."[25]

In August 1986, his fifth season with the Mets, Foster was given his unconditional release. He was batting only .228 and had lost his starting left field job to Kevin Mitchell.

The Chicago White Sox took a chance on the 37-year-old Foster after his release, signing him as a free agent. But Foster's career came to an unflattering end when he batted only .216 for the White Sox with one homer and four RBIs in 15 games before being released again.

It was an inglorious end to a glorious 18-year career in which Foster batted .274, blasted 348 homers and drove in 1,239 runs. Furthermore, he retired with the knowledge that he was part of one of the most lopsided trades in baseball history.

Duffy, whom the Giants had acquired with Geishert for Foster, played 10 years in the majors but finished with a lifetime average of .232 with only 26 homers. Geishert never pitched in the majors.

"I enjoyed my career and what I accomplished," said Foster, "but I like being remembered as an individual that strived to be the best that he possibly could on the field."[26]

Notes

1. Associated Press, 16 July 1976.
2. Ibid.
3. *Los Angeles Times*, 12 July 1976.
4. Associated Press, 25 June 1976.
5. *Sports Illustrated*, 19 September 1977.
6. Associated Press, 16 July 1975.
7. Ibid.
8. Ibid.
9. *Los Angeles Times*, 12 July 1976.

10. Ibid.
11. *Baseball America*, 8 January 1995.
12. *Los Angeles Times*, 12 July 1976.
13. Associated Press, 25 November 1976.
14. Ibid.
15. Ibid.
16. *Sports Illustrated*, 19 September 1977.
17. Ibid.
18. United Press International, 9 November 1977.
19. *Baseball America*, 8 January 1995.
20. *Los Angeles Times*, 6 March 1979.
21. *Los Angeles Times*, 11 February 1982.
22. *Boston Globe*, 18 April 1982.
23. Ibid.
24. Associated Press, 13 September 1982.
25. *Baseball America*, 8 January 1995.
26. Ibid.

"300 Wins Is Nothing to Spit At"

November 29, 1971:
The San Francisco Giants
trade Gaylord Perry and Frank Duffy
to the Cleveland Indians for Sam McDowell

After spending the first 10 years of his major league career pitching for the San Francisco Giants, Gaylord Perry said he was not bitter when he was traded to the Cleveland Indians. But he was surprised.

"I was shocked in a way," said Perry, who was traded with slick-fielding shortstop Frank Duffy for left-handed strikeout pitcher Sam McDowell on November 29, 1971. "I knew Charlie [Fox, Giants' manager] wanted a left-hander bad. I just didn't realize how determined he was. I didn't figure he was ready to give up one of his starting pitchers to get a left-hander, but I guess he was."[1]

The 6-foot-4 Perry had been one of the most consistent pitchers in Giants' history. He twice had been a 20-game winner and had pitched more than 250 innings in each of the last six seasons. He was 16–12 with a sparkling 2.76 earned run average in 1971. The 33-year-old Perry had a notorious reputation as a spitball pitcher, but umpires had been unable to turn up proof he threw the illegal pitch.

McDowell, four years younger than Perry, had enjoyed a productive career in which he had won 122 and lost 109. He had struck out at least 200 batters in five seasons, at least 300 twice. Known as "Sudden Sam," McDowell had led the league in strikeouts those five seasons and had entered the record books as the youngest player to strike out at least 300 batters in a season when he turned the trick in 1965 at age 22. But he was prone to wildness, leading the league five times in walks.

Coming off a 13–17 season with a 3.39 ERA in 1971, the lefty openly questioned the wisdom of the Giants' brass for cutting loose a pitcher the stature of Perry, who had averaged 18 wins the previous six seasons.

"I think the Giants gave up too much to get me," McDowell said. "But

I've known Charlie [Fox] for a long time and he's a fantastic man. If he'd ask me to walk through a stone wall, I'd give it a helluva try. My wish now is to justify the trade so much that we'll be in a World Series next October."[2]

Perry's belief that the Giants were actively seeking a left-hander was corroborated by San Francisco manager Charlie Fox. "McDowell gives us the left-handed starting pitcher we need so badly, a left-hander who can strike somebody out. Then, too, McDowell is 29 and Perry is 33, so the age factor was in our favor."[3]

McDowell, who the Indians said had talked about wanting to be traded, had been coveted by a number of teams. But McDowell admitted to disappointment that the Indians failed to trade him to Pittsburgh, his hometown. Perry, for his part, took the trade in stride.

"I'm not bitter," said Perry, who had tossed a no-hitter against the St. Louis Cardinals in 1968. "I like to think I'm leaving a lot of friends behind when I leave San Francisco and that everything else is forgotten. That's the only way to take it or else I'd be making a lot of enemies and spending a lot of nights wide awake."[4]

One player overshadowed in the trade involving high-profile pitchers was Duffy, whom the Giants obtained in a trade that sent the talented power-hitting George Foster to the Cincinnati Reds. It was the first of two incredibly one-sided trades involving the young shortstop. Duffy, 25, batted only .182 in 34 games with the Reds and Giants in 1971, but Cleveland manager Ken Aspromonte proclaimed him the team's starting shortstop.

"Duffy," said Cleveland general manager Gabe Paul, "was the key man in the deal. We think he is a helluva player, and we told the Giants we would not close the deal without him."[5]

Duffy, however, was still unproven; Perry was not—although he had to demonstrate his skills were not diminishing as he entered his mid–30s. And he would have to prove he could throw his hard slider—and perhaps his spitter—effectively in a new league.

"It'll be strange being out of the National League for the first time," Perry said. "I'm just going to have to get together with guys who played in the American League last year and learn the hitters. Of course, they're going to have to learn about me, too.

"I realize that I'm lucky. I had 14 good years with the same organization. There aren't a lot of players who can say that."[6]

When the 1972 season started, Gaylord Perry got off to a rousing start with the Indians, winning four of his first six decisions. Following Perry's lead, the Indians jumped off to their best start in six years by winning 9 of their first 16 games. Opponents, mindful of Perry's reputation as a spitball pitcher, tried to frustrate and rattle the Indian pitcher at the start of the season. In a game against the Texas Rangers, Texas manager Ted Williams complained that Perry's first pitch of the game was a spitter. But Perry shrugged off that distraction and struck out 12 in the Indians' 12–0 conquest. As Perry showed, he was used to the attention and not one to easily be bothered.

Late in May, Perry was 8–2 and the Indians were the surprising leaders in the American League East. So Perry, who left his heart and family in San Francisco when he was traded, was feeling on top of the world. But he still admitted the trade to the Indians came as a jolt. "I hated to leave San Francisco," he said. "I love the people there."[7]

Perry's wife and four children had yet to join him because the youngsters were finishing out the school term. But the spectacular start indicated there was no doubt that Perry had adjusted to the new league after pitching for the Giants since 1962.

"I like to look at the positive side," he said. "I've been fortunate to get off to a good start."[8]

Perry cited his brother, Jim, a former Indian who was then with the Minnesota Twins, for helping him to baffle the league's batters. And he also credited catcher Ray Fosse. "Ray is the most underrated player in the league," Perry said. "I have complete confidence in him."[9]

Opposing batters were not so kind in explaining Perry's winning tendencies. They repeated the oft-heard complaint that Perry was applying a foreign substance to the ball when he pitched. Perry claimed otherwise but there was no shortage of accusers.

"He puts Vaseline or baby oil or something like that on the ball," New York Yankees outfielder Bobby Murcer said.[10]

During Perry's sixth and seventh victories, Texas manager Ted Williams and Detroit Tigers manager Billy Martin complained to the umpires. Both got nowhere.

To Perry, all the wondering and worrying produced only one result—to help him further confuse batters. "If the hitters are looking for that pitch," Perry said, "they might not be able to hit the others."[11]

The debate over Perry's use or non-use of an illegal pitch intensified as the season unfolded. The reason: Perry was enjoying a Cy Young-caliber year. If Perry were struggling, there probably would be little interest in the charges that he was doctoring the ball. But Perry was winning and winning big. And with the winning came the whining.

Perry was getting a lot of attention from umpires, who frequently checked his uniform, and angry batters and managers. But the complaining did not faze him. "If I didn't like the notoriety, I wouldn't go through all that stuff," Perry said. "I touch my hair, the back of my ear, make a lot of motions. It's all psychological. And when people ask me if I throw it, I don't say. I always tell them I throw what the catcher calls for."[12]

Was Perry "Mr. Innocent"? No way, said Atlanta Braves slugger Hank Aaron, who had faced Perry in the National League. "What a lot of nonsense it is to pretend Perry doesn't use the pitch. He's a master at it. He threw it all these years in San Francisco and he's tearing the American League apart with it. I know what he does.

"If he throws 90 pitches, 88 will be spitters. I've been in the major leagues about 20 years. I know a spitter when I see one."[13]

Perry became baseball's first 10-game winner when he threw a six-hitter against the Minnesota Twins in a 7–1 victory. Perry had only four defeats and a splendid 1.77 ERA. The Indians, however, were not as successful. The Indians were falling fast as their batters struggled. Manager Ken Aspromonte lamented, "We aren't even hitting the ball hard. If I can't get base hits, I expect at least a threat up there."[14]

Despite the lack of support, Perry remained hot in July. He shut out the Rangers for 13 innings before getting help in the 14th in a 2–0 victory. Four of his seven losses were by one run. Cleveland outfielder Buddy Bell summarized the feelings toward Perry when he said, "We want to win so badly for Gaylord that we press. I never saw a ballplayer like him and I probably never will again. He won't let himself lose."[15]

Perry rarely lost. When Perry squeezed home the winning run in a game against the Baltimore Orioles, he ran his record to 17–8 with a 1.69 ERA. The other Indian pitchers had a combined 21–44 record.

In August, Perry suffered his first losing streak, dropping four in a row. Still, Cleveland was playing better and with little more than a month remaining in the season trailed co-leaders Baltimore and Detroit by only 6½ games. A year earlier, Cleveland had been 30½ games out of the lead.

By September, Chicago White Sox manager Chuck Tanner had directed umpires to inspect Perry three times. Each time the umpires reported back to Tanner that they had found nothing suspicious. Tanner was not at all displeased but he did allow that those occasional inspections were done for a purpose.

"The only thing I know," he said, "is we hit the ball hard after every time he was checked. Dick Allen hit a home run once. I figured if the umps would check him, maybe he'd wipe it off and we'd get an edge. If you question him and bother him, he might not throw it as often."[16]

So what did the umpires think? Was Perry loading up or not?

American League umpire Merle Anthony, for one, said Perry was clean as far as he was concerned. "It was Sunday before the All-Star break," said Anthony, who was behind the plate when the Indians played the White Sox.

"I looked everywhere Tanner told me to look: the letters of his uniform, the back of his neck, behind the right ear, his cap, his hair, even his glove inside the fingers. I found nothing but good old sweat.

"He was in the National League for a long time and they damn near undressed him and they couldn't find anything. Tom Haller [of the Detroit Tigers] caught him for years in San Francisco and they're fighting for the pennant. You'd think he'd say something if he knew what he was doing."[17]

"I never really knew," Haller said. "I looked for a sinkerball about 80 percent of the time. When I called for a fastball, I looked for the sinker.

"Anybody who throws a pitch like that for any length of time, he may be able to do it with just a little sweat. He doesn't care about them searching for it. I think he gets a kick out of it."[18]

After winning his 19th game, Perry endured another mini-slump before becoming the majors' first 20-game winner. He finished the season with a 24–16 record and a 1.92 ERA, second to the league's best, 1.91 by the Boston Red Sox's Luis Tiant. Even with Perry's wonderful season, Cleveland could do no better than a 72–84 record and fifth-place finish, 14 games out of first.

If one year was a measure of the trade, the Indians came out like a bandit. Duffy was not a major contributor for the Indians, batting .239 with three homers and 27 runs batted in in 385 at-bats. And McDowell was hardly in Perry's class. McDowell was respectable for the Giants, but hardly sensational, logging a 10–8 mark with a 4.34 ERA as the Giants dropped from being NL West champions in 1971 to finishing 27½ games back in 1972.

Perry further savored the 1972 season when he was named the Cy Young Award winner, garnering 64 points to edge Wilbur Wood, the Chicago White Sox knuckleballer who posted a 24–17 record and totaled 58 points. Perry duplicated the Cy Young feat of his brother, Jim, who was named the American League's best pitcher for the Minnesota Twins in 1970—a year in which Gaylord and Jim became the first brother combination in major league history to win 20 games each.

Winning the Cy Young represented a remarkable achievement for Gaylord Perry because he earned the award pitching for the mediocre Indians. Perry won one-third of the Indians' games and threw a whopping 29 complete games in 40 starts. He did not miss a turn.

Perry credited the American League's grass infield and the skill of his catcher, Ray Fosse, for much of his success. Even though he twice won 20 games for the Giants, Perry called his 1972 season his best because he logged the lowest ERA of his career and eight of his 16 losses "were by one run in low-scoring ballgames."

"The big thing that helped me after moving to the American League," said Perry, "is that they had only one AstroTurf infield—the Chicago White Sox. The rest are on natural grass. The National League has six AstroTurfs, and that made it a little harder.

"I'm a low-ball pitcher and try to get them to hit on the ground. On AstroTurf the ball moves through a little quicker. Grass helps in slowing it down. I'd say the other major factor in my good season was catcher Ray Fosse. I rate him with the best around as far as receiving the ball, setting the hitter up and calling the game. He was one of the big pluses."[19]

For years the center of controversy because of his alleged use of the spitball, Perry finally came clean when he documented his dealings with the spitball in his 1974 autobiography, *Me and the Spitter*. Perry said he used everything on the ball except chocolate syrup for eight years and then he turned straight. He confesses he threw a spitter for the first but hardly the last time in 1964 with the Giants when he was tutored by teammate Bob Shaw, who "had one of the best spitballs I've ever seen."

And Perry added: "I had to learn to load it up, how big a load the ball would carry, where to drop the load, how to grip the ball and how to release it as well as how to control it. And probably the most important, how to hide it from four umpires, three coaches, a manager and 25 players as well as spying executives in the box seats. I spent hours in front of a mirror at home practicing decoy moves."[20]

In 1973, Perry used a series of motions—touching his shoulder, cap and other parts of his body—to keep batters wondering if he was loading up. But Perry did not enjoy the same results as he had in 1972, faltering to a 19–19 record and 3.38 ERA, representing almost a point-and-a-half increase over his Cy Young Award-winning season.

In 1974, Perry returned to top form. He stopped his routine of touching various parts of his uniform because of a new rule allowing umpires to call a ball if they suspected a spitter was thrown. The second time the umpire suspected a spitter was thrown, he could remove the pitcher from the game. "I'm not bothered by my new routine," Perry said. "I had to change to take the pressure off the umpires."[21]

He refused to say in July 1974 whether he still threw the spitball, calling the uncertainty a psychological weapon he could exploit. But whether he threw a spitball or not, the outstanding results were there. Perry won 15 straight games at one point, failing to equal the American League record of 16 when he lost to the Oakland A's on July 8. He finished 21–13, with an excellent 2.52 ERA for Cleveland.

Perry pitched the next three season for the Indians and Texas Rangers, averaging 16 victories. He was not enjoying the success of his banner seasons, but he was still pitching very creditably.

His durability helped him achieve a milestone in 1978. Pitching for the San Diego Padres in their season finale against the Los Angeles Dodgers, Perry became the third major league pitcher to strike out 3,000 batters in a career. He struck out Joe Simpson for number 2,999 in the eighth inning and whiffed Simpson on a called third strike for number 3,000 to end the 10th inning.

The 40-year-old Perry did not get the victory in the Padres 4–3 win in 11 innings, but he finished a magnificent season with a 21–6 record and a 2.72 ERA.

"Yeah, I wanted the 3,000 today," Perry said after the game with Los Angeles. "We open on the road next season and I wanted to do it here. Luckily, this was as good a stuff as I've had all year. The Dodgers weren't giving me anything, were they? Seemed like a half-dozen guys were fouling off two-strike pitches."[22]

As expected, Perry received the Cy Young Award in a landslide vote to become the oldest pitcher ever to capture the Cy Young and the first to win it in both leagues. Perry, who received 22 of the 24 first-place votes, said he felt vindicated after being traded the previous winter by the Rangers for little-known pitcher Dave Tomlin and cash.

"I never felt I had anything to prove to the Rangers, but I'm glad things worked out the way they did. I've always been very close to [Rangers' owner] Brad Corbett, and he told me last year they wanted me in the bullpen. I felt I could start, and I guess I proved that. His people were suggesting all along I either be sent to the pen or traded. I wanted to start. Brad was concerned for my welfare and tried to work out a trade.

"I said I intended to be in somebody's regular rotation and he said, 'You'll have to go to a losing club.' As it turned out, the Padres became a winner (finishing fourth in the National League West with an 84–78 record) and they'll win even more in the future."[23]

Because of a calculation error made near the end of the season, Perry finished with 3,001 career strikeouts, not 3,000 as believed. Perry, who threw a fastball, curveball, hard-breaking pitch, forkball and sidearm curve, said he was helped by the Padres' excellent bullpen, headed by Rollie Fingers. Padre manager Roger Craig called Perry—who won 15 games or more in 13 consecutive seasons—"a great pitcher who uses his whole body to pitch. That way, he saves his arm a lot of work. He has a great natural rhythm."[24]

In 1982 at the age of 43, Perry reached another milestone. As a member of the Seattle Mariners, Perry became the 15th pitcher to win 300 games with a 7–3 victory over the visiting New York Yankees. Perry retired Willie Randolph on a grounder to second for the final out. The crowd of 27,369 at the Kingdome did not stop cheering until Perry returned for a bow. Asked if he thought winning 300 put him among the game's best pitchers, Perry said, "Maybe you guys will start writing about winning 300 instead of writing about that other pitch."[25]

That other pitch—Perry's famed illegal spitter—certainly was on the minds of the Yankees during Perry's 300th victory. New York asked three times to check the ball and three times the umpires did, but without discovering an illegal substance. Perry permitted nine hits—only four through seven innings—walked one and struck out four to improve his career record to 300–241. Perhaps the message on the T-shirt hanging in Perry's locker summed it up: "300 wins is nothing to spit at."[26]

On August 23, 1982, Perry was ejected for the first time in his 21-year career for throwing an illegal pitch. Home-plate umpire Dave Phillips gave the Mariner pitcher the heave-ho in the seventh inning of a game won by the Boston Red Sox, 4–3. Phillips demanded to inspect the ball after Perry threw a called third strike to Boston's Rick Miller. Instead, Mariner catcher Jim Essian threw the ball back to Perry. Phillips, who had warned Perry about doctoring the ball in the fifth inning, ejected Perry without looking at the ball.

On September 23, 1983, Perry announced that he was retiring after 22 years in major league baseball. "The time has come," said Perry, who had just turned 45 years old. "Twenty-five years in professional baseball, 22 in the big leagues, 690 major league starts, 314 wins, two Cy Young Awards. It's all been great."[27] Perry, who was picked up by the Kansas City Royals in July after being released by Seattle, retired with a 314–265 record and 3.09 ERA.

McDowell, for whom Perry was traded, declined quickly after being sent to the Giants. Although he won 10 games for the Giants in 1972, he won only nine more games the rest of his career. In 1985—12 years after he retired—McDowell admitted that his career was undermined by a drinking problem. He pitched in the majors for 15 years, winning 141 and losing 134. Duffy, who was traded with Perry for McDowell, had an undistinguished career in which he averaged .232 during his 10 years in the majors.

Perry's career, on the other hand, was anything but undistinguished. In 1991, Perry was selected to the Hall of Fame in his third year of eligibility.

After his selection, the tributes came out in droves.

From broadcaster Jerry Coleman: "He was the only pitcher who could be behind a hitter three-oh and actually be ahead in the count. He'd throw a fastball down the middle, and it would be three-one. On the next one, the guy would be looking for another fastball, and he'd get a curve that made it three-two.

"Now it was one on one, and Perry would throw one of his other pitches and the hitter was gone."[28]

From former teammate, shortstop Ozzie Smith, who played with Perry on the Padres: "Perry had the uncanny ability of getting them to hit the ball to me. He would turn around to me and motion to go into the hole because he was going to pitch a guy a different way from what our scouting report said.

"He was just phenomenal. The man was a master tactician. He was like a surgeon. He definitely helped my career. He knew how to utilize his infielders to the best of their ability, and that allowed me to utilize what had gotten me here."[29]

Of course, not all were tributes. Some cited his use of an illegal pitch as the key to his success. But nearly all admired his ability to either throw a spitter and get away with it or confuse a hitter with the appearance one was coming.

Said shortstop Garry Templeton: "I know he wetted it up, because he threw some pitches that did weird stuff. If he was in a critical situation, you knew you were going to get the wet one. It would knuckle up here and fall down.

"He used it at least twice in every at-bat, and he knew he could get you out with it. But I'll say this: He was the best I've ever seen at disguising it."[30]

Did he or didn't he?

The man with the absolute answer addressed that subject six years after he retired. "I kept them guessing every chance I got," said Perry. "I made them believe I threw a spitter. Making them think I did was a big advantage to me."[31]

Notes

1. *San Francisco Examiner*, 9 December 1971.
2. *San Francisco Chronicle*, 30 November 1971.
3. United Press International, 30 November 1971.
4. *San Francisco Examiner*, 9 December 1971.
5. *San Francisco Chronicle*, 30 November 1971.
6. *San Francisco Examiner*, 9 December 1971.
7. United Press International, 26 May 1972.
8. Ibid.
9. Ibid.
10. Ibid.
11. Ibid.
12. *Los Angeles Times*, 6 September 1972.
13. Ibid.
14. *Sports Illustrated*, 5 June 1972.
15. *Sports Illustrated*, 24 July 1972.
16. *Los Angeles Times*, 6 September 1972.
17. Ibid.
18. Ibid.
19. Associated Press, 1 November 1972.
20. *Los Angeles Times*, 10 August 1973.
21. Associated Press, 14 July 1974.
22. *Los Angeles Times*, 2 October 1978.
23. *Los Angeles Times*, 25, October 1978.
24. Ibid.
25. *Los Angeles Times*, 7 May 1982.
26. Ibid.
27. *Los Angeles Times*, 24 September 1983.
28. *Los Angeles Times*, 2 August 1994.
29. Ibid.
30. Ibid.
31. Ibid.

"Little Joe"

*November 29, 1971: The Cincinnati Reds
trade Lee May, Tommy Helms
and Jimmy Stewart to the Houston Astros
for Denis Menke, Joe Morgan, Cesar Geronimo,
Jack Billingham and Ed Armbrister*

The Cincinnati Reds and Houston Astros exchanged eight players on November 29, 1971, in a blockbuster trade that featured first baseman Lee May, who had belted at least 34 homers for the Reds each season from 1969 through 1971, including 39 in 1971. Yet, the deal did not make big headlines around much of the nation. Why the relatively skimpy coverage?

The explanation was that on the same day two other big-time trades were consummated. Additionally, the annual major league baseball draft took place and attracted attention away from one of the wildest trading days in the history of baseball's winter meetings.

The rapid-fire wheeling and dealing included the San Francisco Giants' trading of two-time 20-game winner Gaylord Perry and promising shortstop Frank Duffy to the Cleveland Indians for five-time American League strikeout king and 20-game winner Sam McDowell. The Chicago Cubs also got into the act by trading disgruntled but distinguished left-handed pitcher Ken Holtzman to the Oakland A's for fleet outfielder Rick Monday.

So the Reds-Astros trade was somewhat obscured outside of Cincinnati and Houston by other baseball news, but few doubted the transaction would have major repercussions. The Reds and Astros had finished fourth and fifth, respectively, in the six-team National League West in 1971, and both teams desired to shake things up for the 1972 season.

Cincinnati obtained second baseman Joe Morgan, outfielder Cesar Geronimo, minor league outfielder Ed Armbrister, first baseman Denis Menke and starting pitcher Jack Billingham from the Astros in exchange for first baseman Lee May, second baseman Tommy Helms and utility man Jimmy Stewart. May, 28, was the headline player in the trade, finishing third in homers and fourth in slugging percentage in the National League in 1971. None of the five players the Reds acquired had the same stature as May, although Billingham had won 10 games with an impressive 3.39 earned run average in 1971 and Morgan was a lightning-fast athlete who could give the plodding Reds some much-needed speed.

For Cincinnati, the 5-foot-7 Morgan was the big man in the trade. Morgan, 28, was a proven veteran. He was the National League's Rookie of the Year in 1965 when he batted .271, scored 100 runs, walked a league-high 97 times and stole 20 bases for the Astros. Morgan had averaged 44 stolen bases from 1969 through 1971, so there was no question about his running ability. He also had decent power and knew how to get on base, receiving at least 80 walks in each of his six seasons in which he played at least 120 games. Morgan, who batted .256 in 1971, had never batted higher than .285 but his high on-base percentage compensated for that.

What Morgan also offered was insurance in case outfielder Bobby Tolan could not return after two Achilles tendon injuries. The speedy Tolan batted .316 with 112 runs and a league-high 57 stolen bases in the Reds' pennant-winning season in 1970, but he missed the entire 1971 season with a torn Achilles tendon. If Tolan was unable to play in 1972, Morgan would carry the mantle of the Reds' speed game.

The Reds also welcomed the fact that Morgan was a left-handed hitter. "This gives us the left-handed hitting we didn't have," said Reds general manager Bob Howsam. "We made the deal to get the balance we need to make us a contender. We feel we have enough power to win. May had his greatest year last year and we still finished fourth."[1]

The trade, in essence, changed the styles of the Reds and Astros. The Reds had thrived with their power game in 1970 but died with it in 1971. Now the Reds had Pete Rose, Morgan and Tolan, if healthy, as their first three batters and that meant a speedy team. Power hitters Johnny Bench and Tony Perez were primed to drive in the swift table setters. Meanwhile, the Astros, who hit the fewest homers in the majors in 1971, were being billed as a power team behind May, whose 39 homers represented more than half the Astros' total in 1971. Long-ball hitters Cesar Cedeno, Bob Watson, Doug Rader and Jimmy Wynn would surround May in a lineup capable of scoring runs in bunches. That Houston was serious about its power game was made apparent the day of the trade when Astro General manager H.B. "Spec" Richardson revealed that Houston planned to move in the fences at Houston's Astrodome for the 1972 season.

Houston was rolling out the welcome mat for May, who took the news of the trade with grim resolution if not total enthusiasm. "It's the business," May said. "Each club tries to improve its business through trades. If I were a rookie and had a good season and was traded, I'd be upset. But I've been around a while and I've seen players come and go for various reasons."[2] The Astros were able to acquire the powerful May through the lure of Morgan, whom they discarded because they considered him a poor influence on Wynn,

Lee May (above) was a quality player for three seasons after the Houston Astros acquired him from the Cincinnati Reds. But the Astros paid dearly for his services, giving up three players who would play big roles on the Big Red Machine in the '70s: second baseman Joe Morgan (pictured opposite, who won back-to-back MVP Awards), outfielder Cesar Geronimo and pitcher Jack Billingham (photographs courtesy of the Cincinnati Reds).

whose home run output plummeted to seven in 1971 after seasons of 37, 26, 33 and 27 homers.

For Cincinnati, the trade did more than just improve their team's speed. For one, the Reds improved their starting rotation that was in need of help. Billingham, 28, had won a total of 23 games the previous two seasons and had the potential to be a pitching mainstay. Menke, 31, had a disappointing season in 1971 as the Astros' first baseman with one homer and 43 RBIs, but he was being moved to third base on the Reds, allowing Tony Perez, a defensive liability at third base, to return to his natural position of first base. As for the 23-year-old Geronimo, he had played sparingly in the majors the previous two seasons but had good speed, a tremendous arm and the ability to earn considerable playing time.

Most observers believed the Reds got the short end of the trade because of the departure of the big-time-hitting May and the Gold Glove-winning and pesky-hitting Helms, who drove in 52 runs, just four fewer than Morgan, in 1971. Helms, 30, and May had spent their entire careers with the Reds and were regarded as team leaders who held the team together and kept it from turmoil. Still, Howsam was unflinchingly pleased with the players he acquired. "We needed more left-handed hitting, pitching and speed," Howsam summarized. "I really think this is a trade that will help both clubs. I hope that these two teams are battling for number one in the West next year and I think there is a good chance they will. We know what we are giving up in May—and the other players we hated to have to let go, too—but we felt we were in a position to give up some power in order to get what we think we need."

Morgan said he expected to hit better in Cincinnati. "I had a problem picking up the spin [in Houston]," he said. "I think it will be a lot easier to play defensively in Cincinnati."

Still, Morgan admitted he did not relish leaving Houston "because the fans are really great there" although he said he looked forward to playing on what he considered a pennant contender.[3]

When the season started, five teams were regarded as viable West Division contenders—the Reds, Astros, defending champion San Francisco Giants, Los Angeles Dodgers and the Atlanta Braves—all but the San Diego Padres. There was pressure on the new Cincinnati players because the trade cost Cincinnati one of the premier players in the league. But Joe Morgan was not one to bow to pressure. When the season started—albeit 10 days late because of a players' strike—Morgan was brimming with confidence that he would be a major factor on a team that sported such luminaries as left fielder Pete Rose and catcher Johnny Bench. However even with a healthy Tolan, the Reds stumbled out of the gate, losing 7 of their first 12 games while the Dodgers and Astros raced to the head of the pack.

Morgan's talent, though, was evident when he propelled the Reds to one early-season victory, stealing second and third before scoring the winning run in a game against the Pittsburgh Pirates. "I can steal anytime I want to," Morgan chortled.[4]

The Reds had too much talent to be held down for long. In mid–May, the "Big Red Machine" began kicking it into gear and vaulted into the lead for the first time in early June. Bench was enjoying a huge year, shrugging off his lackluster 1971 season and emulating his 1970 MVP season in which he belted 45 homers and drove in 148 runs.

But Morgan was having a big season, too. The Reds' second baseman was running the bases with abandon, hitting well—often with power—and fielding like a vacuum. Tolan was up to speed and Rose was having another banner season to give the Reds three potent players at the top of the order. "You know," said Menke, "we've become a good, good team."[5]

The Astros were no slouches either. May was fitting in well in his new surroundings and making the others around him better. In June, the Astros had become baseball's top run-producers. Houston's only early tailspin came when May was sidelined with a pulled hamstring. But when May returned, so did the Astros' winning ways. May showed he was not adversely affected by playing in new surroundings. "There is no way to pitch to May when he's on a tear," concluded Montreal Expo manager Gene Mauch. "Name your top hitters and he's all of them put together."[6]

As the season progressed, Morgan continued to distinguish himself, even winning the All-Star Game's MVP Award with a game-winning single in the 10th inning. His day-in, day-out exploits helped the Reds move into control of the West Division. The Reds opened a six-game lead over the Astros and a 10-game bulge over the Dodgers by winning 61 of their first 99 games, an impressive winning percentage of more than .600. The keys were Rose, Morgan and Tolan, who were whirling around the bases in dizzying fashion, and the return to form of Bench, who had won the home fans back with 25 homers and 79 RBIs in the team's first 100 games.

Manager Sparky Anderson, who had guided the Reds' 1970 champions, was enjoying the Reds' ingenious ways to manufacture runs. "We are really not the mauling type of baseball team that some people think we still are," Anderson said. "As for those long home runs and huge innings and that ferocious attack we had in 1970, well it isn't quite the same in 1972. We can still hit home runs, but we don't have to rely on them. We play defense a lot better and we'll run at you. We try for any opening we can see."[7]

There was plenty of sentiment around the league that the most valuable Red and perhaps the Most Valuable Player in the league was Morgan, who after 100 games was leading the league in walks and runs and was second in stolen bases to Lou Brock of the St. Louis Cardinals. Morgan seemed to reach base at least twice a game and had fashioned an on-base percentage of .400. Morgan missed only one of the team's first 100 games and was fielding brilliantly, making only six errors. What Morgan had done was exorcise the ghosts of May and Helms in convincing fashion.

Pete Rose, a hitting machine himself, credited his new teammate with being one of the chief reasons for the Reds' turnaround. "When you talk about the Big Red Machine this year," said Rose, "you are talking about Joe Morgan and Johnny Bench. Joe has done an unbelievable job for us, both on offense and defense, and he's in scoring position so often that I keep telling Bench that the only time he should not get a run batted in is when he strikes out."[8]

With 13 homers in his team's first 100 games, Morgan was only two short of his career best in 1969. Although he was getting rave reviews, Morgan—who did not get along with Astro manager Harry Walker—said he believed he was just as good a player when he was toiling for the anonymous Astros.

"When I was growing up, my two favorite players were Nellie Fox of the White Sox and Ted Williams of the Red Sox," said Morgan, an acknowledged student of the game. "I liked Fox because he was a second baseman and admired Williams because he knew how to hit and was an expert on the strike zone. I get so many walks because I'm the type of hitter who isn't strong enough to hit bad pitches for base hits. I need to hit strikes. In many ways, batting averages can be misleading. There are players in baseball who hit over .300 and don't help the team as much as other players who hit .250. The idea is to score runs and that's what I'm supposed to do.

"A batting average is a personal thing. Unless there are men on base, there is little difference between a single to right field and drawing four balls."[9]

On the rare days when Morgan was not contributing, Rose, Tolan, Bench and Perez were providing the clutch hit. But much more often than not, Morgan was in the thick of things when the Reds mounted their rallies. "The kind of year Joe is having reminds me of the kind of season Bobby Tolan had in 1970," Tolan said. "Every time he does something on the bases that leads to a run, I say to myself, 'Hey, that was me two years ago.'"[10]

In August, the Reds continued to roll, although two of their top pitchers, Gary Nolan and Wayne Simpson, were ailing. The Reds' winning ways were a tribute to manager Sparky Anderson's deft touch, the strong offense and an outstanding bullpen led by Clay Carroll and Tom Hall. Falling farther and farther behind, the Astros fired manager Harry Walker and replaced him with Leo Durocher, who had been recently fired by the Chicago Cubs. "We had to make a change," explained Houston general manager Spec Richardson. "We've still got a chance for a pennant and here's Leo, a man who lit a fire under a team that was 13½ games out of first in August [as manager of the New York Giants in 1951] and took them to the pennant."

Walker, not the most popular manager among his players, had one quasi-well-wisher. That was Joe Morgan, who said he felt sorry his old manager got the ax. "I didn't want to see him get fired," Morgan said. "Not now. I wanted to see him finish second to us, then invite him to our party when we clinched it."[11]

The big question in September was not whether the Astros could overtake the Reds, but whether Houston could hold off the Dodgers for second place. The Big Red Machine was clicking on all cylinders and marching inexorably to the pennant behind the dynamic Morgan and the explosive Bench. The Reds' catcher went on another tear in September, blasting three homers, including a grand slam, and driving in 13 runs during one memorable six-game span. Safely ahead, the Reds clinched the division title with a 4–3 victory over the Astros. That the victory came in the Astrodome made it even sweeter for Morgan. "This is the best thing in the world for me," Morgan said.[12]

The Reds ended the season with a 95–69 record, 10½ games ahead of the second-place Astros, who finished percentage points ahead of the Dodgers. A lot of Cincinnati players enjoyed outstanding seasons.

The leaders were Bench and Morgan. The Reds' catcher bounced back from a dismal 1971 season to lead the majors with 40 homers and 125 RBIs. Morgan set career highs with a .292 average, 16 homers and 73 RBIs, topped the majors with 122 runs and 115 walks and was second in the majors with 58 stolen bases behind Brock. Other key cogs in the Big Red Machine were Perez, who batted .283 with 21 homers and 90 RBIs; Rose, who batted .307 with 107 runs; Tolan, who batted .283 with 88 runs; starter Gary Nolan, who went 15–5, with a brilliant 1.99 ERA; reliever Tom Hall, who was 10–1, with eight saves; and reliever Clay Carroll, who posted a major league-record 37 saves.

Morgan, the key player as far as the Reds were concerned in the 1971 trade with the Astros, had come through in MVP-caliber style. But not to be overlooked were the contributions of three other players who came to Cincinnati along with Morgan from Houston. Billingham filled the role of starter in the Reds' rotation with a 12–12 season and an excellent 3.18 ERA. He threw eight complete games, four of them shutouts. Third baseman Denis Menke batted only .233, but he had 50 RBIs and nine homers. And outfielder Cesar Geronimo got into 120 games, batting a respectable .275.

"We all had a lot of nice things happen to us this season," said Bench after the regular season ended and before the Reds' National League Championship Series with the Pittsburgh Pirates, "and they were brought about in part by the fact that we were shaping up at the end of last season. Over the winter, Mr. Howsam [the general manager] made the big trade with Houston. It went down hard with a lot of our fans because we gave up Lee May, Tommy Helms and Jimmy Stewart to get Joe Morgan, Jack Billingham, Denis Menke and Cesar Geronimo. I was at a banquet with Mr. Howsam and when he was introduced, he was booed. That stung.

"I followed him at the mike and told the fans to get ready to watch Morgan have a heck of a year for the Reds. I said if Bobby Tolan could play like Bobby Tolan, they'd just better get ready to watch Cincinnati win the division."[13]

Morgan put up the most dazzling numbers of the players involved in the 1971 blockbuster trade, but Lee May and Tommy Helms of the Astros did not need to apologize for their seasons. Although May's homers dropped by 10 from 1971 to 29, he batted .284 with 98 RBIs, fifth in the league. Helms performed almost identically to the previous year, batting .259 with 60 RBIs and 45 runs.

But it was Morgan who got his team into the National League playoffs, where the Reds were paired against the very tough Pirates, with power hitters Roberto Clemente and Willie Stargell and star pitcher Steve Blass. These were the teams considered the best in baseball and the winner would enter the World Series as the favorite over the survivor of the American League playoffs between the Oakland A's and Boston Red Sox.

Morgan was a force in the playoffs right off the bat, belting two homers in the first two games. But the Reds barely survived the playoffs, eliminating the Pirates, 4–3, in the deciding fifth game, rallying for two runs in the bottom of the ninth with the help of Bench's game-tying solo homer. The World Series, however, was not so kind to Cincinnati, spoiling a storybook ending for Morgan and Bench. The A's pitching was brilliant, muffling Rose, Morgan and Tolan, and Gene Tenace emerged as the unlikely hitting star as Oakland won the World Series in seven games.

But Morgan's impact on the Reds' pennant-winning season was readily apparent. Morgan, now a certified star, was acknowledged in the league's Most Valuable Player voting. Bench earned the award for the second time in three years by garnering 263 points and teammate Morgan was fourth with 197 points. Morgan had as many first-place votes as the runner-up, the Chicago Cubs' Billy Williams, and more first-place votes than the third-place finisher, Willie Stargell of the Pirates.

This was the season that gave Morgan the recognition he lacked while playing for the Astros. It also was the start of something big for Morgan. For Morgan, stardom would turn into superstardom, as he demonstrated he perhaps was the top all-around player in baseball. Beginning in 1972, Morgan enjoyed six straight brilliant seasons.

In 1973, Morgan showed incredible power for his 5-foot-7, 155-pound frame, belting 26 homers to go with 116 runs, 82 RBIs, a career-high 67 stolen bases and .290 average. Cincinnati wiped out a 10½-game lead by the Dodgers in early July with an explosive second-half drive. The Reds won 56 of their last 81 games to claim the division title by 3½ games over Los Angeles, but they were ousted in the National League playoffs by the New York Mets. In 1974, Morgan banged 22 homers, batted .293 and helped the Reds put on another devastating second-half run, although they finished four games behind the champion Dodgers.

But the climax of Morgan's career was still to come. In 1975, Morgan was so hot that he nearly nailed down the Most Valuable Player award in August by ranking among the top five in the National League in hitting, runs, walks and steals and among the top 10 in homers and RBIs. On August 2, manager Sparky Anderson said of Morgan: "Actually, the only thing different this year from Joe's previous three years with us is that he's hitting for a higher average. Up to this point, I've never seen any player play any better than he's played this year. And when you consider everything, from base-stealing and bases on balls to home runs and average, he's been the game's number one offensive player for the last 3½ years."

Morgan reflected back on the trade that brought him to the Reds, to a team that was a winner. "Everything I've done with the Reds," said Morgan, "I did in Houston but not in the same year because I was forced to emphasize different things depending on the manager and the makeup of the club that year.

"Hitting behind Rose, for instance, I always seem to have the first base hole open which means 25 to 30 extra hits a year. And hitting ahead of Bench and Perez means that I see better pitches, giving me both the opportunity to score more runs and set up RBIs for Bench and Perez who are benefited by the pitcher's concern that I might steal."[14]

Morgan, who possessed a distinctive habit of pumping his left arm up and down as he stood at the plate, led the Reds to a 108-victory regular season in 1975 and a whopping 20-game margin over the second-place Dodgers in the West. The Reds then won the World Series championship, a seven-game classic over the Boston Red Sox, for their first world title since 1940. Cincinnati overcame a 3–0 deficit to post a 4–3 victory in game seven. Fittingly, Morgan delivered the winning hit, a run-scoring single with two out in the top of the ninth inning. Morgan later was named the league's Most Valuable Player in a landslide. He received 21½ first-place votes from the 24-member committee and his 167½-point margin over outfielder Greg Luzinski of the Philadelphia Phillies represented the greatest plurality in MVP history in either league.

After being named the 1975 MVP, Morgan said he believed his winning the trophy was good for baseball because it demonstrated the importance of being an all-around player rather than one who could simply swing the bat. And Morgan was inarguably skilled in many areas. He batted at least .300 for the first time in his career in 1975, finishing fourth in the league with a .327 average. He scored 107 runs, led the league in walks with 132, hit 17 homers, drove in 94 runs, stole 67 bases and was the fielding leader among second basemen, making only 11 errors.

It was a dominating season and it was so noted in the MVP voting as Morgan was the only player named on all 24 ballots. "I think the thing that separated me from fellows like Luzinski and [Ted] Simmons and some of the other fellas is that I can do more things than just hit," Morgan said. "This is certainly not a knock at Luzinski, who had a great season, but I think I've shown that I can hit, run the bases and do the job in the field."[15]

The 1975 season gave Morgan the reputation as baseball's most complete player and he lived up to that billing in 1976, enjoying another phenomenal season. He became the first second baseman in 26 years to drive in more than 100 runs. Morgan had career highs with 27 homers and 111 runs batted in, hit .320, drew 114 walks, scored 113 runs and stole 60 bases to become the second National League player to win the Most Valuable Player award in consecutive seasons, duplicating Ernie Banks' feat. The MVP award gave Morgan great satisfaction because it came in a season in which he spurred the Reds to their second straight World Series title, as Cincinnati swept the New York Yankees.

This was the Big Red Machine at its peak and Billingham and Geronimo, who came to the Reds in the Morgan trade, helped fuel Cincinnati's

World Series drive. Billingham was 19–11 in 1974, tied for third in the league in wins, and was 15–10 in 1975. The speedy Geronimo was a steady and productive outfield regular, scoring 73 runs in 1974 and 69 the following year. Meanwhile, the Astros—and May—tailed off after their strong 1972 season and Houston shipped May to the Baltimore Orioles after the team finished fourth in 1974. The following year the Astros finished last and Helms was traded to the Pittsburgh Pirates months later.

After a strong 1977 season in which he batted .288 with 22 homers and 113 runs, Morgan was plagued by injuries in 1978 and 1979. He struggled both years, batting .236 and .250, respectively, and leading management to refuse his contract demands and wounding his pride. Morgan opted for free agency and declared he would sign only with a contender. After encountering few suitors, Morgan signed a one-year, $225,000 contract to return to the Astros, a team that had blown an 11-game lead the previous year.

"I never wanted to leave [Houston]," said the 36-year-old Morgan, who had played for Houston for nine seasons. "That wasn't my choice. I've looked forward to coming back ever since I left. I still have a lot of ability."[16]

It was difficult to believe that Morgan could return to his MVP level with the Astros and Morgan played at less than his best in 1980. Still, Morgan played in 141 games and provided the leadership and timely hits to propel the Astros to a division title, one game ahead of the Dodgers. Morgan batted only .243 but scored 66 runs, stole 47 bases and tied for the league lead in walks. The Astros, however, were ousted in the playoffs by the Philadelphia Phillies.

It turned out to be the last season that Morgan played for Houston. In the off-season, he signed with the San Francisco Giants for the 1981 season. Asked what he contributed to the Astros in his one-season return, Morgan answered: "A pennant." Then he added, "It gave me great satisfaction again to prove that what Joe Morgan is all about is winning."[17]

Morgan made it to the National League playoffs again in 1983, this time as a member of the the Philadelphia Phillies, joining former Big Red Machine teammates Tony Perez and Pete Rose. The Phillies advanced to the World Series but bowed to the Baltimore Orioles in five games. Still, no one could fault the 40-year-old Morgan for the World Series loss. He batted .263 with two homers and one stolen base in 19 at-bats.

Morgan, who was named the the National League comeback player of the year as a member of the San Francisco Giants in 1982, finally retired after the 1984 season with the Oakland A's, his remarkable 22nd season in the majors. Morgan finished with a .271 lifetime average, 268 homers and 689 stolen bases. Billingham, like Morgan, thrived after being traded to the Reds. He won at least 10 games each of his six seasons with Cincinnati and compiled a 75–51 record overall. He was 19–10 in 1973 when he led the league in games started (40), innings pitched (293⅓) and shutouts (seven). He was brilliant in the World Series, allowing only one earned run in 25⅓ innings and winning two games without a loss.

Geronimo was a productive player for the Reds, compiling a 15-year career in the majors, nine of them with Cincinnati. Menke played two years for Cincinnati, batting only .233 and .191. Armbrister, the fifth player the Reds acquired from Houston, played as a reserve outfielder for Cincinnati for five years.

As for the Reds-turned-Astros, May never reached 30 homers again after leaving Cincinnati, but he still was a quality player for the Astros for three years. Traded to the Baltimore Orioles, he led the American League in RBIs in 1976 wth 109. May hit at least 20 homers in 12 seasons and finished with a lifetime average of .267 and 354 homers. Helms played four seasons for Houston, three as a regular. His best season came in 1973 when he batted .287 and drove in 61 runs. Stewart, the final player acquired by Houston from Cincinnati, concluded his career with two seasons as a utility player for the Astros, batting .219 and .191.

Morgan, who was named to the All-Star team in each of his eight years with the Reds and won five Gold Gloves from 1973 to 1977, was voted into the Hall of Fame in 1990 in his first year of eligibility.

Notes

1. *Cincinnati Enquirer*, 30 November 1971.
2. Ibid.
3. *Houston Chronicle*, 30 November 1971.
4. *Sports Illustrated*, 8 May 1972.
5. *Sports Illustrated*, 19 June 1972.
6. *Sports Illustrated*, 12 June 1972.
7. *Sports Illustrated*, 14 August 1972.
8. Ibid.
9. Ibid.
10. Ibid.
11. *Sports Illustrated*, 4 September 1972.
12. *Sports Illustrated*, 2 October 1972.
13. *Sports Illustrated*, 9 October 1972.
14. *Los Angeles Times*, 3 August 1975.
15. United Press International, 19 November 1975.
16. *Los Angeles Times*, 1 February 1980.
17. *Los Angeles Times*, 24 March 1981.

"Lefty"

February 25, 1972:
The Philadelphia Phillies trade Rick Wise
to the St. Louis Cardinals for Steve Carlton

After winning 20 games in 1971, left-hander Steve Carlton experienced difficulties reaching a contract with the St. Louis Cardinals for the 1972 season. The impasse triggered bad memories for Cardinals' owner August A. Busch, Jr.

In 1969, Carlton posted a 17–11 record and became a holdout in the spring of 1970. That year he finally came to terms with the Cardinals on a two-year pact in mid–March, but the three weeks he lost in spring training undermined a potentially glittering season for Carlton, who slumped to 10–19. Remembering the effects of that holdout, Busch ordered general manager Bing Devine to deal Carlton because of the ongoing contract dispute. So on February 25, 1972, the 6-foot-4 Carlton was traded to the Philadelphia Phillies for right-hander Rick Wise. Devine made no bones about the fact that the stalled negotiations were a major factor in the Carlton trade.

"I guess, really, this thing was generated by our differences with Carlton two years ago," Devine said the day the trade was completed. "Having gone through that experience, we could sense a similar situation developing."[1]

Carlton, 27, had been asking for a $25,000 raise on his $50,000 salary of 1971. The Cardinals countered by offering close to $60,000. It was a spat over a mere $15,000 but that is where the two sides locked horns. Neither side would budge.

Wise was also embroiled in a contract dispute. Wise, who pitched a no-hitter against the Cincinnati Reds in 1971, was seeking a near 100 percent raise to $65,000. Phillies general manager John Quinn offered a $10,000 increase.

Carlton and Wise were top-of-the-line pitchers with impressive credentials and the trade made headlines across the nation. Carlton was 20–9 with a 3.56 earned run average in 1971 and was 77–62 in six seasons with the Cardinals.

Wise, 26, had distinguished himself as an all-around standout, belting six homers in addition to leading the league's pitchers in fielding in 1971. His 75–76 record in seven seasons with the Phillies did not seem to reflect his talent. In 1971, he compiled a 17–14 record with a sparkling 2.88 ERA for the last-place Phillies.

So the Phillies and Cardinals had high expectations for their new acquisitions. But both teams had to wait a bit before they could start analyzing the outcome of the trade. Because of a players' strike, the 1972 season opened 10 days late. But when the bell rang, Carlton was ready and he emerged as the Phillies' ace right off the bat. He got the ball in Philadelphia's season opener against the Chicago Cubs and Ferguson Jenkins in Wrigley Field and the Phillies prevailed, 4–2.

In the first two weeks of the season, Carlton also bested the St. Louis Cardinals' Bob Gibson by pitching a three-hit shutout and pitched a one-hitter to beat the San Francisco Giants and their ace pitcher, Juan Marichal. Carlton was taking on all comers—and beating them—en route to winning five of his first six decisions.

Especially delightful was his victory over Gibson and his former teammates. "That is the last team in the world Steve would like to shut out," joked teammate Joe Hoerner, another former Cardinal.[2]

The Phillies, shockingly, were winning most of their early-season games, racing to an 11–6 record. And with an 8–3 victory over the San Francisco Giants, the Phillies climbed to first place for the first time in eight years. "What is this, April?" wondered Philadelphia manager Frank Lucchesi. "It feels more like late August and I'm fighting for the pennant."[3]

While the Phillies were winning in the first month, the Cardinals occupied much of their time on financial matters. Before the season started, St. Louis dumped another economic dissident, pitcher Jerry Reuss—who won 14 games the previous season—in a trade with the Houston Astros for two minor leaguers. Then the St. Louis front office announced that Cardinal players would no longer room alone on the road. This revised roommate system figured to save the club $10,000. So Carlton was just one in a series of Cardinal decisions dictated by finances.

Meanwhile, the Phillies' early hot streak proved to be an illusion. Philadelphia suffered a disastrous May, losing 19 of 26. Even Carlton was snake-bitten, losing five in a row. Carlton could have sued for nonsupport because the Phillies scored only 10 runs for him in those five games.

Carlton, though, helped the Phillies out of the tailspin. Beginning the second week of June, Carlton was a machine, racking up one victory after another and earning the nickname "The Franchise." Carlton won his seventh straight game in early July to improve to 12–6. It gave Carlton seven of his team's 12 wins since May 30.

And Carlton was not just getting batters out. He was striking them out with amazing ease and was the league's runaway leader in that category. Carlton, who possessed pinpoint control, credited positive thinking and strength for his ability to overmatch hitters.

His physical strength, said the 210-pound Carlton, allowed him to blow the ball past hitters. "Strength has everything to do with it," he said. "[Sandy] Koufax wasn't big, but he had a hell of an arm."[4]

Koufax, incidentally, was on the mind of many sportswriters because Carlton's strong start suggested he had a shot at Koufax's season strikeout record: 382 in 1965. But Carlton, who set a major league one-game strikeout record in 1969 when he fanned 19 New York Mets, said records were not the name of the game as far as he was concerned. Rather, winning was.

"I'd rather have 15 or 16 wins right now [than Koufax's record]," Carlton said. "My one thought is to win when I go out there."

Victories, Carlton realized, meant leverage during contract time. "When you put everything [wins, earned run average and strikeouts] together, then you're sitting pretty [during contract negotiations]," Carlton said. "I just come with my three pitches. Each complements the other."[5]

After he produced four-hit victories over the New York Mets and Cardinals, Carlton's personal winning streak reached 12 games. His record stood at 17–6 and he was not cooling off. But Carlton's winning ways were not enough to save the jobs of general manager John Quinn and manager Frank Lucchesi, who were relieved of their duties. Philadelphia won only 26 of 76 games for Lucchesi.

By mid–August, Carlton had won his 14th straight game, improving his record to 19–6. His record was all the more remarkable because the Phillies were playing under .400 ball and had an anemic offense. But Carlton gave up a total of only 15 runs in 15 games to make it easier for the Phillies' near-moribund offense. There was even talk that Carlton could reach 30 victories and that he could surpass the modern-day record of 17 straight victories by the Pittsburgh Pirates' Elroy Face in 1959.

Although the Phillies were fizzling again, their fans could take solace in the fact that Carlton was demonstrating that he was perhaps the league's top pitcher. With 19 victories, Carlton was entertaining hopes for a 25-victory season, a goal he had formulated before the season began while he was still with the more-formidable Cardinals.

And the player for whom Carlton was traded? Well, Rick Wise had won only 11 of his first 23 decisions for the mediocre Cardinals.

Carlton's sterling performance gave the Phillies hope for the future. Paul Owens, the Phillies' new manager and general manager, acknowledged that Carlton would be part of that Philadelphia future. Owens opined that Carlton would not have problems in reaching a settlement during his next contract negotiation. "He can have anything he wants within reason," Owens said. "I told him I'm willing to bet I'll have him signed by Christmas."[6]

Carlton's domination could be traced to his mixture of three effective pitches. Carlton threw a slider, curveball and fastball. Experts cited his slider as the key to his success. After his holdout in 1970, Carlton had scrapped his slider, failing to refine the pitch that had served him so well in the past. But Carlton adopted the slider from the outset of the 1972 season and that decision was paying huge dividends.

"It started to come back in the spring," Carlton said, "and now it is one of my best pitches."

Batters marveled at Carlton's three pitches, each of which was compared to the best in the league. But Carlton was more reserved about listing each of his pitches among the league's elite.

"I admired Sandy Koufax's curve," Carlton said, "but as to be judging my fastball and slider against any other pitcher's, I wouldn't be capable of doing it."[7]

Carlton's winning streak hit 15 before he lost to the Atlanta Braves on an 11th inning, bases-loaded, broken-bat single by Mike Lum. But Carlton could not be sidetracked for long. He won his 24th game on the same day Wise recorded his 15th victory for the Cardinals.

Wise was producing for the Cardinals, but he was hardly in the same league as Carlton. The two pitchers faced each other in late September and Carlton demonstrated firsthand why the Phillies had gotten the better of the trade. Final score: Phillies 2, Cardinals 1. It was Wise's 12th loss in 15 one-run decisions for the fourth-place Cardinals.

Carlton finished the season 27–10, with a remarkable 1.97 ERA and 310 strikeouts in 346⅓ innings. And he accomplished this for the last-place Phillies, who won a league-low 59 games. In other words, Carlton posted 46 percent of the Phillies' victories, an incredible percentage. The 27 victories tied Koufax's all-time record for wins by a left-hander.

Carlton had certainly earned the respect of the Phillies' brass, which was quite pleased with the Wise-for-Carlton deal. "He'll be our first $100,000 player," Owens conceded.[8]

It was hardly a surprise when Carlton was unanimously selected as the league's Cy Young Award winner. Carlton became the first National Leaguer since Bob Gibson in 1968 to win unanimously and was the first Phillies' pitcher to win the award since its inception in 1956. He also was the first pitcher from a last-place club to receive the honor. Carlton led the league in wins—six ahead of runner-up Tom Seaver of the New York Mets—starts with 41, complete games with 30, innings pitched and strikeouts. He completed 28 of his last 35 starts. His eight shutouts were second in the league, one behind Don Sutton of the Los Angeles Dodgers.

After the season ended, Carlton credited positive thinking for his brilliant season and the reason why he did not let the trade to the bumbling Phillies adversely affect him. "With the Cards, I didn't think about going out and getting a lot of runs because we never did," Carlton said. "And I pitched the same way with the Phillies. I just go out and think that I'm going to shut them out. I think a lot more positive now. I know when I go out there, I'm going to win.

"But the big thing is having the opportunity to pitch every fourth day. I needed work and it made me more consistent. Being traded probably was a blessing in disguise."[9]

Wise, for his part, enjoyed a respectable season with a 16–16 record and an excellent 3.11 ERA. His victory total was second on the Cardinals' staff, behind Gibson's 19.

Carlton's phenomenal season enabled him to draw a huge raise for the 1973 season—from $97,500 to $165,000, giving him the highest single-season salary for a pitcher. The money seemed well spent when Carlton got off to a sizzling start in 1973 and renewed talks of a possible 30-win season. Comparisons to Koufax, who retired in 1966 and who had never faced Carlton, abounded.

Phillies manager Danny Ozark, for one, said comparisons of Carlton to Koufax were not all that far-fetched. Ozark, who was with the Dodgers for almost 30 years and had watched Koufax develop, said Carlton has "the same intestinal fortitude Sandy had and the tremendous stamina. And he's got the slider, which Koufax never had."[10]

Carlton had been shadowed by the Koufax comparisons since his rookie season in 1965 when the Cardinals issued him uniform number 32, the same number worn by Koufax, and heralded him as "the next Koufax." But Carlton pointed out that he "didn't ask for the number. They just gave it to me."

And Carlton repeated that he was not focusing on eclipsing any of Koufax's records. "The records mean nothing," Carlton said. "I've just got one goal: win. After that, everything else takes care of itself."[11]

If Carlton desired to be spared the Koufax comparisons, he got his wish the rest of the season. The reason: Carlton could not keep up his early pace and finished 13–20 with a 3.90 ERA. The 20 losses were a league high.

But that season was simply an aberration in Carlton's career. He did not finish below .500 again until 1983 when he went 15–16. In between, he won at least 20 games four more times and also claimed three more Cy Young awards—in 1977 when he was 23–10, 1980 when he was 24–9, and 1982 when he was 23–11—all with the Phillies.

In 1977, Carlton became only the sixth man in baseball history to win the Cy Young more than once. The 1980 honor was a record-tying third time for Carlton, who joined Tom Seaver and Koufax as the only three-time winners. Carlton picked up an unprecedented fourth Cy Young in 1982 at age 37 when he recovered from the worst start of his career. He lost his first four games, but won four of the next five and finished with a flashy 23–11 record and a league-leading 286 strikeouts.

The following year, on June 7, Carlton eclipsed the Houston Astros'

Nolan Ryan as baseball's all-team strikeout leader, as he boosted his total to 3,526. What did Carlton think about the achievement?

Few people knew. Carlton, nicknamed "Lefty," had not granted an interview to the print media since July 5, 1979, although he appeared on some postgame television shows with some friendly colleagues-turned-broadcasters.

Carlton's silence stemmed from what he believed was unfair reporting and a 1979 run-in with a baseball writer at a spring training camp beach party. After claiming the strikeout record, Carlton did not deviate from his pattern, simply doffing his cap when the crowd gave him a standing ovation.

Reporters had to resort to talking to his manager, catcher, other teammates or the opposition to get some insights on him. Carlton rarely wavered from his attitude on interviews. A couple of springs earlier, he had been asked to break his silence and at least discuss the games he pitched. His reply: "Policy is policy," and he walked away.[12]

Teammates said that Carlton's ability to focus on his job and not be bothered by distractions—such as accommodating the media—was a major factor in his success. Longtime catcher Bob Boone said Carlton "had an incredible ability to concentrate. He didn't allow emotions to get in the way of his focus. He trained himself that way. He was a machine."[13]

Once, Carlton was belted in the neck by a line drive off the bat of the Cubs' Billy Williams. Carlton did not flinch. Another time, Carlton was beaned on the neck by a throw from third baseman Kiko Garcia. Carlton's reaction? He acted as if nothing had happened.

That was Carlton's *modus operandi*: Get the job done and do not be bothered by things that he could not control. And Carlton got the job done. Only once in his 24-year career did Carlton go on the disabled list.

Carlton, though, struggled in his final four years, going 16–37. He pitched in only four games for the Minnesota Twins in 1988, his final season.

In January 1994, Carlton was overwhelmingly selected to the Hall of Fame in his first year of eligibility. He was the 25th player elected on his first try. Carlton received 436 of the 455 votes cast, a percentage of 95.8, the fifth-highest percentage in history.

On August 5, 1994, the Phillies honored Carlton, who was inducted into the Hall of Fame a week earlier, before their game against the Montreal Expos. Carlton, who set many Phillies' records and had his number retired by the Phillies in 1989, received a standing ovation from the crowd of more than 40,000.

Carlton, who finished his remarkable career with a 329–244 record, 254 complete games and 55 shutouts, set such Phillies' career records as wins, games started, walks and strikeouts. When he retired, his total of 4,136 strikeouts ranked second only to Nolan Ryan, who had again overtaken Carlton in

1985, and he struck out more batters than any other left-hander. He led the Phillies to the 1980 World Series championship against the Kansas City Royals, winning two games, including the game six clincher, a 4–1 victory.

After the 1994 ceremony in Philadelphia, Carlton, who spent much of his career avoiding the media, held a rare press conference. "I never disliked talking to the press," he said. "I just didn't like abuse and I didn't have to participate in it. I've got a lot of good friends in the media."[14]

Although Wise never turned into the pitcher the Cardinals had envisioned when they traded for him, he distinguished himself as a capable pitcher during an 18-year career in which he won 188 games and lost 181. One of his most memorable moments came in game six of the 1975 World Series when he was a member of the Boston Red Sox. He earned the victory in relief against the Cincinnati Reds in one of the most thrilling postseason games ever. Carlton Fisk decided the game in the 12th inning with a homer off the foul pole.

Notes

1. United Press International, 26 February 1972.
2. *Sports Illustrated*, 24 April 1972.
3. *Sports Illustrated*, 8 May 1972.
4. United Press International, 16 July 1972.
5. Ibid.
6. *Sports Illustrated*, 14 August 1972.
7. *Sports Illustrated*, 21 August 1972.
8. *Sports Illustrated*, 10 October 1972.
9. United Press International, 3 November 1972.
10. Associated Press, 2 May 1973.
11. Ibid.
12. Associated Press, 9 June 1983.
13. *Baseball Weekly*, 2 August 1994.
14. Associated Press, 7 August 1994.

Second to None

January 27, 1982: The Chicago Cubs
trade Ivan DeJesus to the Philadelphia Phillies
for Larry Bowa and Ryne Sandberg

The setting was Wrigley Field in Chicago, June 23, 1984. The sun was shining, the place was packed, and the hated Cardinals were in town to play the Cubs. There was also a national television audience, at a time when that still meant something. As it turned out, it was a perfect day to watch a gifted, young player come of age.

It was a wild and wondrous game, and late that afternoon, the Cubs trailed 9–8 heading into the bottom of the ninth. The Cardinals' Bruce Sutter, one of baseball's premier relievers, was on the mound to protect the lead. Cubs second baseman Ryne Sandberg, who was already 3-for-4 on the afternoon, waited at the plate. Sutter delivered his patented split-finger fastball, and Sandberg launched it into the left-field bleachers to tie the score.

An inning later, after the Cardinals had once again gone ahead 11–9, the Cubs were down to their last out. Sutter was still on the mound. Once again, Sandberg waited at the plate, this time with a runner on base. Another split-finger fastball. Another home run into the left-field bleachers to tie the score.

A few minutes later, when the Cubs emerged with a 12–11 victory in 11 innings, it was obvious that a new star had exploded on the scene. For two years, Ryne Sandberg had merely been the Cubs' promising young infielder, but now he had arrived.

"Sandberg is the best player I have ever seen," Cardinals manager Whitey Herzog exclaimed that afternoon.[1]

"That was a game that really got me going," Sandberg recalled 10 years later. "It changed me as a ballplayer, gave me a lot of confidence. It showed me that I could do something special … be a special player."

The fact that Sandberg could indeed do something special was a surprise even to his biggest supporters. That group included Cubs general manager Dallas Green, who was the driving force behind the trade that brought Sandberg to Chicago. That deal took place on January 27, 1982, and involved three shortstops at varying stages of their careers: Ivan DeJesus going from the Cubs to the Phillies in exchange for Larry Bowa and minor league prospect Sandberg.

At the time, fans and analysts debated who got the better end of the bargain. Bowa, a feisty 36-year-old who had helped the Phillies win the World Series in 1980, was no doubt going to bring a winning attitude to the Cubs. That certainly was needed, considering the Cubs had not won a pennant since the end of World War II. DeJesus was seven years younger, so he was expected to replace Bowa and give the Phillies a solid infielder for years to come.

In the end, neither Bowa nor DeJesus made a lasting impression with his new team. But the 22-year-old Sandberg, the unknown element in the transaction, turned out to be the key individual by blossoming into a franchise player.

The soft-spoken Sandberg was one of baseball's top all-around performers and the game's finest second baseman during the 1980s and early 1990s. He was an All Star every season between 1984 and 1993, and he consistently hit around .300. He even developed a power stroke that allowed him to lead the league in home runs with 40 in 1990.

He also fielded his position with almost machine-like efficiency. In 1990 he set a major league record for infielders (excluding first basemen) by playing in 123 straight games without committing an error. He was the first second baseman to collect nine Gold Glove awards.

Although Sandberg was criticized throughout his career for playing emotionless baseball, in reality it was a cool, self-assured facade. He let his actions on the field speak for him.

"We knew he was going to be a major league baseball player—that wasn't a problem," Green said. "We didn't know he was going to be the star that he turned out to be. I don't think anybody recognized that."

Sandberg himself admitted that, at one time, his goal was merely to be on a major league roster. "I was told I'd never play in the major leagues," he added. "I was told I wasn't good enough, didn't have the fire to play in the major leagues. I heard all of these things coming up."

The reason Sandberg ultimately got his chance with the Cubs to prove everyone wrong was a contract dispute involving Bowa back in Philadelphia shortly after the 1981 season. It was a dispute that really heated up when the outspoken Bowa had some nasty words in public for Phillies president Bill Giles. Paul Owens, the Phillies GM, was told to send Bowa packing.

Green knew all about the Bowa-Giles brouhaha because he had been the Phillies manager from the end of the 1979 season until he took the Cubs' GM job in October 1981. When Green left the Phillies, he took over a Cub team that had finished the strike-shortened 1981 season with a 38–65 record, the worst in the National League. Although Green realized there were many holes to fill in the Chicago lineup, he vowed that he was not just looking for new bodies—he wanted a new attitude. He was determined to acquire players who knew how to win, and Bowa was just that kind of player. A .264 career hitter at the time, he was known for his slick glove and fiery emotions.

Green also knew that one of the Cubs' most marketable players was DeJesus, who had been with the team for five years and had established himself as a steady fielder with decent hitting ability. Although DeJesus was coming off a dismal season in which he batted only .194, he had batted as high as .283 in 1979.

As it turned out, it was a tailor-made situation for the Cubs: If Green offered DeJesus for the unwanted Bowa, he knew he could get more than his money's worth in return. At the winter meetings in December, Green started talking to the Phillies about a Bowa-DeJesus swap.

"I told them I'm not going one-on-one with this deal because I've got the only guy available, and our guy is younger," said Green. "We need to get manpower for the Cubs and it's going to be two-for-one or three-for-one depending on the quality."

At first, Green did not necessarily set his sights on Sandberg to complete the package with Bowa. (Remember, "manpower" was the operative word here.) But Green acknowledged that Sandberg, a shortstop in the Phillies' farm system, was one of the few young players he was willing to accept.

At the time, Sandberg's only major league experience had come during a September call-up in 1981, when he had one hit in six at-bats. But he had looked promising in triple-A ball, batting .293 while stealing 32 bases that summer at Oklahoma City. In his four minor-league seasons, Sandberg had shown everything but long ball potential. In the Phillies' farm system, in fact, Sandberg rated just behind Julio Franco—another shortstop—as the top prospect.

"We desperately needed bodies with speed and defensive ability in Chicago, so we came on Sandberg's name," Green said. "I knew he had good athletic ability and I knew in my mind he could play any position. His defense was impeccable, and his game sense was super.

"We also knew Philadelphia couldn't use him: They had [Manny] Trillo at second and they were going to put DeJesus at short, Schmitty [Mike Schmidt] at third, [Garry] Maddox in center field. So there was no way they were going to be able to use Sandberg, even though he had two great years at Triple-A."

Owens, however, was not willing to part with Sandberg. "I said, 'I can't trade Sandberg. He's going to play in the big leagues,'" Owens recalled. "I offered everybody else in the organization. It went around and around and around. I tried all the young players."

At one point, Green was ready to make a deal that did not include Sandberg. But Green's assistant, Gordon Goldsberry, stepped in and said they should not settle for anyone but Sandberg or promising left-handed pitcher

Mark Davis. Goldsberry was well aware of the Phillies' personnel because he had been a scout in their organization before coming to the Cubs along with Green.

At Goldsberry's urging, Green went back to Owens and made one last plea for Sandberg.

"I told Paul, when I finally talked to him at the end, 'You're going to kill that kid … you're going to send him back to Triple-A and you'll kill him because he's prepared and ready to come to the big leagues. And you're not going to be able to use him for a couple of years with the guys you've got.'

"And I said, 'You just as well throw him into the deal, and if we get those guys, we can work out something.'"

So Owens checked once more with his scouts, who said they honestly did not believe Sandberg had star potential. Upon hearing this, Owens finally relented and gave Sandberg his chance to make it big in Chicago.

When the trade was announced, Sandberg received little mention. As expected, most of the attention was centered on Bowa. One Philadelphia sportswriter noted: "Dallas Green is no dummy. He knows that. And he also knows that for all of Bowa's popping off, for all of his raving and ranting, his screaming and yelling, the guy knows only one way to play baseball—and that's all-out all the time."[2]

When the always-opinionated Bowa heard of the trade, he threw in his two cents. He was right on the money. "Never mind me," Bowa said. "I can't believe the Phillies gave up Sandberg. He'll play for the Cubs right now."[3]

Bowa ended up playing for the Cubs for 3½ seasons and did everything Green expected of him. He was not a major contributor with the bat, but he solidified the infield and showed what it took to win. The big payoff was the National League East championship in 1984, the first time the Cubs won anything since their pennant in 1945. But then Bowa was released midway through the 1985 season, and he soon retired as a player.

DeJesus' stay in Philadelphia was equally brief, just three seasons. Like Bowa with the Cubs, DeJesus was not a major contributor with the bat, but he helped solidify the infield. As Owens pointed out, he was one of the unsung heroes who helped the Phillies reach the World Series in 1983, where they lost to Baltimore.

Sandberg's story, on the other hand, was just beginning during this period.

From the get-go of his relationship with the Cubs, Sandberg showed Green the work ethic he had been looking for. Shortly after the trade, both Sandberg and Bowa showed up at spring training more than a week before the position players were scheduled. Sandberg then went out and proved during the exhibition games that he was indeed ready for the big leagues. "He seems to do what has to be done," manager Lee Elia told reporters at the time.[4]

The only question—the same one that plagued the Phillies—was where to play him. Elia experimented with Sandberg through the first few weeks of training camp, trying him at shortstop, second base, third base and center field. The choices were narrowed a bit when Sandberg did not look as sharp in the outfield as management had hoped. Sandberg then started to settle in at third, where holdover Ken Reitz had fallen out of favor. Sandberg was pretty much set as the Opening Day third baseman when Reitz was given the word on March 28 that he was free to work out a deal with another team.

During that first spring training with the Cubs, Sandberg batted .323. Some reporters even talked about him as a Rookie-of-the-Year candidate.

"I just wanted to make the team," Sandberg said, "but switching the position didn't make me real happy. It seemed like no one had any confidence in me at short, and I was pretty nervous because I didn't know if I could play third."[5]

Once the regular season started, Sandberg's spring training magic seemed to disappear. When it comes to slow starts, Sandberg's was a real classic.

In the season opener against Cincinnati, Sandberg batted seventh and went 0-for-3. He followed that with another 0-for-3 showing against the Reds. In the four-game series that followed against the Mets, he went hitless in 13 at-bats.

It was not until the seventh game that Sandberg got his first base hit, a line single to center against St. Louis. That, however, was his only hit of the three-game series and his average was an anemic .038 with 1 hit in 26 at-bats.

Despite the woeful start, Elia did not give up on Sandberg. Instead, Sandberg was shifted to the number two spot in the lineup. He responded with an 0-for-4 effort against Pittsburgh, leaving him 1-for-30.

As it turned out, that 10th game of the 1982 season was the low point. The following day, he was 2-for-6 and his batting average skyrocketed from .033 to .083. He followed that with a 3-for-5 game against the Pirates. On April 23, Sandberg really let loose by blasting his first two career home runs against Pittsburgh. By the time the month from hell was over, Sandberg's average had inched up to .200.

"Instead of panicking when I went so long without a hit, Lee [Elia] and the coaches did just the opposite," said Sandberg, who was a notorious slow starter throughout his career. "They kept telling me, 'Just do what you can do,' and I blotted everything else out until it happened."[6]

"You've got to give Lee Elia a lot of credit," added Green. "He worked real hard to make sure Sandberg's confidence didn't get down. He stayed with that work ethic. We had to have some patience—we knew that. We weren't going anywhere. We had plenty of time for him to develop."

By the end of the season, Sandberg had very promising numbers. He batted .271, led the team with 103 runs scored, and collected 32 stolen bases.

In the Rookie-of-the-Year voting, he finished sixth behind the Dodgers' Steve Sax, the Pirates' Johnny Ray, the Cardinals' Willie McGee, the Giants' Chili Davis, and the Padres' Luis DeLeon.

During the final month of the 1982 season, Sandberg had switched to second base in place of veteran Bump Wills because the Cubs wanted to experiment with their younger players. At the start of the 1983 season, second base was Sandberg's for keeps. He wound up earning his first Gold Glove, becoming only the second player ever to win the award during his first season at a new position. Offensively, it was another steady-if-unspectacular performance as he batted .261 and stole 37 bases.

Then came the dream season of 1984, which was highlighted by that dream game in June against the Cardinals. At the midseason break, Sandberg was batting .335 with 11 home runs and 52 runs batted in. He made his first All-Star start, signalling that he had passed Sax as the best young second baseman in the game.

By the time the season was over, Sandberg's offensive numbers were eye-popping. He batted .314 and came remarkably close to becoming the first major leaguer ever to finish a season with 200 hits (he finished with 200), 20 doubles (36), 20 triples (19), 20 home runs (19) and 20 stolen bases (32). Again, a Gold Glove was added to the trophy case.

Thanks in large part to Sandberg's excellence, the Cubs finished 96–65 and won the East Division. Although the Cubs lost to the Padres in the playoffs, it did not diminish the regular-season accomplishments. It was their first winning season since 1972 and their best record since winning the pennant in 1945. There were indeed other major contributors—pitcher Rick Sutcliffe came over in an early-season trade and finished 16–1 to win the Cy Young award, and left fielder Gary Matthews provided veteran leadership to go along with his .291 average—but Sandberg was the real pacesetter, and the proof came in November when he was named the league's Most Valuable Player.

As Sandberg noted, the big change in 1984 was his power numbers. He had never hit more than 11 home runs in any previous season, and that came in the minors. Sandberg credited his new-found ability to hit the long ball to manager Jim Frey, who took over in 1984.

"The whole thing with Sandberg was that I tried to develop a different mindset for him," said Frey. "He always pictured himself as the leadoff man or the second hitter. I thought maybe he was shortchanging himself. I tried to convince him that if he changed his technique and mindset, he could be one of those guys who could also hit home runs, drive in runs, be an MVP-type player. I tried to give him the confidence that he could be a different player than he had ever pictured himself being.

"I talked to him about getting the bat out in front and driving the ball. And when you get that pitch you know you can handle, that's the time to crank it. I didn't necessarily talk about hitting it over the left field fence, but I knew that the result would be that some of them would go out of the park.

"I took some criticism from some people in the organization. But I can remember the first time we went out after a ballgame in spring training and had him hit extra. The whole purpose of that drill was to get him to picture himself hitting late in the game with a 2–0 or 3–1 count, where he's gonna sit on a fastball and try to hit it hard and pull it. And after Sandberg hit two or three balls over the left-field fence, I remember Bowa hollering: 'Who's that guy wearing Sandberg's uniform?' This was a different person than anyone had ever seen before.'

"Well, he started to have some success doing that. And then we had that game against St. Louis, and after that, I didn't have to say anything to him anymore."

Frey's teaching method—sort of a "How to improve your self-image in three easy lessons"—seems almost too simple to be possible. But as Frey pointed out, it only works with the right kind of pupil. And Sandberg, with his tremendous natural ability and a willingness to learn, was exactly that.

Sandberg acknowledged that "this was the first time that I had confidence to hit the ball with power."[7]

He maintained that confidence over the next decade, as he continued to hit for a high batting average while steadily increasing his power stats. He hit 30 home runs in 1989, when he helped the Cubs win another division title. Then came 1990 and his league-leading total of 40, which was the third-highest total ever for a second baseman, ranking behind Rogers Hornsby's 42 in 1922 and Davey Johnson's 42 in 1973. All the while, Sandberg never skipped a beat with his flawless, Gold Glove defense.

According to Green, the early scouting reports noted that Sandberg probably would hit 20 home runs at best. But those reports did not measure the intangibles that separate the good players from the great ones.

"He's a very intelligent hitter and a very intelligent player," Green said in 1994. "He learned how to work pitchers and bring the pitchers to his power so that he could hit home runs. And that's what made him a real home run hitter."

"He certainly made himself a hell of a ballplayer," the Phillies' Paul Owens added.

"He wasn't Ted Williams or Willie Mays," said Don Zimmer, who was Sandberg's manager from 1988 to 1991. "But if I gave you a second baseman who would hit 25 home runs a year, steal 20 bases, not make base-running mistakes or miss signs, drive in 100 runs and maybe make four errors, would you take him? He's one of the best I ever saw at second."[8]

A dozen years after the trade, Paul Owens looked back on the Phillies' decision in 1982 to let Sandberg go. Instead of chalking it up as an error of judgment, Owens likened it to another deal the Phillies made—the 1972 trade that brought future Hall of Famer Steve Carlton from St. Louis in a straight swap for Rick Wise. At that time, Carlton was embroiled in a contract dispute with the Cardinals and as a result was chased out of town. The Cardinals' loss was the Phillies' gain.

As Owens noted, when history sort of repeated itself with Bowa in Philadelphia, it was as if the fates were evening things out. "It was a matter of circumstances," Owens said. "It wasn't a deal made from field judgment."

Green agreed: "Everybody in Philly wants to say, 'You stole Sandberg.' They've taken a lot of heat because of the trade, and I think it's unfair because you had to look at the situation. Bill Giles had created the situation where Bowa had to be traded.

"I really think their hands were tied."

Notes

1. *Chicago Tribune*, 24 June 1984.
2. *Philadelphia Inquirer*, 28 January 1982.
3. *Chicago Tribune*, 28 January 1982.
4. *Chicago Tribune*, 9 March 1982.
5. *Chicago Tribune*, 8 July 1984.
6. *Chicago Tribune*, 15 August 1982.
7. *Chicago Tribune*, 14 November 1984.
8. *Chicago Tribune*, 14 June 1994.

The Dynamic "Dude"

*June 18, 1989: The Philadelphia Phillies
trade Juan Samuel to the New York Mets
for Lenny Dykstra and Roger McDowell*

After breaking into the majors in 1985, Lenny Dykstra thrived as a member of the New York Mets. In his first four seasons, he played in two National League Championship Series and helped the Mets claim the World Series title in 1986. The Mets were one of the dominant teams in the mid–1980s and the fiery Dykstra helped make them that way.

But it all changed for the Mets' fleet center fielder on June 18, 1989. That is when the floundering Philadelphia Phillies obtained Dykstra and reliever Roger McDowell from the Mets for two-time All-Star Juan Samuel.

Dykstra, platooning with Mookie Wilson on the Mets, was moving into a full-time job as the Phillies' center fielder. Dykstra, 26, was not pleased about his part-time status with the Mets, so he was buoyed by the fact he was going to become a regular. But the trade still had a big downside. After all, he was leaving the contending Mets for the bumbling Phillies.

The Mets were two games behind the Chicago Cubs in the National League's East Division at the time of the trade. The Phillies, who lost 96 games in 1988, were suffering through another dismal season in 1989.

Still, Dykstra tried to put the best possible face on the trade. "Every team has highs and lows," Dykstra said. "Obviously, this team [the Phillies] can't get any lower. I think I've come at a good time, because there is no way to go but up. I'll be getting a chance to contribute every day and that's all I've wanted. I don't know what it's like to lose. And it's not something I want to learn."[1]

At the time of the trade, Dykstra was batting .270 with three homers and 13 RBIs. He was told he would bat first, giving the Phillies the aggressive leadoff batter they had sought. Dykstra carried the reputation as someone who could reach base, and he gave Philadelphia a potent top of the order with number two hitter Tommy Herr and number three Von Hayes.

The trade for Dykstra and McDowell was one of a series of moves by Philadelphia general manager Lee Thomas, who had promised to shake up the woebegone franchise. Thomas took over his post in June 1988 and watched the Phillies straggle to a last-place finish in the East with a 65–96 record. Thomas observed too many botched plays the second half of the 1988 season not to launch an overhaul.

Mike Schmidt, the Phillies' perennial All-Star third baseman, actually touched off the team's change in direction on May 29, 1989, by retiring, believing his magnificent skills had eroded. Four days later, Thomas dispatched outfielder Chris James to the San Diego Padres for outfielder-first baseman John Kruk and infielder Randy Ready. About two weeks later, Thomas traded prized reliever Steve Bedrosian to the San Francisco Giants for left-handed starting pitchers Dennis Cook and Terry Mulholland. Only a half hour after that trade, Thomas acquired Dykstra and McDowell.

When the dust had cleared, Philadelphia had Dykstra, McDowell, Cook, Mulholland, Kruk and Ready, and if the Phillies failed to improve on 1988's record, at least they would be playing with a considerably different cast. The Phillies' acquisitions recognized that they represented hope for a much brighter future. And even the transplanted ex–Phillies realized that a shake-up was inevitable.

"I know they're trying to make some headway and make things happen and you can't blame them for that," Bedrosian said.[2]

Dykstra—like Bedrosian, Samuel and McDowell—was in the midst of an off-year when he became a member of the Phillies, and the new Philadelphia scenery failed to provide much of a boost. He batted a lowly .222 for the Phillies in 90 games, finishing with a cumulative .237 average, 66 runs and 32 runs batted in for the season. These were not exactly the numbers the Phillies had envisioned when they traded for Dykstra. The Phillies, not surprisingly, landed again in the bottom of the standings in the East with a 67–95 record.

But Philadelphia liked the Lenny Dykstra trade better in 1990. Dykstra emerged as one of the top center fielders in baseball with his relentless, firebrand style of baseball and knack for reaching base via a hit or a walk. There were many outfielders with more speed, a better arm and more power but few could get as much out of their ability as the tough-as-nails Dykstra.

Dykstra, who was nicknamed both Dude and Nails, became the toast of the town by batting .400 for two months, leading the league in batting from May 12 to September 15, breaking up a no-hit bid by John Smoltz in the ninth inning, and demonstrating a dazzling, all-out brand of defense in the outfield.

Playing in 149 games, Dykstra finished fourth in the league in hitting with a .325 average. He stole 33 bases and led the league in hits and on-base percentage. His enthusiasm and aggressiveness became role models. And he made a celebrated appearance on the *Late Show with David Letterman*.

With Dykstra in the lead, the Phillies won 10 more games in 1990 than they had the previous year. The question was: Could the Phillies continue to improve?

In the next two years, Dykstra showed he belonged among the league's elite. The only problem was that Dykstra had diminished opportunities to prove it. Because of injuries and a near-fatal automobile accident, Dykstra played a total of only 148 games in 1991 and 1992.

He missed 61 games in 1991 because of a car crash in which he was driving Phillies' catcher Darren Daulton home from a bachelor party for first baseman John Kruk. After returning to the lineup, he broke his collarbone running into the outfield wall at Cincinnati's Riverfront Stadium six weeks later. Then on Opening Day in 1992, he suffered a broken left arm when he was hit by a pitch by Greg Maddux of the Chicago Cubs.

Still, Dykstra did not disappoint when he was in the lineup. In 63 games in 1991, he batted .297 with 48 runs and 24 stolen bases. Projected over a full season, those numbers would easily have exceeded 100 runs and 50 stolen bases. And in 1992, he batted .301—marking the second time in three years he batted over .300—with 30 stolen bases in 85 games.

To illustrate Dykstra's importance, the Phillies were 76–71 those two years when he played, 72–105 when he did not. The extended absences cost Dykstra $800,000 in incentives, based on at-bats for 1991 and 1992.

When the 1993 season started, the preeminent question facing the Phillies concerned Dykstra. It was not whether Dykstra deserved to be mentioned among the top outfielders in the majors. Rather, it was whether Dykstra could be healthy enough to show he ranked as a marquee player. Philadelphia finished third in the East at 78–84 in 1991 and last in 1992 with a 70–92 record, 26 games behind the first-place Pittsburgh Pirates.

If Dykstra remained healthy, the Phillies hoped they could surprise in 1993. The St. Louis Cardinals and Montreal Expos remained the consensus favorites in the division. The long-suffering Phillies had a lot of convincing to do.

But the Phillies seemed primed for a successful season when they finished the spring exhibition season with a 16–10 record, their first winning Grapefruit League mark since 1987. "There's no question that this team has to believe it can win," Dykstra said. "And to do that, we have to get out of the gate quickly."[3]

And start fast the Phillies did. Philadelphia won its first three games before losing its home opener. It was the Phillies' best start since 1970, and it was accomplished with the aid of two key off-season acquisitions, outfielders Jim Eisenreich and Pete Incaviglia. Catcher Darren Daulton banged four home runs in the Phillies' first six games as Philadelphia took the early lead in the East. The Phillies seemed as if they could do no wrong in the early going, winning eight of their first nine.

It did not seem to matter that Dykstra was off to a slow start. Dykstra was confident he would find his batting eye and he became positively giddy when the Phillies bolstered their bullpen by picking up 1989 Cy Young Award winner Mark Davis in an early-season trade with the Atlanta Braves.

Said Dykstra: "Obviously, they know this is a team that has a chance to win the division. It's great news. There's nothing but positive noise around here."[4]

The Phillies entered May with a 4½-game lead over the second-place Expos and the Cardinals. What worried the Phillies' opponents was that Philadelphia was winning with a struggling Dykstra, who had one hit in his first 19 at-bats with runners in scoring position. If Dykstra ever got into a groove, Philadelphia could turn into a real "Beast of the East."

Dykstra finally emerged from his hibernation in the final week of May, during which he batted .400, scored six runs and helped boost the Phillies into a seven-game lead over the Expos. With his first hot week behind him, Dykstra showed he was just warming up. The Phillies' tobacco-chewing center fielder raised his average to a respectable .278 on June 14, as the Phillies walloped the Expos, 10–3, opening a whopping 11½-game bulge over the second-place Cardinals.

This roaring start was deemed incredible, even to Philadelphia general manager Lee Thomas, the architect of this new juggernaut. "Two years ago, I thought we were getting close if we could stay healthy, but we didn't," Thomas said. "I thought this year we were capable of staying near the top, but I thought that last year too. I knew our pitchers were healthy and I thought that would give us a chance to start off good. I never thought we would get off to this kind of start."[5]

On June 23, Dykstra was beaming when the contract of manager Jim Fregosi, along with that of Thomas, was extended. Fregosi had helped create a relaxed atmosphere in which the Phillies' free spirits—and there were plenty of them—could flourish. "He [Fregosi] has a unique quality I don't think you can find in too many managers," Dykstra said. "He's our friend. We can joke with him. Yet, we know he's the boss. We know where to cut it off."[6]

Another key component in the Phillies' success was the productive group that batted behind Dykstra. They included infielder-outfielder Mariano Duncan, first baseman John Kruk, third baseman Dave Hollins, catcher Darren Daulton and outfielders Pete Incaviglia and Jim Eisenreich. Those players took turns driving in the free-wheeling Dykstra, who was scoring runs at a dizzying pace. He scored at least one run in 15 consecutive games—three short of the National League record set by Cincinnati's Ted Kluszewski in 1954—before his streak was stopped on June 21 by the Braves' indomitable Greg Maddux. On June 27, Dykstra was far and away the league leader in runs with 67, although the Phillies' lead had shrunk to 8½ games over the Cardinals.

As the weather got hotter, so did Dykstra's bat. His average climbed to .296 on July 5, as he scored a whopping 12 runs in one week. But the Phillies could not match Dykstra's blistering pace. The Cardinals pared Philadelphia's lead to 5½ games as the Phillies' pitching—notably starters Tommy Greene and Curt Schilling—faltered. Mark Davis, who the Phillies had hoped would assist the bullpen, demonstrated he was nowhere close to his Cy Young form and was released.

"When you get good pitching, you win. When you don't, you won't," summed up Fregosi.[7]

Ahead by five games at the All-Star break, the Phillies continued to fritter away their lead as the Cardinals crept to within three games on July 19. The Phillies got their first showdown in late July when they played host to the Cardinals. If the Phillies were going to prove they were a legitimate power, this was their chance. Dykstra entered the series red-hot and the Philadelphia fireball maintained his momentum against the Cardinals. Dykstra helped the Phillies sweep St. Louis in the three-game set with six runs and seven hits in 12 at-bats.

The Phillies' lead was now seven games and Philadelphia was blazing—and so was Dykstra, the team's hottest hitter. He compiled a 10-game hitting streak, during which he batted .450 to raise his average to a season-high .309 and improved his league-leading runs total to 96. "I know I've said it before, but that guy amazes me," Fregosi said.[8]

Dykstra was solidifying his credentials as the National League's top lead-off hitter and earning the praise of writers across the country. On August 5, Dykstra scored three runs to pace the Phillies to a 10–4 victory over the Atlanta Braves, as he vaulted past the 100-run plateau with his 101st run in Philadelphia's 109th game. Dykstra appeared headed for the most runs scored by a National League player since the Chicago Cubs' Billy Williams scored 137 in 1970.

The Phillies, though, were no one-man show. Philadelphia produced its fifth starting pitcher with at least 10 victories when Danny Jackson beat the Colorado Rockies on August 24. Curt Schilling also had 10 victories, Terry Mulholland and Ben Rivera 11, and Tommy Greene 12. Even sometimes erratic closer Mitch Williams was finding consistency, earning his 36th save on August 24, in the process converting his 13th straight save opportunity. He failed to hold a one-run lead three days later to break the streak.

It seemed as if Philadelphia was hitting on all cylinders, and the Phillies' 9½-game lead over the second-place Expos with 26 games remaining supported that feeling. Dykstra's gang was simply running wild and scoring runs in bushels. On September 4, Philadelphia set a modern-day National League record by scoring at least one run for the 151st consecutive game, a span that covered two seasons. In fact, it appeared Philadelphia was setting records everywhere. On September 5, Philadelphia became the first team in National

League history to boast three players with at least 100 walks, when John Kruk joined Dykstra and Darren Daulton in the 100-walk club.

All season, Philadelphia was unsure whether it would be Montreal or St. Louis making the fiercest charge. In September, Philadelphia identified its number one enemy: the Expos. Philadelphia appeared to have crushed Montreal's flickering pennant hopes in August when the Phillies swept a three-game set against the visiting Expos. Montreal was left for dead on August 12, falling 13 games behind Philadelphia and playing without top-flight second baseman Delino DeShields, who was out with torn ligaments in his thumb. But there was no quit in Manager Felipe Alou's Expos. Montreal climbed back from a 14½-game deficit on August 20, pulling within five games of Philadelphia on September 12 behind a blitzkrieg-like 18–2 streak.

The division's top two teams met in a pivotal three-game series on September 17, 18 and 19 in Montreal. Dykstra remained confident his Phillies would win the division for the first time since 1983 and dismissed talk of a 1964 repeat—when the Phillies collapsed and could not hold a 6½-game lead with 12 games to play. For Dykstra, it was fine if the Expos were making a run at Philadelphia. The Phillies were ready. "Everybody in this room needs to realize that every team in the league is getting up for us," Dykstra said. "They've already marked it on their schedules. It's their playoffs. We've just got to finish strong. There are 19 games left and it's not over by a long shot."

And Dykstra added, "If you had said at the beginning of the season that we'd be five games up on September 12, you'd have been happy. It could have been better. It could have been worse. But we have to play better to finish the thing off."[9]

Dykstra continued to play magnificently and was embroiled in a Most Valuable Player race with San Francisco Giants outfielder Barry Bonds and three Atlanta Braves—first baseman Fred McGriff and outfielders Ron Gant and David Justice. As of September 12, Dykstra was batting .305, with an on-base percentage of .424, a league-leading 131 runs, 18 homers and 57 RBIs. Bonds, batting .338 with 40 homers and 102 RBIs, had the better statistics, but there was considerable sentiment to give the MVP award to Dykstra, provided the Phillies held on and completed an improbable worst-to-first scenario with a National League East title.

When Philadelphia and Montreal clashed in Montreal, the Phillies held a six-game lead and needed to avoid being swept. The Phillies reached that objective by salvaging the second game of the series, 5–4, as Dykstra scored twice and Greene earned his 15th victory and Williams notched his 39th save. Montreal won the opener, 8–7, and finale, 6–5, to close within four games with 13 to play, but the Phillies foiled the Expos' bid for a sweep and remained in the driver's seat.

Still, Montreal remained in the thick of the pennant fight. "It's like the baseball gods just want us to work a little harder," Dykstra said. "The one thing we didn't want was to get swept and we avoided that."[10]

The Lenny Dykstra Express kept picking up speed in the final days of the season and the Phillies were climbing aboard for the stretch drive. On September 21 against the Florida Marlins, Dykstra turned in a typically electrifying performance that added impetus to his MVP campaign.

Marlin starter David Weathers carried a two-hitter and a 2–0 lead into the bottom of the sixth when the indefatigable Dykstra struck. He knocked in two runs with a double to bring Philadelphia even, 2–2, but the Marlins pulled ahead, 3–2, in the seventh. Dykstra responded with a two-run homer in the bottom of the seventh to provide Philadelphia's eventual winning margin.

"Nothing he does surprises me," Fregosi said. "As great as Barry Bonds is, I don't see how any one player could have done more for his team than Lenny has done for the Phillies this year."

Although winning ballgames was his top priority, Dykstra was fully aware of the MVP race. "I'd be a liar if I said I wouldn't be happy to win the MVP," he said. "Who wouldn't be?"[11]

With eight days left in the regular season, Dykstra already had scored 139 runs, more than any National League player since Chuck Klein scored 152 in 1932. Dykstra also had demonstrated uncharacteristic power with 19 home runs, a far departure from his previous high of 10 in 1987. Furthermore, Dykstra led the league in hits and walks, had stolen 37 bases, and the Phillies were beating back the Expos' challenge and heading for the East title.

As the season wound down, it became apparent that it was just a matter of time before the Phillies clinched the division title. And that time came on September 28 when Philadelphia outscored the Pittsburgh Pirates, 10–7, behind Dykstra, who rapped out four hits and drove in three runs. The next day, Dykstra sat out his first game of the season. He had played in his team's first 156 games.

The Phillies ended the regular season atop the East Division's standings with a 97–65 record, three games ahead of the Expos. Dykstra finished with a .305 average, 44 doubles, 19 homers, 66 RBIs and 37 stolen bases. Additionally, Dykstra accomplished the following:

• He scored 143 runs, more than any National League player since 1932.

• He became the first player in the National League to lead the league in at-bats and walks in the same season.

• He became the third National League player since 1958 to reach base 300 times in a season, joining Pete Rose and Tony Gwynn.

Dykstra's feats were not lost on his manager. "All I know," Fregosi said, "is when he's healthy, we win. When something needs to be done, he gets it done. He's had an MVP-type of year."[12]

The Phillies' next task was to face the three-time National League West Division defending champion Atlanta Braves in the National League Championship Series. These were the same Braves who had run down the San Francisco Giants with a blistering second-half surge. Atlanta had gone 51–17 since acquiring first baseman Fred McGriff from the San Diego Padres. They had finished with 104 victories, one more than the Giants.

The Braves entered the league playoffs as resounding favorites. In fact, the pitching-rich and power-hitting Braves also were favored to win the World Series over either the Chicago White Sox or Toronto Blue Jays, whichever survived the American League Championship Series.

But form and the Braves took a beating in the National League Championship Series. The Braves outscored the Phillies, 33–22, but Philadelphia won the championship in six games. Mitch Williams won two games and saved two others, and the irrepressible Dykstra sparked the offense with team highs in home runs with two, runs scored with five, and hits with seven.

The Phillies earned the right to meet the defending champion Blue Jays in the World Series. Philadelphia appeared overmatched, but the Phillies had appeared overmatched against the Braves too. To upset Toronto, Philadelphia needed come-through efforts from Mitch Williams and Lenny Dykstra. The Phillies got what they needed from Dykstra, who came up big against Atlanta in the National League Championship Series and then positively huge against the Blue Jays. Dykstra put together a blockbuster Series during which he enjoyed being on center stage with all the baseball eyes peering down on the fall classic. Thriving amid the pressure, Dykstra batted .348, scored nine runs, drove in eight, reached base 15 times in six games and was four for four in stolen bases.

Most impressive of all was that Dykstra muscled up to homer four times. In fact, in game four alone, Dykstra homered twice and banged a double off the top of the wall. But it was to no avail. Mitch Williams was ineffective as the Phillies' closer and surrendered the stunning, Series-winning three-run homer to Joe Carter in the bottom of the ninth inning of Toronto's 8–6 victory in game six.

When the National League Most Valuable Player award was announced, the Giants' Barry Bonds earned the honor for the third time in four years. Dykstra was second. "It's no disgrace to finish second," Dykstra said. "It's nice to be rewarded for the work and dedication. There was a little extra incentive for me, too. I had something to prove because of all the things that happened over the previous two years."[13]

As for Juan Samuel, whom the Phillies traded to the Mets to acquire Dykstra and Roger McDowell, he never regained his All-Star form. And the Mets—the National League's Eastern Division champions in 1988—lost considerable luster without Dykstra. In 1989 they finished six games behind the East Division champion Chicago Cubs. McDowell saved 23 games for the

Mets and the Phillies in 1989, saved 22 games for the Phillies in 1990, and saved 10 games for the Phillies and Los Angeles Dodgers in 1991.

Notes

1. *Los Angeles Times*, 20 June 1989.
2. Ibid.
3. *Baseball Weekly*, 13 April 1993.
4. *Baseball Weekly*, 27 April 1993.
5. *Baseball Weekly*, 22 June 1993.
6. *Baseball Weekly*, 6 July 1993.
7. *Baseball Weekly*, 14 July 1993.
8. *Baseball Weekly*, 8 August 1993.
9. *Baseball Weekly*, 21 September 1993.
10. Ibid.
11. *Baseball Weekly*, 5 October 1993.
12. *Baseball Weekly*, 12 October 1993.
13. *Baseball Weekly*, 30 November 1993.

A Power Source
for the Astrodome

August 31, 1990: The Boston Red Sox
trade Jeff Bagwell to the Houston Astros
for Larry Andersen

Late in the 1990 season, the Boston Red Sox looked desperately to shore up their bullpen as they locked horns with the Toronto Blue Jays for the American League East Division title. The Red Sox believed they found the answer on August 31, 1990, when they acquired 37-year-old right-hander Larry Andersen from the Houston Astros at the trading deadline.

The price—third baseman Jeff Bagwell, a top prospect who was still toiling in double A. The 22-year-old Bagwell was not Houston's first choice. Nor its second or third. The Astros made their biggest pitch for one of three minor league left-handers—Dave Owen, Kevin Morton or Scott Taylor—but were rebuffed.

So Houston settled on Bagwell, known as a right-handed hitting machine but with limited range at third. Bagwell had been born in Boston and raised in Connecticut. He idolized the Red Sox legendary outfielder Carl Yastrzemski and dreamed of playing for Boston. But those hopes were crushed when Red Sox general manager Lou Gorman bolstered Boston's chances to fend off the Blue Jays. Four years later, Red Sox fans considered Bagwell— the National League's Most Valuable Player in 1994—as one of the best players the Red Sox have traded, perhaps just behind the legendary Babe Ruth.

The trade came as a huge shock to Bagwell, said his father, Robert Bagwell. "That's when he learned the game is a business. He learned it all at once," he said.[1]

Bagwell admitted in 1994 that he thinks about that turning point in his career. "I don't dream about playing in Fenway Park anymore," Bagwell said. "But I do think about what could have happened. Who knows if it would have worked out. I mean, you get caught up in the numbers game sometimes. I was playing third at the time and I think Scott Cooper or myself had to go."[2]

In July 1994, Gorman defended the trade despite the widespread criticism. "I've always believed that you control 'now,'" Gorman said. "You can't worry about tomorrow. When we made that deal, Jeff Bagwell was only the fourth best third baseman in our organization. We had Wade Boggs, Tim Naehring and Scott Cooper, too.

"No one would have thought he'd be as good as he is now. At the time, he was a prospect. ... I'm sure I'll hear about it the rest of my life."[3]

Gorman's decision paid early dividends for the Red Sox. Andersen posted a 1.23 earned run average in 15 games in a set-up role for Boston, boosting the Red Sox to the division title, two games ahead of the Blue Jays. But the Oakland A's swept the Red Sox in the American League Championship Series. Meanwhile, Bagwell finished second in the double A Eastern League batting race with a .333 average and had 34 doubles, four homers and 61 runs batted in.

Bagwell was ticketed to open the 1991 season in Tucson, the Astros' triple A team, although Astro third baseman Ken Caminiti had played poorly in 1990. But Bagwell got a break in January 1991 when Houston traded first baseman Glenn Davis to the Baltimore Orioles for three unproven players, including pitcher Pete Harnisch. An uncertain platoon of Luis Gonzalez and Mike Simms was expected to fill the Astros' hole at first, but it was Bagwell who capitalized on the opportunity.

Shifted to first base, Bagwell—the jewel of the Astros' rebuilding program—earned a starting job and enjoyed a banner rookie season, batting .294 with a totally unexpected 15 home runs and 82 RBIs in 156 games. He ranked fifth in the league in on-base percentage at .387. For his efforts, Bagwell was selected the league's Rookie of the Year. If Bagwell cut down on his 116 strikeouts, he seemed to be within easy reach of 20 to 25 homers, 100 RBIs and a .300 average. The future looked awfully bright.

Over the next two years, Bagwell established himself as one of the premier first basemen in the league and moved into the elite category in that position along the likes of Fred McGriff and Mark Grace. Although his average declined to .273 in 1992, he improved his homers to 18 and RBIs to 96. Bagwell was also demonstrating he had adapted well to his new position, earning a reputation as an above-average first baseman.

Bagwell continued his ascent in 1993. He played the first 142 games—giving him a streak of 304—before missing the final three weeks because of a broken hand. He posted career highs in doubles (37), home runs (20), stolen bases (13) and batting average (.320). What is more, Bagwell established himself as a superb defensive player. One scouting report on Bagwell read: "Playing in the Astrodome doesn't give a true picture of his power. He's got a picture-book swing and drives the ball. Most of all, he's a gamer. He wants to be in the tough situations."[4]

Bagwell entered the 1994 season with high expectations. Bill James, the master at projecting players' performances, wrote that Bagwell deserved to be among the top five National League Most Valuable Player candidates. "The only thing he needs to do is take one more step forward as a hitter," wrote James after the 1993 season.[5]

Based on such variables as age and past performances, James projected that Bagwell would hit .301 with 18 homers and 88 RBIs. Bagwell had exceeded those figures in 1993, so Bagwell was not under undue pressure to meet unreasonable standards.

Spring training often provides a clue as to what kind of season will follow and Bagwell enjoyed a solid performance in Florida in 1994. Bagwell batted .333 with five homers in 69 at-bats, as the Astros began talking about a championship in the National League's newly configured Central Division. Most observers considered the Astros as the frontrunner in the division, with the Cincinnati Reds and St. Louis Cardinals close behind and the Chicago Cubs and Pittsburgh Pirates trailing.

"[Second baseman Craig] Biggio was the first guy to say it, and he's right," said Terry Collins, the Astros' first-year manager. "This isn't a young team anymore. Now it's time to pick it up a notch. These guys know they belong and they are good enough to win.

"They've just got to do the things they need to do."[6]

Bagwell, batting fourth behind rookie right fielder James Mouton, center fielder Steve Finley and Biggio, came out smoking in the Astros' season opener against the visiting Montreal Expos. Bagwell had three hits, including a two-run homer, to help the Astros rally for a 6–5 victory. As the season progressed, Bagwell showed he was not one to be easily satisfied.

He kept searching for ways to improve and make sure he would not let down despite a strong start in which he batted .333 with two homers and 11 RBIs in his team's first 11 games. But Bagwell claimed that early surge was misleading, that he was far from being in any kind of comfort groove.

"I've been terrible, and I'll be the first to admit it," Bagwell said. "All I've been doing is hitting ground balls that infielders dive over and they go for singles. I'm sure people pick up the paper and think I'm having good days. They aren't good days at all."[7] But even the tough-to-please Bagwell had to be satisfied with the statistics he compiled for April: a .360 batting average, six homers and 26 RBIs. His RBI total was a high for Bagwell for any month in his three-plus years in the majors.

Bagwell tried to explain his hot start as a fluke. "The RBIs are testimony to the way the guys in front of me got on base," Bagwell said. "They made my job easy. The production part of it was great, but it sure was a battle all month. There were a lot of times when I was getting myself out too much."[8]

Bagwell's teammates told a different story. And their explanation contained words like "dedication" and "determination." There was nothing flukey about Bagwell's hitting ability, they said.

"He's a workaholic," said Luis Gonzalez, the Astros' left fielder. "He drives in 26 runs in a month and wants more. That's why he's an impact player in this league. He wants to get to the next level, no matter what he's done."[9]

In early May, Bagwell ranked among the league leaders in most offensive categories. The Astros also were receiving strong offensive performances from Biggio, Finley, Gonzalez and Caminiti and splendid pitching from high-priced veteran starters Doug Drabek and Greg Swindell and rookie reliever John Hudek. With their combination of hitting and pitching, the Astros were holding close to the first-place Reds.

But Bagwell undeniably was the Astros' top gun. Through June 19, Bagwell put together All-Star numbers with a .342 average, 19 homers and a league-leading 65 RBIs. He was on pace to break club records for average (.333 by Rusty Staub in 1967), homers (37 by Jimmy Wynn in 1967) and RBIs (110 by Bob Watson in 1977). Even Bagwell had to admit his torrid streak was pretty impressive.

"Right now, I feel very comfortable," Bagwell said. "When I'm comfortable, things take care of themselves."[10]

Bagwell certainly was in a comfort zone against the Los Angeles Dodgers on June 24 in Houston. He became the second player in Astros' history to blast two homers in one inning, connecting twice in the sixth. He added his third homer of the game in the eighth inning as the Astros routed the Dodgers, 16–4. Suddenly, Bagwell had elevated his status from All-Star candidate to Most Valuable Player candidate.

"This is the best night I've ever had," said Bagwell, who had four hits and six RBIs in five at-bats in his three-homer game. "No question about it. I hit three home runs in a game in college, but this is the major leagues. That wasn't the University of Richmond out there today."[11]

Bagwell's exploits put his name in headlines across the country. He was drawing attention similar to that of Ken Griffey, Jr., of the Seattle Mariners and Frank Thomas of the Chicago White Sox.

Through the Astros' first 80 games, Bagwell had a whopping 77 RBIs to lead the major leagues and put him on pace to become the first National League player to drive in more than 150 runs since the Dodgers' Tommy Davis drove in 153 in 1962. Furthermore, he had already set a personal high with 26 homers and was batting a blistering .352. There even was talk of a possible Triple Crown. Still, some of the talk that compared him with Thomas and Griffey was not what Bagwell wanted to hear.

"I don't put myself in that category," said the ever-humble Bagwell. "I'm just Jeff Bagwell and I'm having a good first half right now. There's still a long way to go."[12]

There was no escaping the fact that Bagwell was enjoying a blockbuster season. And there was no shortage of people to acknowledge that fact. One of Bagwell's boosters came from the opposition—Dodger first baseman Eric

Karros, the roommate of Mike Piazza, the right-handed slugging catcher who was tearing up the league for the second straight year.

So it was quite meaningful when Karros—after watching Bagwell boom three homers against the Dodgers—said: "Wrap up the MVP trophy right now and give it to him. He's the best right-handed hitter in the league, and I can say the best all-around hitter. He's a guy you like to see do well, but not against your own team, because you know that he can swing and beat you."[13]

The plaudits also came from Bagwell's teammates. Said Biggio: "I've never played with a guy who has stayed as hot as he has for as long as he has. He's put a lot of time and effort into hitting and he takes it seriously. Even when he was hitting .330 early in the year, he wasn't hitting the ball well. He was slumping. Then he started getting his swing back and driving the ball."[14]

Bagwell, named to the All-Star team as a reserve, led the Astros into strong contention in the Central Division. On July 1, the second-place Astros trailed the Reds by 2½ games and led the third-place Cardinals by 1½ games.

Bagwell entered the July 12 All-Star Game first in the league in slugging percentage at .698, second in home runs behind the San Francisco Giants' Matt Williams with 27 and first in RBIs with 82. Bagwell expressed surprise at his newly developed power; entering the season, he had 53 homers in three seasons, an average of less than 18 per season. "When I was in the minors," Bagwell said, "I thought I might be able to hit 27 in the big leagues, but not 27 in one half."[15]

Bagwell's phenomenal season seemed to just get better. In a week span from July 18 through 24, Bagwell blasted four homers, scored 11 runs, drove in 10 and batted .462. One of Bagwell's homers—against the Cardinals on July 18—helped the Astros rally from an 11-run deficit to a 15–12 victory, the greatest comeback in league history.

Bagwell blasted his 30th homer on July 23 against the Pittsburgh Pirates, becoming only the third player in Astros' history to hit 30 in a season. It was Bagwell's 18th homer in Houston's Astrodome, tying the club record set by Lee May in 1974. "I would have been happy with 25 home runs this season; thirty is a surprise to me," said Bagwell, who had four hits in four at-bats in the game.[16]

Bagwell's effort certainly impressed Pirates manager Jim Leyland, just one of a growing number of believers. Leyland said Bagwell was the top MVP candidate. "He's a lock right now, but it's only July 23," Leyland said. "If the season is over now, he's the MVP."[17]

Bagwell's emergence was becoming one of the biggest baseball stories of 1994. He was producing numbers that ordinarily would translate into a Triple Crown winner. But with Tony Gwynn chasing after the magic .400 batting average, Bagwell's pursuit seemed confined to leading the Astros to the division title and earning an MVP trophy.

Bagwell was still lagging behind Ken Griffey, Jr., Frank Thomas and Matt

Williams in national exposure, but manager Terry Collins recognized that Bagwell was growing in stature each day. "We're not one of the high-profile teams," said Collins, "so Jeff hasn't gotten as big a name as Griffey or Thomas or Williams. But I tell you, he's going to have it. Everybody's going to know about this guy before he's done."[18]

Bagwell was pounding the ball using an unorthodox wide stance, with his legs positioned slightly more than shoulder-width. Bagwell would settle into a crouch that offered the pitcher a tiny strike zone. As the pitch would come in, Bagwell would lift his front foot slightly, then plant it and uncoil with a ferocious upper cut. He could drive the ball to any field.

Teammate Kevin Bass said Bagwell had perfected his mechanics, making hitting elementary. "He's only 26 and he's figured it out," said Bass, a veteran outfielder. "My swing can get a few rattles in it at any time. You hear about tight cars, how they never get a rattle. Jeff's a tight hitter. He's like Will Clark, Wade Boggs, Kirby Puckett—you see the same mechanics night after night. Sure, he makes adjustments, but he makes them in his mind. His swing is solid."[19]

Bagwell took the compliments quietly. His focus was a team focus—helping the Astros try to track down the Reds. Individually, Bagwell worked hard every day to improve. He watched as much baseball as he could on television to gain further knowledge.

"Too many guys coming up don't think they can learn any more," Bagwell said. "As far as I'm concerned, I don't think you ever quite master this game. A lot of people think they've got it all down. They'll tell a coach, 'I know the game.' Nobody ever knows everything about this game."[20]

Amazingly, Bagwell's torrid season got even hotter. He belted another four home runs with seven RBIs and a .429 average the last week of July to give him 36 homers, 105 RBIs and an eye-popping .366 average.

As the season moved into its fourth month, Bagwell found himself performing under the backdrop of a possible players' strike. With the baseball owners declaring the necessity for a salary cap, major league players pointed to August 12 as the date a strike would begin unless both sides could reach an agreement on finances.

Facing a 3½-game deficit on August 1, the Astros understood the urgency of putting together a winning streak. Houston then won six consecutive games to close to within one-half game of the Reds. Bagwell was of course, the catalyst. By August 5, Houston's 110th game, the powerful first baseman had set club records for homers, RBIs and extra-base hits.

"I was aware of the home run and RBI records and I started thinking about it too much the last couple days," Bagwell said. "Now I can relax and get back to business as usual. I might never have a year like this again, but I've had two-thirds of it. If you have the greatest year in the world and don't win anything, what good is it?"[21]

The Astros' march to overtake the Reds took a severe blow on August 10, two days before the strike date. That was the day Bagwell was hit on the left hand by a pitch from Andy Benes of the San Diego Padres. The resulting broken bone was expected to sideline Bagwell—the major league leader in RBIs—for three to five weeks.

"I can't believe this happened to me two years in a row," said Bagwell, who had broken a bone in the same hand the previous season. Still, Bagwell showed he retained a sense of humor about the incident. "I'm going for all 10 fingers and a couple of toes," Bagwell joked. He was hit in the third inning but the tough-minded Bagwell didn't leave the game until he took a called third strike in the fifth inning.[22]

Benes expressed deep regret about the injury. "I'm disappointed he's hurt," Benes said. "I'm disappointed that a guy of that caliber is injured on a ball I threw. I'm extremely disappointed. I can't overemphasize that sentiment.... I threw a 2-and-1 fastball in and he swung at it, so I tried it again and it ran up and in.

"Even when he was on third base, I asked if he was all right and he said, 'Nope, I'm not.'"[23]

The quick exit wound up stopping Bagwell's 18-game hitting streak. Bagwell was taken to a hospital for X-rays, but he was back in the clubhouse by the game's end. Houston had won, 3–1, and coupled with Cincinnati's loss to the Dodgers, left the Astros one-half game behind with one day remaining before the start of the planned players' strike.

But that was little solace to Bagwell, who was batting .368 with 39 homers and 116 RBIs in 110 games. "It's disappointing, strike or no strike," Bagwell said. Nor did the Astros' spirits improve the following day when Houston suffered an 8–6 loss to the Padres to remain one-half game out of first.[24]

That defeat turned out to be the season finale for the Astros, who sat around helplessly as the baseball strike, indeed, began August 12. Surprisingly, to most experts, the strike lasted through the end of the regular season, forcing the cancellation of the playoffs and World Series.

Shortened season or not, the postseason honors were handed out and there was no surprise when Bagwell was selected the league's Most Valuable Player. He was a unanimous selection, joining Orlando Cepeda in 1967 and Mike Schmidt in 1980 as the only unanimous National League winners.

And Bagwell had the statistics to back up the award. In his fourth season, he was the league leader in RBIs (116, tops in the majors), slugging percentage (.750), runs (104) and second in batting average (.369), home runs (39), hits (147) and on-base percentage (.451). Although he finished only four homers behind the Giants' Matt Williams, Bagwell wasn't a Triple Crown threat at the end because the Padres' Tony Gwynn was way ahead in average, finishing at .394.

When told of his MVP honor, Bagwell was in a celebratory mood. "I'm proud of what I did and a little worried about doing it again," Bagwell said. "People always said I was a guy who might hit 25 to 30 home runs. I hit 39. That's a little scary to me. I had 116 RBIs by August 10. I feel I played as well as I can, which makes next year a real test for me. We're going to find out how good I really am."[25]

Williams, the Giants' third baseman who led the major leagues in homers with 43, finished second in the voting and Montreal Expo outfielder Moises Alou was third. With Bagwell injured two days before the start of the strike, the Astro first baseman was asked whether he had the strike to thank—at least partially—for winning the award.

Responded Bagwell: "I can see that point. On the other hand, I think I would have been well enough to play the last month and would have had the opportunity to improve upon my numbers and help the Astros win the division.

"Either way, I think I'd have come out a winner. People may say that the award doesn't mean as much because of the shorter season, but I'm not going to say that. I'm honored and grateful to win it."[26]

Bagwell, who had a base salary of $2.4 million, received a $500,000 bonus for winning the award. He was named *The Sporting News* Player of the Year and picked up his first Gold Glove for making only nine errors in 1,051 chances, for a .991 fielding percentage.

And whither the three players the Red Sox refused to trade to obtain Larry Andersen and instead gave up Bagwell? Dave Owen and Scott Taylor were out of baseball by the time Bagwell had earned his MVP award. And Kevin Morton enjoyed marginal success in 1994, toiling as a starting pitcher for the New York Mets' triple A team in Norfolk, and compiling a 5–8 record with a 3.74 earned run average.

As for Andersen, he endured a series of injuries after leaving Houston but continued to pitch well in relief the next few years for the San Diego Padres and Philadelphia Phillies. Andersen, known as a free spirit with a highly irreverent sense of humor, addressed his role in the Bagwell trade in December, 1994.

"All I knew at the time of the trade was that he had led the Eastern League in hitting," Andersen said. "You didn't know what the guy was going to do. He was just in double A. It's easy to look back at it after the fact. When he first came up, he had a couple of holes and if you pitched him right, you could get him out. Now he's filled those holes with some pretty good spackling.

"I told him he owes me something, and that was before this year. The least he could do was put gas in my rental car when I came to town, but after this year and his new contract, I want a new car. You can't be any more of a complete player than he is. He is just a fabulous player all the way around.

"I've never even sniffed a thought that he thought more of himself than just being a good hard-nosed ballplayer, and that is refreshing. He's the type of guy you hope keeps going. You pull for those guys."

"Up until this year I thought the highlight of my career was the 1993 World Series [with the Phillies], but now it's getting traded for him. If he continues to play like he's capable of, he is going to make my name a household name."[27]

Recognizing that they had something special, the Astros rewarded Bagwell with a spectacular contract in September 1994. The Astros signed Bagwell to a $27.5-million four-year deal with three option years. It was a deal with an average annual value of $6,875,000, the fifth-highest in the majors. It was a contract richly deserved by the National League's newest superstar.

Notes

1. *Baseball Weekly*, 2 August 1994.
2. Ibid.
3. Ibid.
4. *Bill Mazeroski's Baseball '94.*
5. *The Bill James Player Ratings Book* 1994.
6. *Baseball Weekly*, 5 April 1994.
7. *Baseball Weekly*, 26 April 1994.
8. *Baseball Weekly*, 10 May 1994.
9. Ibid.
10. *Baseball Weekly*, 28 June 1994.
11. *Baseball Weekly*, 5 July 1994.
12. *Baseball Weekly*, 12 July 1994.
13. Ibid.
14. Ibid.
15. *Baseball Weekly*, 19 July 1994.
16. Associated Press, 23 July 1994.
17. Ibid.
18. *Baseball Weekly*, 2 August 1994.
19. Ibid.
20. Ibid.
21. *Baseball Weekly*, 16 August 1994.
22. Associated Press, 11 August 1994.
23. Ibid.
24. *Baseball Weekly*, 23 August 1994.
25. *Los Angeles Times*, 28 October 1994.
26. Ibid.
27. *Baseball Weekly*, 10 January 1995.

How the West Was Won

*July 18, 1993: The San Diego Padres
trade Fred McGriff to the Atlanta Braves
for Melvin Nieves, Vince Moore and Donnie Elliott*

It did not take long for the Atlanta Braves to reap the benefits of acquiring first baseman Fred McGriff from the San Diego Padres a little past the midway point of the 1993 season. In his first game as a Brave, McGriff blasted a home run to propel Atlanta to an 8–5 victory over the St. Louis Cardinals. The following day, McGriff did it one better, clubbing two homers in the Braves' 14–2 victory over the Cardinals.

But even with McGriff's immediate lift, one question remained: With 2½ months left in the season, did the Braves have enough time to catch the rampaging San Francisco Giants? Behind left fielder Barry Bonds, third baseman Matt Williams, starting pitchers John Burkett and Bill Swift and reliever Rod Beck, the Giants appeared firmly in command in the National League West Division. And they showed no signs of slowing their pace.

The Braves were nine games behind the Giants before McGriff joined the team, but his arrival allowed the anemic Braves' offense to develop instant muscle. He was recognized as probably the premier first baseman in the National League, ahead of even the venerable Will Clark, who was suffering through a subpar year with the Giants.

The powerful 6-foot-3 McGriff had clouted an impressive 171 homers the previous five years to top all major leaguers. He belted a National League-leading 35 for the Padres in 1992 when he became the first player to capture the home run title in each league. McGriff had 31 homers for San Diego in 1991, and playing for the Toronto Blue Jays, 35 in 1990, an American League-leading 36 in 1989, and 34 in 1988.

McGriff came to the Braves carrying a .275 batting average, with 18 homers and 46 runs batted in. The Braves' platooning first basemen, Sid Bream and Brian Hunter, had combined for a mere eight homers and 35 RBIs, so there was no question the Braves were much-improved at that position.

McGriff was feeling at home even before he swung a bat for the Braves. "We have a ways to go, but it will be exciting," said McGriff after the trade.

"It will be a challenge and I'm getting closer and closer to [my hometown of] Tampa."

With the announcement on July 18, 1993 that the Braves were obtaining McGriff for three prospects, Atlanta's side rejoiced. "[McGriff] is an impact player," Atlanta manager Bobby Cox said. "Any club can certainly use a guy like that. We certainly can."[2]

Atlanta's pitchers, who were not receiving much run support, found considerable delight in the acquisition of McGriff. "It's sort of like when we got [Greg] Maddux [before the year began via free agency]," said Atlanta pitcher Steve Avery. "That was a sure 15 wins. Now we have somebody who will give us 30 homers and hit .280."[3]

While the Braves were eyeing a run at the Giants, the Padres were looking at their bottom line. They were 36–57, 25 games behind the Giants and two games ahead of the last-place Colorado Rockies, a first-year expansion team.

Tony Gwynn, the Padres' star right fielder who was enjoying another banner season, was dumbstruck at the trade in which San Diego obtained three minor leaguers: outfielders Melvin Nieves and Vince Moore and pitcher Donnie Elliott. Nieves and Elliott were assigned to triple A Las Vegas and Moore was sent to class A Rancho Cucamonga.

"You trade somebody like Freddie McGriff, you expect to get some quality in return," Gwynn said. "We'll have to wait and see what's going to turn out with these guys. I think the fact that none of them are coming here doesn't speak all that well.

"I'm frustrated. I can't understand why we're doing what we're doing."[4]

What the Padres were doing was evident. The McGriff trade was a dollars-and-cents decision for San Diego. Three weeks earlier, the Padres had dispatched third baseman Gary Sheffield, the National League batting champion and nearly the league's Triple Crown champion in 1992, to the Florida Marlins. It marked the first time that a club had traded separate home run and batting champions from the previous season.

McGriff, the highest-paid Padre, was earning $4.25 million in 1993, Sheffield $3.11 million. The trade left San Diego with 11 players making the minimum $109,000; eighteen were not making more than $165,000. Until the Padres unloaded McGriff, the club had not conceded their trades of big-name, big-money players (starting with the trade of pitcher Craig Lefferts the previous year) were economically motivated. But San Diego general manager Randy Smith admitted finances were indeed a major reason for McGriff's departure.

And Padre president Dick Freeman, without releasing figures to substantiate his claims, said the franchise lost $7 million in 1992 when the club drew 1.7 million fans and hosted the All-Star Game. And through the All-Star game in 1993, the attendance at Padre home games had dropped 13.9

Due to financial problems, the San Diego Padres traded slugger Fred McGriff (above) to the Atlanta Braves for three prospects—Donnie Elliott, Vince Moore and Melvin Nieves—in 1993. The Braves cashed in immediately as McGriff led them to the division championship (photograph courtesy of the San Diego Padres).

percent. "Never in my wildest imagination did I think our financial situation would be this precarious," Freeman said.[5]

McGriff expressed disbelief that both he and Sheffield could be traded. "I'm 29, getting close to 30, but Gary is 24," McGriff said. "That's pretty young I would've figured that I would've been traded before him. From what they've been telling me, it's basically money. I never thought it would get to the day where I made too much money and it became a bad situation."

The Padres expressed satisfaction that they secured three highly regarded prospects despite reports that they preferred one of the Braves' three most publicized minor leaguers: shortstop Chipper Jones, first baseman Ryan Klesko or catcher Javier Lopez. Smith insisted the Padres were more interested in the switch-hitting Nieves, 21, than Klesko—both of whom projected as big power hitters.

"We were salivating over Nieves," Smith said. "We thought he was one of the two best prospects in their organization. He could be a Ruben Sierra or Bobby Bonilla-type player."[7]

Smith said Elliott was the Braves' top pitching prospect from double A and above. Moore was considered the Padre center fielder of the future.

As for McGriff, he became the Brave first baseman of the present. Atlanta hoped he could catch fire from the outset. Eerily, fire became the main topic in McGriff's first game as a Brave. McGriff blasted a two-run homer against the Cardinals, but it was overshadowed by a fire that broke out at Atlanta-Fulton County Stadium 90 minutes before game time. The contest was delayed 1 hour 58 minutes as firefighters extinguished a blaze that began in a mezzanine box and spread to several others adjacent to the press box. Only one person was hurt in the blaze, a firefighter who was overcome by smoke.

It was quite an eventful debut for McGriff, who drove to Atlanta from Tampa earlier in the day. "With the fire and driving from Tampa—what a day—I need some sleep," McGriff said.[8]

McGriff apparently got sufficient rest that night because he took center stage the next day by belting two homers, a double and driving in three runs to lead the Braves past the Cardinals. In two days, McGriff had three homers. He certainly had adjusted to his new surroundings.

A day later, the Giants demonstrated they were not intimidated by the McGriff trade by defeating the Philadelphia Phillies, 4–1, to take a season-high 10-game lead over the Braves, who had blown a three-run lead in the ninth to the Pittsburgh Pirates. Still, the Braves' mood was confident despite the shattering defeat. Atlanta general manager John Schuerholz, who pulled off the McGriff trade, declared his team was primed to make a charge at the Giants.

"My view is through eyes that are getting dust kicked in them by a relentless leader—who won't drop back and keeps doing everything it needs to do," Schuerholz said. "On the other hand, we've had what for us is a month's worth of production in the three or four games McGriff has been with us.

"And if we keep getting that offense with the caliber pitching we've had all along, we can still make a run for it. I mean, all we need to do is pick up a game a week, not lose a game."[9]

For that to happen, McGriff had to remain in a groove and his long-ball-hitting teammates—third baseman Terry Pendleton and outfielders

David Justice and Ron Gant—had to join in. Without McGriff, the Braves had the lowest batting average in the league and ranked near the bottom in runs scored.

But that was all before the McGriff era. In McGriff's first week with the Braves, Atlanta scored at least 10 runs in four consecutive games for the first time since the team moved to Atlanta in 1966.

McGriff was hitting but so were his teammates. Justice batted .542 with two home runs and seven RBIs in McGriff's first week. Mark Lemke, a weak-hitting second baseman, batted .536 that week. The long-dormant Pendleton, the league's Most Valuable Player in 1991, went on a tear with two homers and a .407 average, giving every indication that he was getting over his slow first half. Gant belted two homers and drove in eight runs. Shortstop Jeff Blauser batted .308 with three homers.

McGriff jump-started the sputtering Braves' offense, leading Atlanta to eight wins in his first nine games as a Brave. The Braves began to slowly chisel into the Giants' lead. McGriff batted a robust .360 with four homers in his second week on his new team, helping Atlanta pull within 7½ games of San Francisco by August 1. All told, McGriff had a remarkable six homers in his first 35 at-bats.

"He has given us a shot of B-12," said Atlanta center fielder Otis Nixon. "He's relaxed our big guns. When you have terrific pitching like ours, it adds more pressure when you don't hit. But the attitude has changed with Fred. We definitely think we can get back in this thing."[10]

Despite McGriff's contributions, he found himself subject to speculation that he might be dealt after the season ended to pare the Braves' payroll. After all, the Braves had grade A prospect Klesko eagerly awaiting his chance at first base. But Schuerholz tried to squelch the rumor, calling the talk ludicrous. "Who in their right mind would not want him on our club after the impact he has made? We got him for the short run and the long run," he said.[11]

The Braves had McGriff under contract through 1994 and held an option for 1995. McGriff, for his part, expressed little concern. The decisions about his future could wait. "I really haven't talked to anybody about it," he said. "I haven't been thinking about it."[12]

On McGriff's mind was the Braves' relentless pursuit of the Giants. On August 18, the Braves closed to within 6½ games with a 3–2 victory over the Los Angeles Dodgers for their eighth straight victory. The next day, McGriff homered to help Atlanta to a 5–4 12-inning victory over the Dodgers, but the Giants also won. On August 20, the Dodgers ended the Braves winning streak at nine with a 7–5 victory. Meanwhile, the Giants remained hot, defeating the Pittsburgh Pirates, 6–3, to move 7½ games up.

The Giants were 81–40, 41 games over .500 for the first time since they won a three-game National League playoff over the Dodgers in 1962 to finish that season 103–62. The Braves' challenge was being rebuffed by a Giant team that refused to buckle. Atlanta desperately needed to make some fast gains when the teams tangled in two series of three games each that would begin on August 23. The Giants welcomed the opportunity to put themselves out of reach of the Braves.

"We think we can put an end to their winning ways," declared Giant reserve Todd Benzinger.[13]

But the Giants failed miserably in San Francisco. The Braves won all three games in the series, punctuated by a 9–1 rout in the finale that left the deficit a less-than-insurmountable 4½ games. Atlanta collected 16 hits—six homers—in that farewell game as McGriff and Justice belted back-to-back homers in both the first and fifth innings.

The two homers boosted McGriff's home run total to 30, with 12 coming as a Brave. Justice and Gant each had 31, giving the Braves three players with 30 or more homers for the first time since 1973, when they had three with at least 40 (Davey Johnson, 43, Darrell Evans, 41, and Hank Aaron, 40), the only time that has happened in the major leagues.

The Giants were in a race and they knew it. While the Braves had greatly upgraded their offense for the stretch run, the Giants put first baseman Will Clark on the 15-day disabled list because of a knee injury. Further misfortune befell the Giants when starters Bud Black and Trevor Wilson came down with injuries. The Giants tried to deal for distinguished veteran Dennis Martinez of the Montreal Expos, but the Braves blocked the trade by claiming Martinez on waivers. Although Martinez was able to void the move to the Braves and remained with the Expos, Atlanta still came out ahead by denying the Giants a chance to bolster their sagging pitching corps.

The Braves chopped another game off the Giants' lead when they won two of three games in the last head-to-head series between the contenders. The Braves still trailed by 3½ games, but the Giants were unmistakably teetering. Still, the Giants spoke with confidence. "Anyone with a lead still has that advantageous position," asserted Giant manager Dusty Baker. "From now on, it all depends on how each of us plays. The Braves are hot, but they've still to play hot Montreal and Philadelphia, which is hot too. I like our position. I wouldn't trade it for nothing in the world."[14]

But the Giants were having difficulty staving off the Braves' charge, and on September 10 Atlanta surged into a tie for first with a 3–2 victory over the Padres. McGriff, enjoying his return visit to San Diego, blasted a three-run homer the next day to power Atlanta to a 13–1 victory and into sole possession of first place, one game ahead of the Giants, who lost their fourth straight game.

As the Giants' losing streak stretched to eight games, McGriff maintained his torrid pace, raising his average to .290, an increase of 15 points since he left the Padres. On September 15, the Braves opened a four-game lead with a 3–2, 12-inning victory over the Cincinnati Reds. Now it was the Braves who appeared headed for a runaway.

But the Giants were far from dead. After all, they had the magnificent Bonds, whom they had signed to a six-year, $43.75 million contract before the season. And Bonds, whose recent slump coincided with that of the Giants', was coming out of his cold spell with a vengeance.

Behind Bonds, the Giants regained the momentum and pulled even with Atlanta on September 30, winning the first game of a four-game set with their archrivals, the Dodgers, in Los Angeles. On the same day, the Braves fell to Houston, 10–8, despite McGriff's two-run homer and two other hits.

The season came down to the final three games, with each team at 101–58. The Giants had three more games against the Dodgers in Los Angeles, while the Braves had three home games against the Rockies, who were 0 for 10 against the Braves in 1993.

A one-game playoff loomed if the teams couldn't shake their rival over the next three days. The Braves appeared to have the edge because the Rockies—despite a significant second-half improvement—seemed overmatched against Atlanta's top-notch pitching and explosive offense. And the Dodgers, 80–79, were bent on deriving some satisfaction out of a disappointing season by sandbagging the Giants' pennant hopes the way San Francisco had done numerous times to Los Angeles.

Playing a few hours before the Giants' game, the Braves extended their domination over Colorado with a 7–4 victory, highlighted by the rejuvenated Pendleton, who had five RBIs to boost his total to 80. "I should have 180," said Pendleton afterward. "I just haven't done my share. In fact, Fred McGriff came up to me today and said he was tired of carrying me." Pendleton then laughed at the recollection of that good-natured jab.[15]

The Braves' win was no laughing matter for the Giants, who counterpunched with an 8–7 decision over the Dodgers. Bonds solidified his MVP credentials with two home runs and seven RBIs.

The next day the co-leaders prevailed again. The Braves cruised to a 10–1 victory, Maddux's 20th win. The Giants held off the Dodgers, 5–3, to make it three wins in a row over Los Angeles in the four-game series. McGriff drove in one run with a double in the Braves' rout to give him 100 RBIs. He joined teammates Justice (119) and Gant (115) in the 100-RBI club. The Braves, averaging 5.8 runs during the 67 games with McGriff, were 50–17 with their new first baseman and 53–19 since the All-Star break.

One game remained in the regular season, with a tiebreaker game in San Francisco appearing very possible. The Braves had an ace in the hole with Tom Glavine pitching and the dependable left-hander paced the Braves to a 5–3 victory, his 22nd win. McGriff drove in one run and scored another, but the hitting star was Justice, who clouted his 40th home run. All Atlanta could do now was wait for the conclusion of the Giants' game with Los Angeles and hope Dodger veteran right-hander Kevin Gross could outduel Giant rookie Salomon Torres. A few hours later, the Braves were celebrating with their third consecutive division title.

The Dodgers, exposing the Giants' patchwork pitching, romped to a 12–1 victory behind Gross' complete game and Mike Piazza's two home runs. "We were hoping the Dodgers could win one," said Braves manager Bobby Cox, "and the way they did it made the wait less difficult."[16]

The Giants ended the season with a terrific 103–59 record, but it fell one game short of the Braves. "We just ran out of innings," said Bonds, who finished with a .346 average and a league-high 46 home runs.[17]

But Bonds was not enough to negate the great impact that Fred McGriff had on the Braves. McGriff finished the regular season with a .291 average, a career-high 37 home runs and 101 RBIs. He became the 12th player to hit 30 homers in six consecutive seasons. For Atlanta, McGriff batted .310, clubbed 19 homers and drove in 55 runs in 68 games. Even more important was the beneficial effect he had on his new teammates.

McGriff became the Braves' cleanup hitter when he came to Atlanta and a domino effect was created. Gant was moved from fourth to third in the order, Pendleton was dropped from third to sixth and Justice remained as the fifth-place hitter. All four prospered because none of the four could be pitched around and all recognized there was no pressure on any of them to carry the load.

McGriff subscribed to the belief that his new teammates swung a hot bat on his arrival because of a new mental attitude. "All the guys are very talented," McGriff said. "It's not like they never hit and all of the sudden I come and they start hitting. Nothing I did physically helped them hit, but from a mental standpoint, I'm sure it took pressure off a little bit."[18]

Next stop for the Braves was the National League Championship Series against the Philadelphia Phillies, a team known for its charisma and characters but an underdog against Atlanta in the best four-of-seven series. After all, the Braves had the best starting staff in baseball with the foursome of Greg Maddux, Tom Glavine, Steve Avery and John Smoltz, the power of Fred McGriff, David Justice and Ron Gant, the speed of center fielder Otis Nixon and the steadiness of shortstop Jeff Blauser. The Braves also were on a mission to claim the World Series championship that had eluded them the previous two seasons. The addition of McGriff had given the Braves the respect and admiration of the baseball community.

While the Braves flourished with McGriff in the regular season, they flopped with him in the Championship Series. Not that it was McGriff's fault. McGriff, the consummate professional, led all Braves with 10 hits in the playoffs, batting .435. But the Phillies, despite being outscored, 33–23, won the series in six games as reliever Mitch Williams won two games and saved two. Whether Atlanta was mentally and physically exhausted after its great second-half drive or it was a matter of being outplayed, the Braves did not perform up to standards at critical junctures.

It was a disappointing end to a magnificent season and it was the third straight time the Braves had failed to win the World Series after claiming their division title. But the Braves decried the notion that they were losers because they had been defeated by the Phillies, a team that had won 97 games during the regular season.

"We accomplished a lot," Smoltz said. "But sometimes that's overshadowed and taken away from by not winning the World Series, and that's what's frustrating about sports—how the Buffalo Bills [losers of four straight Super Bowls in the 1990s] can ever be looked upon as failures. And I'm sure we'll be thrown in that category.

"I don't think that's a fair assessment. In other words, the perception says if you only go to the World Series once in 20 years and win it, that's better than going 10 times and only winning once or losing all 10 times. You can take that for what it's worth. But I think we're one of the great teams in the past 10 years."[19]

The addition of Fred McGriff helped create that dominating team, which came out of nowhere to eclipse a powerful Giants' team. "It almost turned out to be a great story," said McGriff, who finished fourth in the National League Most Valuable Player voting behind Bonds, Phillies outfielder Lenny Dykstra and Braves' teammate David Justice. "If we had made it to the World Series, it would have made it a great, great story."[20]

McGriff enjoyed another banner season in 1994 for the Braves, batting .318 with 34 homers and 94 RBIs. It was the seventh straight season in which McGriff smacked at least 30 homers and it was achieved despite the season ending almost two months early because of a players' strike. Still, McGriff had his usual share of highlights. One of the biggest came in the All-Star Game when he hit a two-run pinch-homer in the bottom of the ninth off closer extraordinaire Lee Smith to tie the score and pave the way for a National League win in extra innings. McGriff was named the All-Star Game's Most Valuable Player for that clutch homer to the opposite field. "I've played seven years in the big leagues and I've hit a lot of homers," McGriff said. "This is a nice little feeling. It's the stuff you dream about."[21]

Meanwhile, two of the players for whom McGriff was traded were called up by the Padres in 1994. Pitcher Donnie Elliott got into 31 games for San Diego, all but one in relief, and finished with an 0–1 record and 3.27 ERA. Outfielder Melvin Nieves collected 19 at-bats for the Padres and batted .263 with one homer and four RBIs. Nieves showed promise in the minors, hitting 25 homers with a .308 average for triple A Las Vegas.

But the futures of Elliott and Nieves appeared uncertain, while one thing appeared definite about Fred McGriff. He was headed in the direction of the Hall of Fame.

Notes

1. Associated Press, 19 July 1993.
2. Ibid.
3. *Baseball Weekly*, 27 July 1993.
4. Ibid.
5. Ibid.
6. Associated Press, 19 July 1993.
7. *Baseball Weekly*, 27 July 1993.
8. Associated Press, 20 July 1993.
9. *Los Angeles Times*, 25 July 1993.
10. *Sports Illustrated*, 9 August 1993.
11. *Baseball Weekly*, 17 August 1993.
12. Ibid.
13. *Baseball Weekly*, 31 August 1993.
14. *Baseball Weekly*, 14 September 1993.
15. *Los Angeles Times*, 2 October 1993.
16. *Los Angeles Times*, 4 October 1993.
17. Ibid.
18. *Baseball Weekly*, 12 October 1993.
19. *Baseball Weekly*, 26 October 1993.
20. Associated Press, 17 March 1994.
21. *Baseball Weekly*, 19 July 1994.

Index